SO-ALF-584

Suzy Gershman

BORN TO SHOP

FRANCE

The Ultimate Guide for
Travelers Who Love to Shop

2nd Edition

MACMILLAN • USA

For my French family: PA and Thierry, Marie Jo
and Gerard, Domy and Richard, Danielle and
Dominique, Patricia and Walter, Jill and Yomi,
Pierre, Laurent, Alec—and all my Philippes.
Bisous à toutes et grosses mercis.

Prices in this book are listed in either U.S. dollars or French francs, written as F. The conversion rate used for exchange in these pages has been 6 F = US$1. When you travel, the rate of exchange may be different. Please note that prices in euros in France are more or less on par with the U.S. dollar; to get the euro price from French francs, divide by 6.6.

Macmillan Travel

A Simon & Schuster Macmillan Company
1633 Broadway
New York, NY 10019

ISBN 0-02-862360-6
ISSN 1088-8519

Editor: Leslie Wiggins
Production Editor: Michael Thomas
Copy Editor: Faren Bachelis
Map Editor: Gail Accardi
Design by George J. McKeon
Page creation by John Bitter and Natalie Evans

Manufactured in the United States of America

CONTENTS

MAP LIST

TO START WITH

Welcome to a new edition of one of my favorite books, our France edition which is not to be confused with *Frommer's Born to Shop Paris*. We publish the Paris guide and this book in alternate years to keep you as up to date as possible. This edition will be more helpful for those who will be driving around the French countryside, visiting the Riviera and Provence, or enjoying a cruise of either Mediterranean or French Atlantic ports.

I think you'll find that this book is much more, uh, French. This is the intermediate class. I assume that you speak or read a teensy bit of French. I assume you have been to Paris before, possibly many times. This book is for the family, the couple, the pals who are visiting several French destinations. You are seeking more France than Paris offers—a more intimate experience, with the people, the land, the food, and the stores.

If you're going to be just in Paris, or if you think you will confine your serious shopping to Paris, you'll find that *Born to Shop Paris* is more detailed. The Paris chapter in this book is for people who will be in and out in a day or two and who have already had the opportunity—or will soon have the opportunity—to shop in the countryside.

Originally I did my research on driving trips orchestrated through family and friends, because I was afraid to drive in France. I've now overcome that childishness and adore the freedom on the road. I do thank the people of France for their patience in teaching me how to fill the car with gas (*sans plomb*—unleaded), and my French friends, especially on the Riviera, for teaching me the tricks that helped make me a little bit French. Yes, I now drive with my Visa card between my legs so I am ready to pay the tolls on the highway—my friend Richard taught me this, as well as many other things.

Richard and his team at Noga Hilton Cannes have been a big help with this edition: I thank them all. Thanks also go to Ken Yellin at Concorde Hotels and much of the Concorde team in France—my new family stretching across not only Paris but almost all of France; to Fran Natale and Alice Gentils, at Societe Bains de Mer of Monaco, and my beloved Dario dell Antonia, minister of tourism for Monaco. I stayed at many Relais & Châteaux properties throughout France. Each was more divine than the next—you can read more about them in these pages.

There's much new hotel research in the Paris chapter, so I send thanks to the team that worked with me: Franka Holtzmann and Bernadette Skubly Butts, of Hôtel Ritz; Dominique Borri, the general manager of the Meurice; and Gabrille Hirn at The Bristol.

The French Government Tourist Office in New York helped me immeasurably with research and plans, as did tourist offices in many French cities; big hugs of thanks to Judith Richards in Lille who drove me to the Porthault factory and introduced me to smelly cheese tarts, Spot, and much, much more. *Merci bien* to Robin Massee and Marion: Someday *nous sont faire fete ensemble.*

Finally, some special thanks—*avec beaucoup de bisou*—to my old friend Alain Ducasse, whose tips are found woven into many portions of this book. I fell in love with him years ago, way before his six stars! He now adds tips to three portions of this book: Monte Carlo, Provence, and Paris.

I might not write as well as M. Ducasse cooks, but I think you'll find nine stars worth of information within these pages. *Bon appétit!*

Chapter One

· · · · · · ·

THE BEST OF FRANCE AT A GLANCE

FRENCH LESSONS

· ·

Paris is a special place unto itself. Far more than just the City of Light, it has many wonderful and beautiful things to see, to eat, and to buy—but it is not France. In many ways, it is the opposite of the rest of France.

You will find passion and fashion and style by the mile in Paris, but you will not find the soul of France. Therefore, I have devised this quickie overview chapter to give you a fast look at what I consider to be some of the best bets in the French countryside. Everything listed in this chapter is outside of Paris.

Obviously I haven't been to every village in France, and this book does not cover the entire country. What you have here are some highlights that might help you flash forward to the best addresses if you are in a mad rush. *Vite, vite!*

Who knows, you could be between screenings at the Cannes Film Festival. Or you could be between *couverts*. Straighten your black tie, fluff up your bosom, put on your Ray-Bans, and get out your highlighter pen.

THE BEST SOURCE FOR POSTCARDS

· ·

KING PHOTO
11 bd. Gambetta, Nice

I'd been thinking that Monoprix did a great job with postcards at 1.60 F (25¢) per card but, voilà, here are postcards for 1.30 F (22¢) and they're great. They have an insert of an old poster of the area (different choices) and a photo teamed together.

THE BEST MAKEUP & PERFUME SHOP

· ·

SEPHORA
Stores in Paris and the provinces

There are Sephora stores all over France and each varies depending on the real estate. The flagship on the avenue des Champs-Elysées is probably the best one, but there are good ones in most major cities.

Many Sephora stores are on two levels and come complete with a kiddie play area downstairs or in the rear of the shop. All of the merchandise is organized by color in the front of the store and by brand around the sides of the store, with fragrance in a different part of the store. Fragrance is alphabetized and no one line has more space or adverts over any other line: It's very democratic. There are tons of testers and paper strips so you can spritz until you cease to breathe.

The house line of bath products is not only fabulous but is issued in miniature sizes perfect for travel or gift-giving. Sephora provides an electronic *détaxe* at the cash register if you qualify (see chapter 3).

THE BEST MONDAY IN FRANCE

· ·

Hitting the Flea Markets in Cannes and Nice

This is a doubleheader for true flea market devotees: You can do the half-hour between the two cities on a train. Monday flea markets are held year-round, so there's none of this closed-on-Monday business.

While the Cannes Monday *brocante* market (Marché Forville) isn't that big or splendid, it's very nice and funky, and prices are quite good. Combine it with the 250-odd dealers at the Cours Saleya in Nice and you'll have yourself one fine day.

There are oodles of other flea markets in France, but many of them are more expensive; Provence is charming, but you pay for it.

THE BEST FRUIT & FLOWER MARKET

· ·

Cours Saleya
Nice

Any day of the week except Monday (see above), the Cours Saleya in Nice is awash with striped awnings and tables heaving with locally grown fresh produce. Buy flowers, candies, olives, honey, and more.

THE BEST FACTORY STORE

· ·

Porthault
19 rue Robespiere, Rieux-en-Cambresis (near Lille)

Porthault sells goodies at a fraction of their retail price. It's very hit or miss and you must pay in cash, but this is not only worth the drive, it's worth a trip to France. The only drawback: The person to whom you give a Porthault gift must understand its value. I got a table set for my girlfriend Wanda in Paris and she was delighted and over the moon; I bought a baby gift for an American who gave me a weak thank you.

Runners Up:

JEAN VIER
St. Jean de Luz (near Biarritz)

Jean Vier, the maker of Basque-style country linen, is located right outside Biarritz. This factory store is a winner for many reasons. It's situated in a restored farmhouse that is a full showroom and is simply to die for in a breathtakingly gorgeous, magazine-spread sort of way.

Another plus is that the bargain back room has genuine bargains and markdowns, which is more than you can say about some of the other big-name French fabric factory stores.

LES OLIVADES
See page 358.

THE BEST THALOSOTHERAPIE PRODUCT
. . . .

THALAMANCHE BAIN MOUSSANT
St. Malo

Thalosotherapie (seawater spa treatments) is the rage in France (see chapter 5). I paid a whopping $30 or so for the 500ml size of Bain Moussant Aux Algues, which not only smells of the sea but floats me out to sea every time I soak. When I emerge, I swear I am Venus.

THE BEST SOAP
. . . .

MARIUS FABRE
148 av. Paul Bourret, Salon-de-Provence

My friend Alain Ducasse turned me onto this brand; it's a small firm in business since 1900. You don't have to go to Salon-de-Provence to buy it; there is distribution in most Provençal-style shops, especially in the area between Nice and Cannes.

BEST MULTIPLE TO OPEN ALL OVER FRANCE

. . . .

L'Occitane
Stores throughout France

I don't know who pumped the money into these guys, but suddenly they have shops everywhere—not just in France. They carry an enormous line of soaps, bath products, beauty products, and household scents, such as candles, incense, and room sprays. My friend Betsy says they make a long-lasting lipstick that is one of the best she's ever tried. I like the little tins of soap; they cost 28 F ($6)—you get the soap and the tin. The Shea butter is good for very dry, winter hands. It's a great place for doing all the gift shopping in one swoop.

THE BEST COOKIES

. . . .

Mere Poullard
Mont St. Michel (and elsewhere)

These simple butter cookies will slay you. They are nationally distributed throughout grocery stores in France; I buy mine in Paris at the grocery store attached to Bon Marché on the Left Bank. You can get a small box, which makes a great gift, for less than 10 F ($1.70). A regular box costs 25 F ($4.20), and a tin costs 50 F ($8.30).

THE BEST CHOCOLATE

. . . .

Bernachon
42 cours Franklin Roosevelt, Lyon

Okay, so it's no surprise that Bernachon would end up on my list—he's on everyone else's list too. But when I say chocolate, I'm thinking of a rich, creamy chocolate eclair. Better than sex.

THE BEST CONFITURE SHOP

. . . .

MAISON DE LA CONFITURE
Gassin (outside St. Tropez)

Note that I didn't say they have the best confiture in France—that would be harder to pick—just that they have the best shop. Maison de la Confiture has many wild, weird, and wonderful flavors and combinations, and all the jam jars are topped with little squares of Provençal fabric. It's simply heaven.

THE BEST IN-FLIGHT DUTY FREE

. . . .

AIR FRANCE
Not only does Air France have a very good selection, but it sells a number of French luxury brands that aren't offered on other carriers and at excellent prices.

THE BEST IN-FLIGHT DUTY-FREE GIMMICK

. . . .

DELTA
Delta awards passengers a $20 duty-free gift certificate, which you redeem immediately on the plane when the duty-free cart rolls past.

YOU'RE GOING TO BUY ONLY ONE THING IN FRANCE (AND THE DOLLAR IS STRONG)

. . . .

- Hermès tie.
- Hermès scarf.
- Bottle of scent not yet introduced in the United States.

YOU'RE GOING TO BUY ONLY ONE THING IN FRANCE (AND THE DOLLAR IS WEAK)

- Used Hermès scarf.
- Smaller bottle of scent, possibly less scent in the mixture (if not parfum, then eau de parfum; if not eau de parfum, then eau de toilette; and so on).
- Bottle of good wine to bring home and drink at some future date when you need it (you'll know when).

YOU HAVE TIME FOR ONLY ONE-STOP SHOPPING

Try any branch of Monoprix or Prisunic or get thee to a *hypermarché,* the French version of a modern dry-goods store attached to a grocery store.

THE BEST KITSCH OUTSIDE PARIS

This wasn't meant to be funny and not everyone thinks it is funny (kitsch has that problem), but personally, I think this is just the best: Joan of Arc (Jeanne d'Arc) coffee, sold only in Rouen, the city where Joan was burned at the stake. It's French roast.

THE BEST GIFTS UNDER $5

- Latest edition of a French magazine, preferably *Elle,* which costs about $2.50. There's also *Top Model,* which is great for teens.
- Calissons. Candy-covered almonds, sold everywhere in Provence for about $3 a box.

- Savon de Marseille. A 400-gram block (the bigger-size square) costs about $3.
- Coffee. My friends Ken and Kim both swear by Carte Noire brand, which can be bought in any supermarket.

THE BEST GIFTS FOR LOVED ONES

- Bottle of wine, vintage year dated when a child was born or when you were married—you get the idea. Conversely, a wine that will be at its peak on a special date (a 21st birthday, a 50th birthday, and so on).
- Crystal heart form one of the famous French crystal houses such as Baccarat or Lalique. They're 40% less in France, with greater savings if you buy several and qualify for *détaxe*.
- Scented candle with exotic scent, such as one from Marriage Frères in Paris, about $50. There are candles for less at other stores. I'm also big on Diptyque, about $35.
- Longchamp folding shopping bag or weekend tote; prices range with size and style. The new weekend bag, at 690 F ($115), is fabulous.

THE BEST PROMISE TO COME

Promise her anything but give her Arpège? Well, almost. Forget the perfume and instead bring your honey (him or her, we're not chauvinistic about these things) the menu from a famous French restaurant and the promise that on the next trip, he or she can come along.

By the way, Arpège is a Michelin-starred restaurant in Paris.

THE BEST GIFTS FOR KIDS

- Monoprix has a small toy selection, but it is well stocked with Legos and often has models not available in the United States.
- Little girls (and big girls too) love perfume miniatures and samples, as well as makeup and small-size toiletries. Hoard the ones you get for free; buy miniatures if they are well priced (some are collectors items and cost a fortune; watch out); and stop by Sephora for its adorable bath and fragrance collection in tiny sizes.
- Books in French, especially storybooks that you already have in English, make wonderful gifts for children. All Disney stories are available in French. Do not buy videocassettes, as they are in Secam, not NTSC, and will not be compatible with your VCR.
- Build-it-yourself paper cutouts of French landmarks.
- Souvenir with the child's name on it in French. If you can't get an exact match, find a similar name and give the child a French pet name. You can even pick a saint to go with it and then celebrate the saint's name day with your children.

Chapter Two

. . . .

FRENCH DETAILS

WELCOME TO FRANCE

. . . .

I did it! I did it! I drove in France! It was easy! It was fun! And if you do, too, it will free you to discover a whole new France and a whole new you!

Speaking of freedom, we now sit on the cusp of the franc and the launch of the euro, which will free you when you cross borders to neighboring countries, expand your French horizons, and lead to even more shopping opportunities. *Vive la différence!*

So welcome to France, the France where you can drive and take it all in, where the highways and the back ways are yours to explore. Indeed, if you think France is Paris, it's time to start packing, start driving, or start thinking (and drinking) Champagne (and champagne).

While the shopping in Paris may be quicker and easier than in any other city in France, you don't really get the picture of what France is if you stick to the big cities.

And *francly,* my dear, if you're looking for a price break, you want to get to some of the out-of-the-way places and even into a few factories. Yep, they've all got back rooms and markdowns. Wait till I tell you about my factory scouting trip to Lille!

France happens to be filled with bargains. I don't care how high or how low the dollar goes, or how much you're bitching and moaning about a poor exchange rate. There are still buys to be had that will thrill you for years to come. And I won't take *non* for an answer.

If you think France is prohibitively expensive and the Riviera out of sight in all respects, I'm here to tell you I have just done it all, seen it all, shopped it all (again), and some of the best bargains in France happen to be on the Riviera. France can be expensive, but it can also be a bargain. Don't quit without learning more.

When I welcome you to my France, it's a whole other place than the expensive—or the rude—country you may have heard about. My France is filled with people ready to please, white asparagus laid out in neat rows, and more olives than you can count. In my France, you buy your olive oil right from the barrel (after tasting it, of course).

So *bienvenue*, my friends, grab hold of your map, prepay your train pass or your rental car in the United States, and hit the road, Jacques. France and all its bounty await you. Bargains are out there; they may be hiding sometimes, but they're yours for the finding.

Welcome to a country filled with charming old towns, geraniums and window boxes, luxury hotels, perfume buys and beauty programs, Provençal fabrics, and heaps of raspberries nestled into little handmade *paniers* (baskets).

Oh yes, did I welcome you to the France of wine, to the France of rows of vines draping the roadsides, of tiny bubbles in a glass, and of châteaux so cozy that you'll come away with a proprietary feeling?

Welcome to a country where every local market is a photo op, where the dime store still has plenty of affordable goodies, and where all you really need to be permanently chic is a single Hermès scarf or tie (which can be bought from a *dépôt-vente*, a shop that sells used designer status goods).

Welcome to a country that will fill your senses with wonder and wash your soul in passion.

KNOW BEFORE YOU GO

. . . .

If you want to have money left over for shopping, you have a fair amount of homework to do before you set foot in France. The bargains are not just lying around; you're going to have to work for them. The cost of living in France is high, so you have to think French-style in order to save.

Many bargains are related to special prices for tourists when goods or services are prepaid in U.S. dollars before the journey even begins. You may also want to buy traveler's checks in French francs before you get to France (see chapter 3). There are deals for tourists and deals for locals and you need to know when you should be which.

While there is a French Government Tourist Office, with offices in various U.S. cities, that offers some super materials, I have been knocked out by the brochures, maps, and paperwork sent to me by local tourist offices throughout France. All are available in English. Don't be shy about writing or faxing directly to France.

Information, Please

If you have an ongoing interest in French travel, there are two sources of information I recommend: Club France, a service offered by the French Government Tourist Office, and *France Today*, a newspaper published in the United States in English.

A membership in **Club France** costs about $70 for a single membership; call ☎ **800-881-5060,** ext. 27, for more information or to join. Membership entitles you to a discount card and a bulletin filled with tips and coupons for complimentary drinks and other goodies.

France Today is a great newspaper, and I'm not sure which I enjoy more, the editorial content about

France or the ads, which often have specific travel and trip info. There's also a classified ad section if you want to rent a house or get personal in French. A 1-year subscription is about $40 in the United States; $50 outside the United States. Call ☎ **800-999-9718** for more information.

Electronically Yours

You can spend years on the Internet looking up travel information on France. Hotels, airlines, and travel agents all have their own Web sites, which can give you a glimpse of locations and deals. All the stores have Web sites, even **Tati!** (www.tati.fr). Each issue of *France Today* has a column called "Web Watch," which highlights some of the best Web sites with information about France. I personally search for "Bonjour Paris" on the America Online website, which does cover more than just Paris (AOL keyword "Bonjour").

Also remember generic U.S. travel sites that will have information on many places and will always have some information on France—try **www.hotdeals@traveleisure.com** for a bulletin on money-saving deals. The bulletin comes in subscription form, but it is free and includes weekly updates.

Here are a few more addresses you might want to check out; obviously Web sites come and go at rapid pace.

www.culture.fr (Wisdom from the French Culture Ministry)

www.paris.org (Pictures of Paris)

www.info-france-usa.org (The French Embassy in the United States)

www.monaco.mc/usa (The Monaco Tourist Bureau in New York keeps you up-to-date. No recipes from Ducasse.)

www.jetvacations.com (The large tour operator gives fares plus packages)

www.kemwel.com (My chosen car-rental agency with great prices on long- or short-term rentals, and yes, cars have automatic transmission)

www.hotelweb.fr (Book hotel rooms from Sofitel, Novotel, Mercure, Ibis, and so on)

www.placedemode.com (French and English reporting on the fashion scene from Paris)

www.worldmedia.fr/fashion (French fashion reports)

www.meteo.fr (French weather report)

SEASONALLY YOURS

The biggest secret to eating, sleeping, and shopping in France is not related to how much goods and services cost in France or the United States or what happens to the dollar and the franc or the dollar and the euro—it's simply seasonal. The prices on most items change with the climate in France.

Most destinations have two seasons: in and out. Summer is traditionally thought of as "in season." Everyone who travels knows that winter is "out" and thus always cheaper than summer.

However, France does not play by the same rules.

In France there are four seasons, and almost all hotels have four different price categories for the very same room: high, very high, low, and shoulder.

In Cannes, there is one season called Festival. During this season, which covers the Film Festival in May and all large conventions, rooms are actually scalped and prices are raised sky-high. Summer's "high season" is a respite compared to Festival prices.

As much as I don't like to talk about it, I must also point out that there is what I call Tragedy Season. This means that some weird act of God, or terrible thing (a bomb, a hijacking, a strike), has occurred, causing people to not travel and, thus, pressuring hotels and restaurants to drop their prices. Tragedy seasons can be terrible things, but the chances of them happening to you are usually small, and the bargains to be had are usually large.

Besides the fluctuation in hotel room rates, menu prices also change in various seasons. Similarly, if prices in stores aren't raised outright during peak seasons, at the least your bargaining position with the proprietor changes according to the flow of tourists.

Please note that by tourists I don't just mean Americans. When the French school holidays take place and families travel to resorts, the prices are raised for French tourists as well. Know when French school holidays fall, because they will affect your freedom to travel and get deals. The tourist office now prints a free wallet-sized card that lists all of the French school vacations, as well as train station phone numbers. In Paris, you can pick one up at the tourist office in the Carrousel du Louvre.

True, some of the cute little shops are closed in resort towns when the season passes. But we're talking down-and-dirty here: Do you want to pay top dollar for the privilege of shopping every store in town, or will you take a town with fewer tourists, lower prices, and the real soul of France?

The seasons in resort towns vary with the parts of the country. When it's "in" season in Cannes, it may still be out of season in Deauville. When rooms are top dollar in Cannes, with surcharges up the wazoo, prices are dirt cheap in Paris, where they'll throw in everything but the hotel's terry Porthault bathrobe. (Not to fret about that one, we've now got the address of the Porthault factory.)

Big cities traditionally have low room prices in July and August and on weekends throughout the year. Also note the French celebrate many holidays and *vacance* days (try getting any work done in the month of May). During these times hotel rooms in big cities go begging while resorts are sold out. Plan your travel accordingly and you can save.

GETTING THERE

. . . .

From the United States

Here are a few of the tricks I've discovered:

- **Jet Vacations** did go out of business, yes, but it's been reborn with pretty much the same deals, though it's no longer a division of Air France. Call ☎ 800/JET-0999 to book seats at "chartered" rates. The catch is that Jet Vacations doesn't use charters for these flights; it uses regularly scheduled flights and you still get a discounted price. You can either book just the flight, or book packages that include airfare and hotel. It has two packages that are so incredibly low you will blink twice at the price—ask about the "Affordable Paris" and "Affordable Provence" tours, which include airfare plus hotel and still cost under $1,000. *Mon Dieu!*

- If you are traveling from the United States to a city in France other than Paris or Nice, you will need to connect in one of these two cities, because they are the only two gateway cities in France for traffic originating in the United States. Air France also works with Air InterEurope, which supplies French domestic service. When you buy an Air France transatlantic ticket, you are entitled to specific programs and passes that may lower your airfares. Ask!

- Air InterEurope is no longer the only regional game in town. Discount regional airlines are popping up like mushrooms in springtime—and creating so much fear that even British Airways and Virgin Atlantic now have discount airlines as branches of their own firms. These lines serve French airports and destinations. Compare prices, passes, and deals with Air Liberté or TAT, which is a division of British Airways, as well as Air Littoral and AOM. Many of these regional airlines have deals advertised only in Europe or in

France; I tore an ad for AOM from a French magazine—it says something about its Carte Detene, which brings down the round-trip price of a Paris-Nice ticket from 2,170 F to 1,040 F ($362 to $173)—quite a savings.

- Delta has a fabulous nonstop flight from New York to Nice, which is superb for getting to the Riviera or if you are driving into Provence or any southern destination, but there are a few caveats. During the summer season, this flight is so popular that it is often full or blacked out for upgrades with frequent flyer mileage. Even out of season, this flight can jam up months before departure, so get your reservations in as soon as possible.

    Delta also serves Paris from numerous U.S. gateway cities. You can connect from Paris to other parts of France on different airlines, by train, or in your little ole rental car.

- If you plan to travel by cashing in your frequent flyer miles, note that during the off-season various airline programs discount their mileage. I was just offered two economy tickets to Europe on Delta for 70,000 miles (the regular price for one ticket is 50,000 miles). My American Airlines bulletin had a list of specific cities with sale- priced tickets (mileage sale, that is) and Brussels—a suburb of Paris as far as I am concerned—was one of the sale cities.

- If you think you'll just book in one airport and out another and pick up easy or inexpensive transport between cities, I beg you to think twice and to read the "Getting Around France" section below. France isn't a very big country, but it's plenty big when it comes to driving or taking the train from Nice to Paris or Lyon to Bordeaux or Marseilles to Biarritz. And it's plenty expensive when it comes to buying a one-way plane ticket between cities. Try every trick you can think of when you price fares. Often buying a round-trip ticket with a Saturday night stay and throwing away one portion of the ticket is the least expensive plan.

- Low-cost airlines keep trying to make it in the big bad world of commercial fare wars and competition; many of them quickly go out of business. Others are cheap but offer no-frills flights with way too many thrills. Still, **CityBird** has low-cost flights from the United States to Brussels, and both **Tower** and **Air Europa** serve Paris.

From the United Kingdom

Travel from Great Britain to France has always been a breeze; the opening of the Chunnel has made it even breezier. This is the case not for the obvious reason, but because of the demand factor: Airlines and ferries are now engaged in price wars and promotional deals geared to woo travelers away from the new convenient train services, Le Shuttle and Eurostar, and both are booked through Eurostar, 1-800-RAILEUROPE. With all these deals, the public has more and more options, and price possibilities, for easy or inexpensive (or both) connections from the United Kingdom.

Furthermore, if you buy a BritFrance train pass from **BritRail** (☎ 800/677-8585), you get a major discount on your Eurostar ticket or tickets. (I paid $118 for a first-class ticket that would have normally cost $150.)

The Chunnel offers two types of service: Eurostar, which is regular passenger service on a deluxe train, and Le Shuttle, which offers you the opportunity of driving your car (or rental car) right to France. Several car-rental companies even have packages that allow you to rent your car in Britain and drop it off in France.

There are three kinds of service on the passenger train, at three different prices: economy, first, and premium. There are also promotional fares, especially in winter. I recently bought a phone card that entitled me to a discount coupon for Eurostar!

If you are traveling to a few destinations in continental Europe, look into the British Airways (BA) Airpass, which is actually a series of discounted coupons based on a zone system.

If you're into collecting mileage points, you may want to book your tickets based on mileage promotions. My BA Executive Report sent me a notice that I could earn triple mileage points on intra-European flights from the United Kingdom to France or Germany (in Club Europe seats, mind you).

BA's low-cost airline is called **Go** and Virgin has **Virgin Express,** which serves Nice as well as Brussels. You may have to call overseas to get fare quotes from these carriers, or go online.

From Other European Locales

Using a point of entry outside of France, even for mainly French travel, is also attractive if your trip includes some other international destinations or if you are bargain hunting and like the looks of some of the Swissair, British Airways, Sabena, Iberia, Alitalia, or Lufthansa deals and promotions.

With most French cities, you have to go to a travel hub to get to the United States anyway. Don't take it for granted that Paris is your best hub. From Nice to the United States, you don't have to use the Paris axis—try Sabena via Brussels or on KLM via Amsterdam. KLM is in a partnership with Northwest Airlines. New airline partnerships, merges, consolidations, and alliances can make combination routes easier and less expensive; this is especially true if you are trying to get in and out of an American gateway city that is not New York.

GETTING AROUND FRANCE

By Plane

Air InterEurope has some fabulous promotions for Americans, including two types of passes: one for

The Regions of France

multiple trips within France and one that allows you to use the pass for up to 30 days and allows four flights within France and two flights outside of France. For a cost of about $500 each, these passes are a sensational value. For reservations in the United States, call Air France at ☎ 800/237-2747.

As with the British Airways system, each pass actually consists of a series of discounted coupons. You must buy a minimum of three coupons; each coupon is good for one connecting flight. The price of the coupons can depend on the time of year, the distance flown, or what type of promotional schemes are available. Air France and Air InterEurope have a promotional rate of around $99 per coupon through a program called Euroflyer. Euroflyer coupons are only sold in conjunction with an Air France transatlantic ticket.

Air France also has air passes for unlimited travel that work much like train passes. For about $330, you can get Le France Pass, which will allow you any seven flights in a 1-month period. Again, passes can only be bought in conjunction with an Air France transatlantic ticket.

In conjunction with Hertz, Air France also offers a fly-drive package for travel within France that includes an Air France air pass and a few days of car rental.

Student and youth passes are also available.

A handful of small regional carriers have also recently sprung into being. They specialize in getting you to and from smaller cities in and around France while avoiding Paris connections. The major cities served are Bordeaux, Nice, Marseille, Strasbourg, and Toulouse. But getting to other cities can be easy and cheap too: I just bought a round-trip ticket from Nice to Lyon on Air France for $132, a very good deal in France and possibly less than train fare.

Also note that it costs less to fly on certain days of the week, and other airlines also offer all sorts of promotions. Look through French magazines and newspapers even if you can't read French; if you see a travel ad with good prices get your hotel concierge to translate.

Le Round-Trip Trick

Very often it costs less to purchase a round-trip ticket (with a Saturday night stay) and simply discard the unused portion of the ticket, since one-way fares can be so high.

And while we're trading secrets here, here's another one if you are flying into Paris. The airfare to Paris from Nice via either of the two Paris airports is the same. *But* it's really not the same, since taxi fare to these airports differs by about $30 to $50! Book yourself out of Orly, and you'll get there faster and save money to boot. Also note that many of the small regional airlines don't use the bigger airports—make sure you know which airport your flight departs from.

By Car

Dreaming of driving all over France with your honey? What a nice dream. To keep it from being a nightmare, you might want to check out a few facts, like how many marriages have been saved by train passes. Seriously though, folks, driving in France can be fun. My husband and I had a bad journey once, but my last trip, during which I drove myself, was fabulous.

Car rentals that are arranged in the United States and are prepaid in U.S. dollars are far cheaper than any on-the-spot rentals you can arrange in France. All the major car-rental agencies have deals for day-, week-, or month-long stays that are competitive.

I've found that Kemwel's plan—which uses Citer in France—is the best deal. Every time we've used them, we've been thrilled. They do have a 3-day minimum, but don't let that slow you down; sometimes their 3-day minimum is less money than 1 day with another firm!

Renault Eurodrive (☎ 800/221-1052) has an excellent program in 27 European countries, though I've never tested it myself because I love Kemwel so much. Also note that this plan caters to longer rentals with plans beginning at 17 days. Note that you can order a cell phone to go with the car rental; it costs 25 F ($4.20) per day and then 5 F (85¢) per minute for calls within France—obviously more for calls outside of France.

Be sure to check out drop-off fees carefully. Hertz has cut drop-off fees between major European cities to a mere $55. This is a vast improvement. Kemwel has no drop-off fee for cars returned anyplace within France. However, Kemwel does have a drop-off fee between countries, so if you picked up your car in Nice and returned it in Brussels, your drop-off fee would be four times higher than that offered by Hertz.

Also find out what perks you get with the rental. Budget provides drivers with complimentary

WorldClass Budget Savings Books with discount coupons inside. They also publish driving routes and directions to take with you on your assorted itineraries across France. Kemwel sometimes offers phone cards with $25 international phone credit to use when calling home from abroad. Hertz offers what it calls Affordable Phone rates that come with a free one-class upgrade in France.

Here are some other hints: Don't assume that mileage is unlimited, that your car has automatic transmission, or that the price quoted includes tax or value-added tax (VAT). Ask and compare. Do not assume you and your luggage will fit into a Type A car. Or even a Type B. Make sure you get the help line number for the country or regions where you will be driving, and find out if there is English-language help available.

Picking up rental cars at major French airports (and returning them, as well) can be easier than using car return offices at local French train stations. Much easier.

Finding the train station in a major French city can ruin your vacation. Note that the bigger the city, the more train stations it has. The bigger the city, the more parts of town you have to drive through to get to the train station, the more one-way streets and chances to get lost, and the more stress. In one city, we actually hired a taxi driver whom we followed to the train station.

Avis currently holds a lease with the train stations in France, so Avis is the only car-rental agency actually in train stations. This means that you just may go nuts finding the place to return your car when you think it's in the train station—and the U.S. arm of the agency has told you it's in the train station—but, in fact, it's only near the train station.

If you need the car for 3 weeks or more, consider a lease package, which actually can be less expensive than renting. Kemwel has a lease plan, as does Renault.

When you pick up your car in France, do not congratulate yourself if you are upgraded to a larger

Car-Rental Companies at a Glance

Avis	☎ 800/331-1084
Budget	☎ 800/527-0700
Europcar	☎ 800/CAR-EUROPE
Eurodollar	☎ 800/800-6000
Hertz	☎ 800/654-3001
Kemwel	☎ 800/678-0678
Renault Eurodrive	☎ 800/221-1052

car free of charge. The larger the car, the less easily it will make the corners in medieval towns.

In order to drive in France, you need a few maps—both the very detailed kind and the big overview kind. My friend Pascale-Agnes says that no map is worth buying save Michelin because they are updated every year (spend the money for the most current one) and have the newest auto routes marked. Since more and more autoroutes open every year, there can be dramatic changes from year to year.

You should also learn what the basic pictograms mean ("Honey, what does that sign with the little line through it mean?"). Picking up a few French phrases, such as *cedez le passage* (yield), won't hurt you either.

When driving in France, consider traveling with a teenager, a graduate of MIT, or a mechanical genius. We had difficulty adapting to the fact that our brand-new Citroen had a computer code needed to start it and only our teenage son could remember what to do. (I learned it! I learned it!)

There are fly-drive packages that include airline tickets and car rental and fly-train-drive packages that include airfare, a certain number of days of train travel, and car rental. With this second package, you can use the train to get out to the countryside and then pick up the car for the good stuff and the wonderful back roads. These packages always cost less when arranged in the United States.

Parking is almost never included in the price of a hotel room, even a hotel in the boonies. In Cannes, parking through a major hotel costs 100 F ($17) or more a night; in Bordeaux, it's a mere 50 F ($8.50).

Speaking of parking, it is virtually impossible to do so in France. Should you be so lucky as to find a space, there are different types of spaces with different systems for paying. Make sure you understand the rules and the systems (see chapter 5).

By Train

If you don't want to worry too much about details, you can buy a train pass for France, for Britain and France together, or for any variation or combination of European countries in different types of time frames. If it's Tuesday, this must be Belgium . . . or something like that.

If you're like me and can't stand the thought of being cheated or not getting your money's worth, you need to understand a few tricks about these train passes.

Train passes are incredibly convenient and easy to use. That ease may be worth dollars and cents to you. I've learned to never knock convenience, even if you have to pay for it.

French train passes usually include the needed supplements for TGV (high-speed train) travel. I mention this because general Eurail passes and some other country passes do not include supplements, or they have conductors who like to gyp tourists by asking for extra supplements, so it is a pleasure to not have to worry about this in France.

Train passes only equal their cost or save you money if you use them on long hauls or if you plan your travels carefully. Having a train pass good for 5 days of travel is downright stupid if your travels are all day trips from Paris or short hops to places such as Versailles, Chartres, Reims, or even Lyon. The train pass costs far more than the individual legs would cost if you just walked into a French train station (or travel agent) and bought the tickets.

If you do plan to use a train pass for day trips and short hops, a second-class ticket is less money than a first-class ticket and usually offers all the comforts you need. First-class tickets are worth the difference in price if you are traveling a great distance, if you have a lot of luggage, or if you need extra isolation from the insults of the real world.

If you are undecided as to which offers better value, a train pass or a few single-leg tickets, try to get some idea of the train fares on big-haul trips.

Note: Train passes and/or train tickets in France pay for passage but do not guarantee a seat! If you're smart, you'll make a seat reservation for every single train trip you take. Smarter yet, you'll do this in France, not in the United States. You pay an additional fee for reservations, but this fee is dramatically less within France. Reservations in the United States cost $10 each. Reservations in France cost about $3.50 each, depending on the time of day and the class of train you are booking. You may change a reservation for free (as many times as you want) before the departure time of the reservation you are holding. The concierge of any good hotel can get the reservations for you. Reservations are required for all TGV and other high-speed trains.

I have traveled by train in France using both methods: I have bought my ticket in France and I have bought my ticket ahead of time in the United States. While it's easier to buy the ticket in the United States, it's also more expensive. Again, the amount you pay cannot accurately be calculated until you average in stress factors, your abilities in French, and your basic travel savvy and/or survival skills.

My rule of thumb is pretty simple: If I am on a very involved trip with lots of travel, much luggage, and a lot of time pressure, I travel first class and I book in the United States, either through **BritRail** (☎ 800/677-8585), for combined Britain/France travel, or through my travel agent, who gets the tickets via **Rail Europe** (☎ 800/438-7245). If the timing is tight and I am very busy, I also make the reservations in the United States, even though the deal is pretty outrageous: You are charged $10 per reservation, plus a $10 mailing fee, plus a $10 purchase protection fee. This is $30 for something that would normally cost you $3.50 in France.

For trips that are more involved than simple day trips, I pick up the tickets a day before travel. I also take time to check out the train station so that I can see where handcarts are, where taxis arrive and depart, and what the general layout of the station is.

I almost missed a train in Lyon once because I didn't check out the station beforehand and arrived only to discover that this particular station has no handcarts because of its architectural style. Furthermore, porters are hard to come by at this station. If you have more than one suitcase, you can miss your train while looking for someone to help you. You may not find this amusing.

If you are spending the night on the train, even with a train pass, you pay an additional fee for a bed (*wagons lits*) or a bunk (*couchette*). A bed usually costs about $125 more, and there is a huge difference between a wagon lit and a couchette; don't learn the hard way (see chapter 5).

Now then, here's the part I know you are wondering about. If you are traveling alone in a *wagons lits,* will you get the whole cabin to yourself or will you be booked with a total stranger? Total stranger it is.

Finally, no matter what type of ticket you use for a train in France, make sure you *composter* (validate) your ticket before you get on the train. There is a hefty fine for not doing so and playing dumb American will not get you out of having to pay it.

Composter is such a perfect verb for this act that it is hard to translate—hmmm, I guess it means "punch your ticket with an electronic hitching post." To do so, note that all tickets or reservation cards have a magnetic strip on the back of them. See that electronic post by the entry to each train platform? It looks like a modern hitching post. Place the ticket, with the magnetic strip up, into the slot the only way it fits. The machine will automatically chomp on your ticket and spit it out. An electronic nick has been punched out of your ticket, and you have now been accounted for. Congratulations, you have composted.

By Bus

While I haven't considered traveling around France à la Greyhound, regional buses are a great option in places such as the south of France, where the cities aren't very far apart and the buses are scenic, cheap, and frequent. For example, consider taking the bus when traveling from Nice to Cannes, or from Avignon to Tarascon. Also note that there is no train service between St. Raphael and St. Tropez, so a bus is a handy idea there.

Also consider getting to airports by bus. If you can handle it, this will save you a lot of money, especially in the Nice area, where the taxis from the Nice airport to nearby cities are outrageously expensive. I'd explain why they are so expensive, but I might end up with a pair of cement Charles Jourdan shoes.

By Boat

Be it cruise ship, yacht, or barge, there's no better way to get around France, because you don't have to park the sucker yourself and you aren't in a train station looking for a porter or a handcart.

I have developed a travel rule that states that the amount of pleasure a specific destination in France gives you is directly proportional to how difficult it is to find a parking space or how bad the traffic jams are. When you arrive by boat, you usually arrive in—or are taken by the boat to—the cute part of town. I call it The Cute.

Antibes can be anyone's favorite city in France if they arrive by yacht. You step off the pier into The

Cute. Try driving around like an idiot looking for The Cute and then finding a parking space near The Cute. Ditto St. Tropez. You can't imagine how much nicer your trip to key tourist cities will be if you arrive by boat.

Aside from the cruise ships that regularly call in the south of France, some companies also offer a regular schedule of French Atlantic ports of call. I made the following trip with Silversea—from Lisbon to London with four stops in France. Yummy yum yum. This is a great way to see a lot of the smaller towns and special places you might not have taken the time to drive to. And when the chef from Le Cordon Bleu comes onboard to cook, oh my.

Also note that there are various barge trips around France that give you the benefit of arriving by water and often even eliminate the crowd problem by choosing ports that are less congested than Antibes and St. Tropez. Some 200,000 people per year barge around France.

Die-hard shoppers please note that some of these barge trips specialize in antiques and plan journeys so that you barge all night and shop all day. They also arrange to ship home your furniture. These trips are most often in Burgundy, where prices on furniture are the least expensive.

The barge trips move slowly, often feature a good chef, and are almost always sold as inclusive packages with air, land, meals, and so on. Shore excursions and tips are extra.

For barge trips, try **Abercrombie & Kent** (☎ 800/323-7308); **European Waterways** (☎ 800/217-4447); **French Country Waterways** (☎ 800/222-1236); **JET Vacations** (☎ 800/JET-0999); or **Kemwel** (☎ 800/678-0678). **Le Boat** (☎ 800/922-0291) has an incredibly fancy brochure that not only features barge trips, but also offers an entire catalogue of yachts to rent.

I studied many barge brochures and discovered that some companies offer specific tours that are less expensive if you buy the barge portion directly from the supplier and pay for your own round-trip airfare. Run the numbers with several firms if price is a consideration.

PHONING AROUND

Rather than use any of the U.S. telephone company direct dial deals, which have fees attached to them, I simply buy a French phone card at any Tabac or news kiosk and use the pay phones, even to call the United States. Dial 00 for an international line and then the country code (1 = United States; 44= United Kingdom; 377 = Monaco, and so on) and then the phone number, with area code if you are calling the United States.

HOTEL DEALS IN FRANCE

Here are a few tips:

- The easiest way to book hotel rooms on a multidestination trip to France is through any of the hotel associations or chains that have hotels all over France or in the cities where you are going in France or Europe. One phone call can get it all done.
- The best way to get a deal on a hotel room is to either contact the general manager of the hotel directly and ask him or her for the best price or to book through the chains and associations, asking if they have prices frozen in U.S. dollars and/ or any promotional deals that offer extras or discounts. That failing, sometimes calling the hotel directly (once you know the best offer from their reservation system) will get you a better rate.
- The extras can be anything from full breakfast (a better value than continental breakfast), to a free night for every 3 nights you pay for (or every 5 nights or 7 nights or whatever), to airport transfers. American Express is very aggressive these days about getting its hotel partners to offer perks

to guests who book and pay with American Express cards. Many extras, such as airport transfers, are offered through AmEx's programs. Ask.

- Do not expect your travel agent to know every trick in the book or to be responsible for saving you money or getting you the best possible deal. Travel agents can be terrific—use a good one—but be willing to do some legwork yourself by using on-line information services and toll-free numbers and looking at brochures (one picture may save you from a mistake).

- On-line services are getting more and more sophisticated. Sure you can get price information, but many hotels also give you a tour of their rooms through photos on-line.

Hidden Hotel Deals

Because hotel chains are run by big corporations, confusion and misinformation can occur between hotels and their associates, or between your travel agent and the hotel reservations toll-free switchboard. For that reason, I suggest you consult several sources for information on the best hotel deals and clip ads from newspapers and magazines so you can refer to specific offers.

Here's an example of a hidden hotel deal I recently encountered:

I was booking a room for my husband and myself for a few days in Cannes in August. I know that no hotel manager will cut a deal in August, because he's going to sell every room he's got and then some. I therefore asked the general manager of the Noga Hilton, in Cannes, if the Hilton World of Summer Savings program was the best possible deal. At \$249 per night (advertised in *The New York Times*), this sounded pretty good to me for an in-season price. Since Inter-Continental was advertising The Carlton at \$292, I thought \$249 sounded like a fine bargain.

Mais non, said the GM, who suggested I book a Cannes Summer Fun Package. At \$268 per night (plus $50 per night supplement for the month of August), I would be paying $328 per night but getting two full breakfasts each day and two chaise longues on the private beach (which normally sell for $25 per chaise per day).

Because the $249 rate does not include tax and service, the real Hilton World Summer of Savings rate would be about $275 per night. With the Cannes Summer Fun package, I'd be spending almost $10 a night less and saving about $90 a day on breakfast and chaise longues. Even with the August supplement, I'd be saving money.

In short, the bargain was hidden, as are most bargains in France.

It can be almost impossible to compare the confusing and often conflicting hotel offers that are out there. You may have to go directly to France to get information. The bottom line is ask questions, and then ask more questions.

Hotel Chains in France

Almost every hotel, no matter what chain, has a promotional rate for weekends. Paris hotels usually discount July and August, while resort hotels may add surcharges for summer or for August.

If you are traveling with children, modern hotels are usually bigger and will have more beds in a room as well as more space. We stayed in several hotels with lofts so that three or four could indeed sleep in one room. It is harder to find a château room that fits a family of four.

Here is a list of the major chains; specific hotel recommendations can be found in each of the destination chapters. Note that Paris has been invaded by the big American chains in the last year or two.

CONCORDE HOTELS I have now stayed in almost all of the Concorde Hotels (☎ 800/888-4747) across the south of France. Maybe we just got lucky, but all of our hotels—and I booked eight different ones—were super. Some were the stuff of which dreams are made. It is a little unsettling to go from one Concorde Hotel to the next day after day, since the styles vary so much. But I don't think I've found an easier-to-work-with association of hotels with a consistently high quality of product.

To be fair, along with the quality of the actual product is the quality of the service I got on the telephone. My reservations agent not only knew her stuff, but she explained various nuances in the deals and how to make sure I saved the most money.

HILTON   There are only five Hilton hotels in France (☎ 800/HILTONS), so Hilton makes more sense if you are visiting France and the surrounding area: Brussels, Barcelona, and Geneva. Indeed, if you look at a map, Geneva is almost in France and is a practical solution for some overnight visits.

Hilton's best service to the public is that it delivers a product you can trust at a fair price. Better still, it often has sensational deals frozen in dollars. Its Paris hotel at under $200 a night is a steal. You can also get London-Paris and Paris-Cannes package prices and even Eurostar tickets with hotel packages in any of the three major Eurostar hub cities (London, Paris, and Brussels). Hilton also has a few hotels at airports that are good for layovers.

INTER-CONTINENTAL   One of my secrets for being able to afford to stay at a luxury hotel in Paris is the Inter-Continental chain (☎ 800/327-0200). While it doesn't have a lot of hotels in France, if you are only going to Paris and to Cannes, you may be quite happy with one phone call.

LEADING HOTELS OF THE WORLD   This is my main squeeze and frequently the only phone number I need anywhere in the world (☎ 800/223-6800; www.lhw.com; e-mail: hrihotel@idt.net). It has some overlap with Concorde; several of my Concorde choices are also members of Leading Hotels of the World. If prices are past your budget, check out its corporate plan.

PRIMA HOTELS   Prima is a small international chain offering luxury properties of a more intimate scale for a little less money than Leading Hotels

(☎ 800/447-7462). In St. Paul de Vence it has the Mas d'Artingy, a swoon-for villa; there are five famous hotels in Paris.

RELAIS & CHÂTEAUX   Its catalog of fine châteaux hotels with wonderful chefs is a dream come true in itself (☎ **212/856-0115**; fax 800/ 860-4930; www.relaischateaux.fr). I've never gone wrong with one of its 415 properties and consider the catalog to be one of my bibles, especially when planning a driving trip through Provence or the French countryside.

SOFITEL This is a major French chain, owned by Accor, and it has hotels all over the world, but particularly in France (☎ **888-422-2332**). I'm especially keen on its three- and four-star hotels, which were small older hotels that have been taken over, redone, and offer good value for money. There are several in Paris with excellent shopping locations—near the Arc de Triomphe, near rue St. Honoré, and on rue Scribe (it's the Hotel Scribe in fact, quite a grande dame), a block from Galleries Lafayette. For reservations and information call toll free 888-422-2332.

ROMANTIC PROPERTIES   This is an association of hotels organized by E&M Associates in New York, which offers combinations of hotels and packages in any number of cities, all chosen for romantic impact (☎ **800-223-9832**). It represents hotels in France, Italy, and the Caribbean. All are of the Relais & Châteaux type, although there are big hotels in Paris that I know and approve of (Raphael and Regina, for example).

Chapter Three

. . . .

MONEY MATTERS

CURRENCY EXCHANGE

. . . .

Whether we're talking dollars to francs or dollars to euros or francs to euros, the bottom line is still the same: To get the best rate of exchange, use a credit card rather than cash, unless you happen to have bought local currency at a better rate than the one existing when you are spending.

Here are some other tips:

- Keep watching your credit card bills after you return home. Watch for accurate charges and refunds. Don't be alarmed if it takes a while for smaller towns to post your billings with your credit card company—it can get quite laid back in the French countryside. I bought a dress one May in Galeries Lafayette in Nice; it appeared on my January bill the next year. Now there's a float.

- I buy traveler's checks in French francs at my local AAA Motor Club and therefore do not pay a fee for cashing checks or exchanging money once in France. I am tied to a rate of exchange, of course, but I usually find that to be a plus.

- When figuring out how much anything costs, divide by the rate you paid for the money, *not by what the newspaper says the bank rate is*. The bank rate is meaningless unless you own the bank.

- Prepay for anything and everything possible in U.S. dollars. If you do prepay, make sure you have the vouchers and the paperwork with you.
- Also, if the dollar gains strength after you prepay, don't beat yourself up over the fact. Let it go; have a good time anyway.
- Avoid those cute foreign machines that look like ATMs but ask you to insert your cash (meaning U.S. dollars or whatever you have on you from the last country you visited) in order to receive the local currency. The commission can be outrageous!

  I once needed money for the grocery store and inserted a $20 bill into one of those automatic change machines. I got back $10 worth of local currency and a receipt explaining that I had paid a $10 commission for the privilege. Ouch! Know an ATM from a change machine!

- Do use real ATM machines as a simple way to obtain cash. Your bank will charge a fee (usually $1 or so per pop), but this is still a good way to get a very good rate and handy cash.

YOU & THE EURO

As we go to press there is still much debate about what exactly will happen when the euro is fully launched. It's now thought that the currency will be so strong that all world markets will be forced to realign, which will naturally affect the value of the U.S. dollar, sending it down. Start shopping now if you want to save money.

Here are some of the basics. The European Union has voted to be represented by a single currency, the European Monetary Unit (EMU), to be called the euro. As of 1999 all European computers must carry this symbol on their keyboards. The symbol for the euro will look like this: €

Exchange Rates for the Euro

COUNTRY	CURRENCY	DOLLAR RATE	EURO RATE
Austria	Schilling	$0.08	13.91
Belgium	Franc	0.0271	40.78
EU	ECU	1.1	-
Finland	Mark	0.1841	6.01
France	Franc	0.1666	6.63
Germany	Mark	0.558	1.98
Ireland	Punt	1.4058	0.80
Italy	Lira	0.000566	1958.0
Luxembourg	Franc	0.0271	40.78
Netherlands	Guilder	0.495	2.23
Portugal	Escudo	0.00545	202.72
Spain	Peseta	0.00658	168.20

*Keep in mind, these exchange rates will fluctuate. Make sure to check the current exchange rates before you leave for your trip.

On January 1, 1999, the euro became the official currency in many of the 15 member nations, and all countries must list prices in euros and in local currency. The rate of exchange has already been fixed and follows below in chart form. For 2 years, the existing national currencies will be accepted along with euros. Thereafter, *adios* to the old and *bienvenue* to the new.

Those travelers who stash currencies (I personally have a United Nations worth of coins in a desk drawer) will be able to take their funds to any bank in any EU country and exchange for Euros in the year 2001. If you find this annoying, think of how much easier your travels will be when you no longer have to keep changing money.

ATM MACHINES

· ·

Before you leave home, ask your bank or bank card company about automated-teller machines (ATMs) in foreign destinations; check to see if your personal identification number (PIN) will work on a foreign machine. You will get an excellent rate of exchange with these machines. MasterCard publishes a free booklet on shopping with your ATM card (☎ 800/999-5136).

It is believed that in the next few years new ATMs will give you the choice of receiving money in local currency or euros until local currency becomes unwieldy and only euros are used.

DÉTAXE

· ·

If you are making a big purchase or a series of smaller purchases that may add up, go for a value-added tax (VAT) refund.

VAT is called TVA in France and it's a whopping 20.6%. You are entitled to a refund of about 15% to 18% if you spend 1,200 F ($200) (or more, *mais oui*). The refund is called *détaxe*.

Some stores let you accumulate receipts and spend the 1,200 F over a 6-month period; others want it spent at one time. Since 1,200 F is about $200, you certainly wouldn't mind a little bit of a refund. It may take a little thought, or merely a few minutes in Hermès, but take the time to ask for the refund form; then do the paperwork and process your claim at the airport as you leave the EU.

The refund is only granted to visitors who live outside of the EU and who take the goods out of the country within 3 months of purchase. The goods must be shown to customs officials when you depart the EU; if you travel beyond France to another EU country before returning to the United States, you claim the refund in the last country you visit—even if you didn't buy anything there.

While the refund can be given to you in cash at the airport, you will probably lose money on the exchange rate. The best way to get a refund is to have it credited directly to your credit card. Mark the appropriate box on the refund forms.

Major French department stores have offices that handle the refund papers at the time of your purchase. Outside of Paris, retail staff may not speak English and may not be familiar with the paperwork. Allow at least 20 minutes in a department store for the paperwork; longer in summer.

Stores that sell luxury goods (including perfumeries) are far more familiar with the refund process and can usually supply the papers—and a lesson in how to fill them out, if needed—in a minute or two.

Please note, however, that the détaxe requirement is 1,200 F ($200) net, which means, for example, that if you are shopping at a perfume store that grants tourists a 25% discount, you must spend around 1,700 F ($283) before you qualify for the refund.

Détaxe Warnings

You may convince yourself to make a purchase based on the fact that you think—or the salesperson convinces you—that you will get a 20% refund on the tax-back scheme. This is rarely true. At the big department stores they tell you up front that all you get back is 13% because of the fee charged for doing the paperwork; other firms aren't as honest. It's very rare to get the full refund!

TIPPING TIPS

. . . .

The price of tipping in France has gone up, especially in Paris and resort destinations. Tips are related to the local value of the currency, not what they translate into in dollars. Because times have been tough in France, people are more dependent on tips and in some cases the amount expected for a tip has doubled in the last 2 years.

- I tip 10 F ($1.70) per suitcase to the bellhop who handles the luggage.
- I round up my fare in a taxi to add on a few francs as a tip, but I don't give a percentage. I never give less than 5 F (85¢).
- I give 5 F (85¢) for hailing a taxi or 10 F ($1.70), depending on weather conditions and the change I have on me.
- I give 5% more at the hairdresser so that the total tip has been 20% (the 15% that's included plus my additional 5% cash).
- In restaurants, I always leave extra cash because I don't think the waiters get any of the inclusive stuff. I usually leave 50 F ($8.50) in cash as an additional tip (on a dinner bill for two people); if it's a seriously fancy place and the service has been stellar, it's 100 F ($17). If it's just a snack or a lunch or not a big deal, 20 F ($3.30) will do. On a cup of coffee or something small, 3 F to 5 F ($50¢ to 85¢).

U.S. CUSTOMS & DUTIES TIPS

To make your reentry into the United States as smooth as possible, follow these tips:

- Know the rules and stick to them!
- Don't try to smuggle anything.
- Be polite and cooperative (up until the point when they ask you to strip anyway).

Remember:

- You are currently allowed to bring in $400 worth of merchandise per person, duty free. Before you leave the United States, verify this amount with one of the U.S. Customs offices. Each member of the family is entitled to the deduction; this includes infants. You may pool within a family.

- You pay a flat 10% duty on the next $1,000 worth of merchandise.
- Duties thereafter are based on a product-type basis. They vary tremendously per item, so think about each purchase and ask storekeepers about U.S. duties.
- The head of the family, who need not be male, can make a joint declaration for all family members. Whomever is the head of the family, however, should take the responsibility for answering any questions the Customs officers may ask. Answer questions honestly, firmly, and politely. Have receipts ready, and make sure they match the information on the landing card. Don't be forced into a story that won't wash under questioning. If they catch you in a little lie, you'll be labeled as a fibber, and they'll tear your luggage apart.
- Have the Customs registration slips for your personally owned goods in your wallet or easily available. If you wear a Cartier watch, be able to produce the registration slip. If you cannot prove that you took a foreign-made item out of the country with you, you may be forced to pay duty on it.
- The unsolicited gifts you mailed from abroad do not count in the $400-per-person rate. If the value of the gift is more than $50, you pay duty when the package comes into the country. Remember, it's only one unsolicited gift per person for each mailing. Don't mail to yourself.
- Do not attempt to bring in any illegal food items—dairy products, meats, fruits, or vegetables (coffee is okay). Generally speaking, if it's alive, it's verboten. I also shouldn't need to tell you that it's tacky to bring in drugs and narcotics.
- Antiques must be 100 years old to be duty free. Provenance papers will help (so will permission to export the antiquity, since it could be an item of national cultural significance). Any bona fide

work of art is duty free whether it was painted 50 years ago or just yesterday; the artist need not be famous.

- Dress for success. People who look like hippies get stopped at Customs more than average folks. Women who look like a million dollars, who are dragging their fur coats, have first-class tags on their luggage, and carry Gucci handbags, but declare they have bought nothing, are equally suspicious.

- Laws regarding ivory are new and improved—for the elephants, anyway. You may not import any ivory into the United States. Antique ivory must have provenance papers to be legally imported.

- The amount of Customs allowance is expected to change or be modified into a different type of declaration. If you are a big shopper, check before you leave to see if there's any news.

Chapter Four

. . . .

SHOPPING STRATEGIES

Any shopping spree in France needs to be as organized as the assault on the Normandy beaches, simply because the truth of the price structure in France is not what you think it is.

Also, if you are driving, France may not be any bigger than you think it is, but it's still a little larger than Texas. Paris and Nice are not around the corner from each other. Distances can be farther than you think, so your trip needs to be planned in advance and thought through in terms of dining, shopping, and hospitality opportunities.

You may also be going to so many places in France that you truly don't know where to invest your money or when it's time to pounce. For example, I was recently in the south of France with one of my Born to Shop Tours, and this multibillionaire tycoon takes me aside and says, "Suze, how can you really honestly bring us to the south of France and tell us to buy anything here. There aren't any bargains in the south of France."

Wrong!

I've now done careful price comparisons all over France and can honestly tell you that Cannes is not only the shopping capital of the south of France, but it is the bargain capital of the tourist trail. Prices are raised artificially in all resort cities, but prices in Cannes—where there is a substructure of real life—are often 10% to 20% lower on the same merchandise than elsewhere in France. You think you're going to tool around Provence and fill up your car with cute little treasures? You're going to find them for less in Cannes and the surrounding area.

You think you're going to go to flea markets and antique vendors in the middle of nowhere in France and pay far less than you would in Paris? You will. But the prices in Antibes are 20% less than the prices on l'îsle sur la Sorgue, a village I bet you've never even heard of that is nonetheless famous for its weekend flea market and antique-dealer secrets. The prices in the flea market in Lyon, *mon Dieu,* are they ever cheap too.

For the most part, France is an expensive country and the cost of living is outrageously high. People come to America to shop; they don't go to Cannes to shop. Every local has a trick to save over the cost of living in France: my girlfriend who lives in Biarritz goes to Spain to do her grocery shopping, and my friend Richard mails me his shopping list so I can send things to him in France.

The shopping in France is tricky. The things to buy are those items that are significantly cheaper than they would be in the United States or those items that just aren't available in the United States (and therefore fall into the I-don't-care-what-it-costs category).

As a general rule, new French designer goods are only a buy if they are on sale and you qualify for the *détaxe* refund, or if you luck out on a special duty-free deal. In fact, depending on the dollar, you may find that French goods cost less in the United States. (Gently worn designer goods can be another story entirely; see chapter 5.)

THE BEST BUYS OF FRANCE

Here's a list of the best buys in France arranged alphabetically by category of goods:

Cosmetics

You'll get the best price possible if you make one giant haul and combine your cosmetic and perfume shopping at one discount shop (not at the airport duty free!) where you get a whopping 40% off the French retail price and meet the requirement for détaxe.

Even if you don't qualify for détaxe, you can get a 10% to 25% discount on French prices in almost any good store in France, and you will save money on certain brands (but not all!). Chanel is one of those brands that offers a savings; my foundation is actually half price when I buy it in France. Many of the best buys, however, are on French brands that aren't available in the United States.

Don't worry if you hear guff about the abolition of duty-free shopping in 1999; this is for travel within EU borders only.

Foodstuff

It's no secret that you can happily eat your way across France. Even if you are on a budget, you can eat quite well by going to the markets and grocery stores for your daily *pique-nique* and for your gift shopping. You needn't have Dijon on your itinerary (poor you) in order to buy mustards—they're available in every supermarket in France for about $3 a jar. Be sure to buy a type that's not easily found in your grocery store at home. I go for Maille's "Provençale" flavor. It's orange, so you can't miss it on the shelf.

Other inexpensive but great items include honey, especially from the south of France and Provence, and *calissons* (sugar-covered almonds), which are easy to pack and cost a mere $3. *Warning:* Make sure the honey is French, not Chinese—this is the latest scandal reported in *Gault Millaut,* the foodie magazine.

If you find yourself in the south of France, olives are a way of life. They also make great gifts because they come in airtight sealed bags for about $3 each. Olive products, such as *tapenade* (see chapter 5), also make for a fabulous gift for the fans back home.

No conversation about olives is complete without telling you to pick up a few cans of local extra-virgin olive oil. They are a little hard to take home, but I do have a few tricks (see chapter 5). Olive oil is a souvenir that keeps on giving until the last drop.

Perfume

Not only is French perfume cheaper in France, but new brands are launched in France usually before they hit the shelves elsewhere, even in the rest of Europe and the United Kingdom. For the person who has everything, a bottle of perfume that isn't yet available in the United States is a unique and special gift. Also note that French perfume is made with potato alcohol, not denatured alcohol, so it wears longer on the skin. Even if there is no price savings, French fragrance is a good buy because of the chemical differences.

THE DOLLAR & THE DOUGHNUT

. . . .

If you happen to fall into one of those black holes during which the dollar is moving around, especially if it happens to be moving down, you may find that prices on French goods are less at home. I once bought a Lacoste shirt for 390 F (at that time, $80 on my AmEx bill). This same shirt sold for $65 at any branch of Saks in the United States.

Even savings on goods that may traditionally be less expensive if bought in France rather than in the United States will even out quickly if the dollar falls below the established rate for that fashion season. A falling dollar will decrease whatever savings you may have garnered to zilch.

Fortunately, this is not an overall rule and doesn't apply to all goods. It very much varies from line to line, so don't cancel your trip to France—just pay attention to prices at home before you leave.

THE MOSCOW RULE OF SHOPPING

· ·

The Moscow Rule of Shopping has been a basic tenet of each edition of every *Born to Shop* guide since the series began. While I very much believe in this concept, and am about to spell it out for those of you who are new to the notion, I must also warn you that I have been shocked to find that prices in France vary so much that if you follow the Moscow Rule of Shopping, you may feel like a fool. I therefore have added the Cannes Contingency (see below).

Now then, if you happen to be shopping in Moscow, even in these enlightened times, you'll note that there is only one concept that pervades the air: Buy it when you see it because it won't be there when you come back.

Likewise, I have always suggested to shoppers that they buy something they love when they see it because they are never really going to get back to that town or that store, and the opportunity will haunt them if they don't pounce. Of course, this policy breaks down on touristy items, which are a dime a dozen, but the basic tenet is a simple one, and I continue to believe in it.

However, throughout the research of this book, I was struck by a few amazing facts:

- Paris is still the shopping and style capital of the world. If your trip ends in Paris, that's where you do your serious shopping. That way you don't have to schlepp everything all over the country with you. However, Paris is more expensive than the provinces for things like shampoo and real-life items. Buy these before you get to Paris.
- Provence is so incredibly overpriced that unless you don't care about price tags, you are

overpaying if you buy anything there (see the Cannes Contingency below).

- Outside of Paris, do your shopping in the south of France, preferably in the Nice-Cannes-Grasse triangle, which includes Antibes.
- Regional specialties should be bought locally and preferably from the maker or the factory, except in Provence (this includes the outrageously over-priced Souleiado factory, which I suggest you boycott).

THE CANNES CONTINGENCY

I'm the last person in the world who thought Cannes would offer bargains. If I hadn't been researching this book over a period of years, I would think that what happened to me when comparing prices there was an anomaly. It does not appear to be so.

We all know that Cannes is the style center and shopping headquarters of the Riviera. We all realize that when I tell you there are designer resale shops and stores that sell big-name designer clothes with-out labels at a discount, it makes sense considering the profile of the city of Cannes.

What I found absolutely shocking is that prices in Cannes and the surrounding area turned out to be basically 20% less than in Provence for many categories of other goods. Okay, a minibar Coke in Cannes is 25 F ($4.20) and a Coke on the street in Avignon is 15 F ($2.50), but from Baccarat to Souleiado, from antiques to brocante, I found ask-ing prices lower on the Côte d'Azur.

MAGIC MOMENTS

Unless you are willing to pay for the magic of a moment, do your regional shopping with care. Tour-isty items cost more in touristy, honey-pot cities. Real-people items, such as things from the dime store and the drugstore, cost less in the larger provinces.

MY CHEATING HEART

. . . .

Also understand, especially before you head off to France, that some French products are going to cost less in the United States, and some gifts "from France" can actually be purchased in the United States.

Or, if you find yourself in a bind, you can often dash out and buy a French product in the United States and convince someone that you bought it especially for him or her in France.

It just so happens that I give a lot of inexpensive little gifts to various business contacts. On my last trip back from France, I truly didn't buy enough gifts for my assorted friends and obligations. I hurried off to my local discount store, where I found plenty of Christian Dior ties for $13.99.

Likewise, at T.J. Maxx I found Perlier brand bath foam for less than it costs in France.

When you're buying gifts and goods in France, don't pay extra just for having bought it on your trip. Buy it because you love it or you need it or you know someone who will adore the thought. But look before you leap, and don't fret if you have to fill in a few gaps when you get home.

SHOPPING MANNERS

. . . .

Americans are very quick to complain that the French are rude. What few people understand is that, because of numerous cultural differences, we are rude to the French. They are merely reacting to our bad graces.

Shopping manners are especially important. Americans tend to want to be invisible in a store and only want help or attention when they decide they are interested. To the French shopkeeper, you are a guest in his "home"—whether you buy anything or not is secondary.

Therefore, the minute you walk into a French store, you should make eye contact with a person and greet him or her in French and by gender. Not just *"Bonjour"* but *"Bonjour, madame"* or *"Bonjour, monsieur."* When you leave, say your thanks and your good-byes. Anyone can manage this much French.

SHOPPING HOURS

Shopping hours for Paris and for the rest of France are two completely different topics. While hours are discussed in each chapter, the regular rule of thumb for France (not Paris!) is that stores are closed all day on Sunday and on Monday until *après-midi* (that means they open around 2pm or 2:30pm on Monday).

In the summer season, some retail shops in some towns are open on Sunday from early morning until 1pm. You have to ask around to find them.

Outside of Paris, stores traditionally open around 9am, close at noon, and then reopen after lunch around 2pm. The farther south you go, the more relaxed the hours can get.

Paris has more sophisticated business hours. Most stores do not close for lunch in Paris and most are open on Monday mornings. Very little is open on Sunday though, even in Paris.

SUNDAY SHOPPING

As I write the above sentence, my friend Richard Duvauchelle is faxing me an article from *The European* about the changes in Sunday shopping in France. It seems that despite the fact that there are fines from the government, more and more stores are paying the fines just to be open on Sunday because their customers demand the extra shopping hours.

Richard Branson (my other Richard) started some of the brouhaha by opening his two Paris Virgin Megastores on Sunday and by agreeing to pay the fines. He now claims that he does 20% of his business on Sunday, and the volume is almost equal to that on Saturday. So it's not just tourists who want to shop on Sunday!

While there is more and more Sunday retail in Paris (get a look at the Carrousel du Louvre if you want to see Sunday shopping), the provinces are closed except for a pharmacy or two here and there. Flea markets dominate the shopping scene on Sunday outside of Paris. But don't be surprised if laws come along that allow the *hypermarchés* to open on Sunday. In fact, it's my bet that when economic strength comes to France through the euro (make that *if*) and the rest of the European Union allows Sunday shopping, France will loosen up on its blue laws. It took Britain a long time to get to it; France will eventually follow.

SHOPPING SCAMS

· ·

The only times I have ever noticed that someone was trying to cheat me by giving me the wrong change have been in the south of France. In any part of the world where there are a lot of tourists, you have to expect that a small part of the service population will try to take advantage of you, especially if you have a foreign accent. Always count your change and always pay attention.

Chapter Five

· · · · · · · ·

HOW TO BE FRENCH

Okay, you don't really want to be French. You just want to know enough to not make a fool of yourself, to have a good time, and to prevent being cheated, laughed at, or scorned.

While you would have to live in France longer than a week or two to get into the cultural differences and to begin to understand French thinking, you can take my crash course to learn some of the most basic facts of life.

You'll find that French people aren't rude at all, but they live by a series of rules and social codes that are very different from American (and even British) rules and codes. When we don't know their rules, French people are offended—or amused. If they are offended and show it, we assume they are rude.

If you plan to sail through France without interacting with the people, you may do fine. Otherwise, I suggest you *bonne* up.

Below I have composed a brief dictionary of French life and style. It includes some important French lessons, such as how to tell the difference between the menu and the *carte* (among other things).

Once you know how to act you'll be ready to shop, so this chapter also includes an alphabetical rundown of the major French boutiques and chains.

AN ALPHABETICAL GUIDE TO FRENCH
LIFE & STYLE

. . . .

À VOLONTÉ Ever since the recession, this has become a big marketing trend in French restaurants, especially family restaurants—all you can eat. Certain dishes (often the oysters and the chocolate mousse) are priced at a flat rate, and you can just keep shoveling it in.

A/R (ALLER/RETOUR) It means round-trip and is usually written after a price for an airline or train ticket. Do not assume that a one-way fare is half of a round-trip fare.

AUCTIONS Christie's is the world's second largest auction house, doing over 6 billion francs in business last year alone. It has offices in several French cities and handles assorted big-name, big-time auctions. This is the first English auction house to be owned by a Frenchman!

If you prefer the small-country kind of auction or the funky stuff, France has a tradition of accessible auction houses that are not nearly as intimidating as Christie's and Sotheby's. My friend Christian goes to country auctions every weekend and fights with dealers for the best buys in the country. In Paris, all the funky estate business goes to L'Hotel Drouot, which even publishes its own magazine. In Aix, check out Hours de Valaurie Hotel de Ventes, chemin de la Vierge Noire; in Cannes, Isally, 31 bd. d'Alsace. In Marseille, it's Hotel de Ventes Trabo Borde, 19 rue Borde.

Of course, there are other sorts of auctions. Among the most famous is a wine auction held on the third weekend in November in the town square of the medieval town of Beaune, in Burgundy. The annual event, celebrated since 1859, raises funds for the local hospice and serves to set the regional wine prices for that year's harvest. It's a big mob scene of tasting and touring, and you don't have to bid in order to join the party. Call ☎ **03-80-26-21-30** for dates and details.

AUTOROUTE   France is connected by a series of highways that are the closest thing to an American freeway, a British motorway, or a German autobahn. In some cases, the autoroute only offers one lane in each direction, but in most cases the roads are similar to American highways.

Autoroutes are designated by the letter *A* before their route number. They are pay roads, and also can be marked *péage*. The tolls are very steep—it costs about 30 F ($6) to get from Cannes to Nice on the péage. And that's only a 20-minute ride. Tolls may be paid in cash (french francs only) or by credit card.

BCBG (BON CHIC BON GENRE)   It means preppy and is usually used to describe a style of clothing.

BEAUJOLAIS NOUVEAU   A brilliant marketing plan to get people to drink young wine. The new wine is uncorked on the third Thursday of November, usually around the 15th. The exact date, which varies each year to add to the fun, is announced and celebrated throughout France. Festivities begin around 5pm the night before the big day, with the official sale beginning as the clock turns to midnight on the day stores may legally make the first sale.

So, if the third Thursday of November is the 15th, then the party starts on Wednesday the 14th and lasts until midnight, at which time the stores open and the party continues.

The event has become international in the world of spirits and is even big in Paris. It's not unusual to spot *Le Nouveau est Arrivé* signs here and there—even in New York.

BIDET   If Mother told you it was for washing your socks, she lied. Even if Mother told you the truth, she probably didn't tell you how to use it. I mention this because I was shocked at one of the finer details: You stand facing the wall. The rest is pretty basic.

BOURJOIS   Dime-store brand of makeup sold at every Monoprix, Prisunic, and department store in France. The line also has some international distribution and, while not currently available in the United States, it can easily be found in the United Kingdom at Boots.

Not only is the makeup affordable (and less expensive in France than elsewhere), but it possesses its very own secret: Chanel makeup is made in the same factories. There are differences between the two brands, of course, but they aren't as big as the price difference.

BROCANTE   There is an enormous difference between a *brocanteur* and a person who sells antiques, so heads up everyone. An antique dealer sells *antiquités*, which are important pieces from previous times. *Brocante* is junk. It is usually sold at flea markets or during the brocante day at the local *marché*. It is sold by anyone and carries no particular provenance or value.

CAPOTES ANGLAISES   Slang for condoms.

CARRELAGE   French for tile; French for "Stop the car honey, it's time to shop." You'll see this word as you drive around Provence and the south of France.

CARTE   We all know that à la carte means off the menu, or at least that's what it means to an American. To the French, the menu is the list of the set meals for the day, and the carte is the rest of the offerings. In short, what you think is the menu is really the carte!

CENTRE VILLE   It's downtown. Follow that sign. Every now and then it's written as *ville propre*.

CHAMPAGNE   Mere alcohol doesn't thrill me at all. But start singing about the night they invented champagne, and let me sing along, off-key, and explain it all in simple terms.

First, Champagne is a *département* of France, a very particular part of the French map and some very specific real estate. If the grapes aren't grown in this zip code, then the bubbly they make just ain't champagne.

The word has become synonymous with the type of sparkling wine made in the Champagne region, but no wine can actually legally claim to be "champagne" unless the grapes grew to maturation in Champagne. Thus, you have scads of champagnelike drinks that aren't really champagne; they are made with the *méthode champenoise*.

And if you think that's confusing, add to the whole brouhaha the fact that Yves Saint Laurent created a fragrance he named "Champagne" (for the woman who sparkles). The name fizzled in court. It is now illegal for Saint Laurent to use that name for that scent in certain parts of the world. However, because of this, perfume bottles with the name "Champagne" inscribed on them are collectibles already worth some 800 F ($144). Should you want to buy the scent, it is now called simply "Yves Saint Laurent." But any duty-free shop will know what you mean if you ask for "Champagne."

CHARIOT   French word for the luggage handcart at train stations and airports. Sometimes they are free, and sometimes they require a 10 F piece ($1.80).

COCA-COLA   Just ask for *un Coca*. If you're on a budget, forget it. The average price of a Coke in a hotel minibar or a bar in any decent hotel in France is $5 per. You can buy a six-pack of Coke in any grocery in France for about $4, but very few people bring their own Cokes to Sennequir, the leading cafe in St. Tropez.

COMITÉ COLBERT   Organization of luxury-goods makers of France. Many of the firms are centuries old. The organization holds annual events and promotions (in France and in the United States) to extend an understanding of the workmanship involved in luxury goods and why they are worth the price. Any ads or window stickers that refer to membership in this very exclusive club assure you that you are buying only the best France has to offer.

M. Colbert himself made lace in Alençon in the 1660s before rising to more prominence. He brought to France the best lace makers from Venice and Flanders and marketed his lace as the best in the world. Thus, the idea of deluxe was born, and it remains an essential component of French retailing, marketing, style, and pride. For more than 300 years, French generations have been raised to respect the *produit de luxe* and the names that make them. Advertising helps too.

CONDOMS   There is a large and extremely visible campaign to promote the use of condoms in France. Condoms by law must be sold in single units in all pharmacies. They are also sold in machines all over France. Although there are a number of slang words for a condom, the most widely used expression is the proper word, *un préservatif.*

Laboratoire Wyeth France offers a small plastic compact with a lift-up mirror. Underneath the mirror is a place to stash an extra condom or two. And it's free; ask at a pharmacy.

COOKING CLASSES   For gastronomy classes at **Le Cordon Bleu** in Paris, call ☎ 800/457-CHEF (in the U.S.).

The **Ritz-Escoffier École de Gastronomie Française** in Paris (at the Hotel Ritz, of course) has its own cooking classes and even offers a program for kids (☎ 800/996-5758 in the U.S.). One look at the brochure and you will be in heaven. There are also 1-night lectures and events; this is not just a ladies' thing.

Besides Le Cordon Bleu, the most famous cooking school in France is probably **La Varenne,** which has a school in America and is run by a British couple, so you won't have any language problems. A weeklong class in Burgundy costs about $3,000 per person. The fee includes accommodations, all food, tuition, visits to local markets, and a few dinners out at Michelin-starred restaurants (☎ 02-86-63-18-34; fax 02-86-63-01-33). You can also call its American offices for dates and details (☎ 202/337-0073).

Patricia Wells, the most famous American cooking expert currently in France, offers cooking classes in her home in Provence. You can fax her directly at ☎ **919/846-2081.** You cook in her home and stay in a nearby hotel.

Kathie Alex is another American living the dream: She packed up, moved to Provence, and studied cooking in the great kitchens of the south. Now she has her own classes in Bramafam in a house that once belonged to Julia Child. You have morning classes in the kitchen but also make side trips to the markets, especially in Cannes, which is just 20 minutes away. Book by faxing ☎ **04-93-60-10-56.**

During the summer, the **Noga Hilton Cannes** offers cooking classes for kids aged 8 to 10. During the rest of the year, you can cook with a pastry chef in the Chef for a Day plan. Chef Pierre Cebeillac can be faxed at ☎ **04-92-99-70-11.**

As for tours:

Annemarie Victory (☎ **212/486-0353**) is a travel agent in New York who specializes in a wide range of international deluxe specialty tours, including a variety of top-flight gourmet food and wine-tasting tours in France.

France in Your Glass (☎ **800/578-0903**) specializes in wine tours mostly but also offers some cooking and eating tours. A variety of tours are available, including day trips, weekends you can add to your own trip, and even kitchen visits.

European Culinary Adventures offers country kitchen tours. Tours range from a barge trip or stays at local inns to visits to farms, vineyards, and local suppliers with the marvelous Kate Rattiffe (☎ **800/852-2625** or **508/535-5738**).

COPPER (CUIVRE) French cooking is widely associated with copper pots, which have been used locally for centuries because of the evenness of the conduction. Villedieu-les-Poêles, a small town near

Mont St. Michel, is known for the best copper pots in France, but you can find fabulous copper pots for sale at any brocante in France.

If you want to buy directly from the source, head for l'Atelier du Cuivre in Villedieu. They've been in the Guinness Book of Records for the size of their pots. The town supplies many famous chefs as well as the omelette pans for my favorite haunt in Mont St. Michel, La Mere Poulard.

When buying copper pots, judge the quality of the pot by how thick the copper is, making sure the copper is the same thickness all over. Check to see if the pot or pan has been patched or repaired. Look to see how the handle(s) is(are) attached and if the rivets go into the inside of the pot (bad). Remember that it takes more than a little elbow grease to clean up an old copper pot.

COUCHETTE   If the first phrase you ever learned in French was *"Voulez vous a coucher avec moi* (Will you go to bed with me)," you haven't booked an overnight train in France. Yes, a couchette is a bed, but in train parley, it's a bunk bed, and there are usually six—stacked three and three—in each train.

I do not know a lot of details, because it's been explained to me that anyone over the age of 25 is too old to travel this way, and I have always booked the *wagons lits,* which is a real bed in a real sleeping car.

CREPES   To an American, any French pancake is a crepe. Actually, there are two types: meal crepes, which are usually made of buckwheat flour, and dessert crepes, which are made of white flour. Dessert crepes are the type you are probably thinking of, and they taste awful with Roquefort cheese.

DÉGRIFFÉ   A *griffe* is a signature, or a label, in France. Clothes sold without labels, à la Loehmann's, are sold *dégriffé;* the stores that sell them are also called dégriffé. This is another way to spell "bargains" in French. Not all dégriffé shops sell designer names by a long shot. Every now and then, though, you'll find one that advertises itself as *haute*—this means it sells designer clothing.

DÉGUSTATION   Most fancy restaurants have a tasting menu (*menu dégustation*) whereby you are served many courses and get to taste a lot of textures and talents of the featured chef. Beware that these events usually take forever and offer far more food than God ever intended a human to eat. Furthermore, you can wait up to an hour between courses if you get unlucky. I'm not saying don't do it, I'm saying watch out and have plenty of time on your hands. Elastic waistbands also help.

DEPARDIEU   Any time, any place. Your country or mine.

DÉPÔT-VENTE   A used-clothing store, often specializing in designer resale. There's a handful of resale stores in Paris, in Cannes, and in the bigger cities of France that will make you swoon with the selection and fair prices. Others specialize in antiques.

DUCASSE   Any time, any place. Your kitchen or mine.

DUTY FREE   Forget everything you ever knew or hoped was true about duty free, partly because France has a slightly different system from other countries and partly because duty free will be outlawed for EU residents by 1999 and is therefore in the process of becoming the basis of a new discount network.

Now then, Paris has a slew of makeup and perfume stores that are a combination of duty-free discounters that offer far better discounts (a total of about 40% off) to non-EU residents. My favorite is Catherine, which offers a total of 45% off (see chapter 6). More traditional to all of us are duty-free stores at airports or the duty-free offerings now made on airplanes.

ELECTRICITY   There's no shortage of electricity in France (nuclear power!), but there is a shortage of people who have recovered from their post–World War II deprived childhood. Don't be shocked if the lights are off in the hallway. Feel around to find the switch and voilà—limited lighting on a timer.

ESCOTA Access card used in the south of France to pay tolls on the highway, like a Discovery card with benefits and discounts for the cardholder. Call Escota to apply for your card (☎ **04-92-97-40-40**). Note, the card pays tolls for Riviera and Provence, Esterel and Alpes areas only. If you are spending any time in these parts or are a regular visitor, it may make sense for you.

EURO One euro equals 6.6 F ($1).

FAIENCE Hand-painted ceramic earthenware identified with country France. Some regional painting styles are more famous than others, especially those made in Marseille in the 1860s. The designs mostly consist of flowers on a white background. French faience is decidedly different from Italian faience and is usually simpler with a larger portion of white background. There is a museum of faience in Marseille.

Expect to pay approximately $20 to $25 for a new plate. Antique wares are considerably higher. Because they are earthenware (clay, not porcelain), they do break easily, so pack with care.

The major French faience cities are Rouen, Nevers, Gien, Nîmes, and Moustier Ste. Marie. Salernes is thought of as the capital of tiles, whether earthenware or hand painted. However, deep-water trade to Brittany also affected local pottery there, so that northwestern Atlantic France has its own regional faience and pottery styles, which are best known to Americans through Quimper.

As for basic design points: Moustier is mostly known for story-telling pictures; Quimper has peasant figures; and Rouen has Arabic-influenced lace-edged patterns with arabesques and elaborate borders. Note that Gien faience is not earthenware but white paste, similar to English bone china. Gien patterns are very elaborate and are partially transferred by copper engraving (like English Staffordshire) and then hand painted. This gives a much more sophisticated image than what you get when a local artisan paints a cock in the center of a plate.

They do not make faience in the French city of Fayence, but they do make pottery in Faenza in Italy. You just never know.

FESTIVAL INTERNATIONAL DU FILM (FIF)   Held in Cannes for 2 weeks in the middle of May (the dates vary slightly each year), the Film Festival takes over the town. While it will be virtually impossible to get a decent hotel room in Cannes during the festival, you can write ahead for movie tickets and get a room in Nice. Write **International Film Festival,** Service d'Accreditation, 99 bd. Malesherbes, 75008, Paris, France; or fax ☎ **01-45-61-97-60.** It's virtually impossible to get into the official competition screenings, but there are so many other screenings that it's worth a shot. Don't forget your tux and dark glasses, darling.

FÉVE   The word in French actually means "bean," but shoppers know this as a collectible best found in a French flea market. To celebrate Epiphany, French bakeries make cakes (*galette des rois*) in which an ornamental bean is placed. If you get the piece of cake with the *féve,* you are the king or queen and get to wear a paper crown. The féve itself represents life and death. It's a symbol representing fertility, goodwill among humankind, happiness, and peace.

Not only is this popular with French children, but various firms market different types of féves for promotional purposes. When Disneyland Paris opened in 1992, many bakers made féves with Disney characters on them. A more traditional féve would be one of the figurines from a crèche. Tiny porcelain féves can be bought at flea markets and are collectors' items. Syros (a publishing house) has a series of books in French for collectors, including one on féves.

FRANC   The unit of currency used in France is technically a French franc, as there are also Belgian francs and Swiss francs. Can be written correctly in prices either as F or FF.

FRENCH-KISSING   They don't call it French-kissing in France, and they certainly don't have a verb "to French." This doesn't mean they don't do it.

FRENCH LESSONS   It's my goal to open my mouth and speak French like an angel. My tutor says I need intensive training in situ, but after my 10 days of French immersion at Dartmouth College, I'm not sure if I can take any more immersion. I may just sign up to be an exchange student. Nonetheless, I have a list of French language schools in France gathered from ads in the *International Herald Tribune*.

France Langue   Paris and Nice locations; intensive French; classes offered year-round; accommodations available. In Paris, call ☎ **1-45-00-40-15;** fax 1-45-00-53-41. In Nice, call ☎ 04-93-13-78-88; fax 04-93-13-78-89.

Institut de Français   On the Riviera, with 8 hours of study per day and two meals; classes offered year-round (☎ **04-93-01-88-44;** fax 04-93-76-92-17).

Paris Langues   Small groups for adults; 1-week sessions (☎ **1-45-65-05-28;** fax 1-45-81-26).

Sorbonne French Language   In Paris; all levels; classes offered year-round (☎ **1-40-46-22-11;** fax 1-40-46-32-29).

Universite Aix-Marseille   This is the most famous school for Americans; all levels; intensive programs in the summer (☎ **04-42-23-28-43;** fax 04-42-23-02-64).

FRENCH LETTERS   More condoms.

FRENCH MAGAZINES   To subscribe to French magazines in French (from France!) at your home in the United States, call **Express Mag** (☎ **800/363-1310**). French *Elle,* which comes out weekly, costs about $180 per year. The women's supplement to *Le Figaro, Madame Figaro* (also weekly), is over $400 a year, exactly what it would cost you to buy it every week in France—you just don't get the Saturday newspaper that comes with it.

FROUFROU   This is a legitimate style in France and it means just what you think it means: Overbearingly decorated with swags, bows, ribbons, ruffles, and the like.

FRUITS CONFIT   Close, but you're wrong—this is not jam (confiture) made of fruits. Fruits confit are essentially jellied fruit, a regional specialty in the south of France. Instead of being dried, the fruits are soft and a little gooey—often covered with a sprinkled-sugar crust. Their natural liquids have been drained and they have been immersed in fresh sugar water for about a month. Nonfattening, of course.

GALETTES   Literally means "cookies." What is most notable about them is that each region of France has its own specialty galette. An important part of your research as you travel will be to test them all. The differences in taste are usually related to the proportion of butter in the batter, which ranges from about 18% to 35%.

GAS   Not only does gasoline cost a fortune in France and not only is the price always rising, but you may not find it when you need it. There simply aren't as many gas stations in any given neighborhood as there are in suburban America.

Now then, the French buy gas on a regular, usually weekly, basis, whether they need it or not. They top off the tank as a ritual. This is usually done in conjunction with a family shopping expedition to the nearby *hypermarché*, which always sells gas and usually has discount prices, or at least, better prices than at regular retail.

If you are driving across France, you will do well to watch the tank and start thinking about where you can fill 'er up when you have a quarter of a tank left. This will allow you to be a little bit choosy and to plan your course to include a stop at the gas station area of a hypermarché. You will usually need to follow signs to get to one, which will be off the *autoroute* but not sufficiently far as to be avoided. It just takes planning.

Should you find yourself really turning into a French person, you will check your gas tank as you pass a hypermarché (or the advertisement for one) and see if you should top if off while it's convenient to do so. And remember, unleaded gas is called *sans plomb*.

GIBIER   Game; as in game season in late fall and early winter when restaurants feature game and stores may even get into the act with either promotions or window displays. I once saw a store window filled with stuffed rabbits wearing clothes! These were real dead rabbits, not plush toys. The entire concept of game season takes France by storm, especially in the more northern regions.

GÎTE   This is a small cottage, the home of a real person, or a funky place that you can rent in lieu of a hotel. There are agencies in France that rent them to Americans, although you are taking blind chances. Since there are approximately 60,000 properties offered for rent, the French government does not regulate them or the listing firms. *Bonne chance!*

GRANDS MAGASINS   No, this isn't a particularly thick or overly fancy issue of *Vogue*. The big department stores are called les grands magasins. Sometimes ads don't list specific suppliers but simply say les grands magasins. Mostly this means Galeries Lafayette and Au Printemps.

H$_2$O   It's water, and in France when we Americans drink it from a bottle it can either be *plate* (flat), which is also called *sans gas,* or *avec gas,* which is the bubbly kind that makes you burp.

Many people order bottled water by brand name to indicate they know the terrain and the types. Say Evian or Vittel to indicate that you like flat bottled water. If the house does not carry these brands, the waiter will counter with the brands of flat water the house offers. Say Badoit or Perrier, and you'll get the bubbly water list.

Recently, brand-name bottled water companies have begun to extend their lines by marketing other products, such as spritzing water, beauty and spa products, and deodorant. Vichy and Vittel each have their own lines of skin care products, sold in dime stores all over France. There's even an actual store in Evian that sells not only many Evian water products, but merchandise bearing the Evian logo as well.

HERBS DE PROVENCE   Sold in bundles, jars, or even glass containers, these spice gift packs are a mixture of the indigenous herbs of Provence and include rosemary, thyme, bay leaves, and savory— often crushed and blended but sometimes sold as dried twigs.

HONEY   Provençal honey is considered the best in France because the bees were buzzing around the lavender before they made their little combs. Look for the label "miel de lavande." Those marked "label rouge" are considered the best quality.

HYPERMARCHÉ   Americans may have supermarkets and even warehouse clubs, but no one has hypermarchés like the French do. A handful of French hypermarchés tried to make it in the United States and failed. To this day, I do not understand why.

One of the greatest adventures in retailing (in the world) is a trip to the hypermarché. These giant supermarkets rival the original concept of a general store but are all modern convenience without a smidgen of French charm.

Part of the hypermarché is a grocery store, part of it is a hardware store, part sells dry goods, such as clothes and linens and household equipment. There's always a gas station outside, and usually a car and tire center as well.

There may be as many as 50 checkout lanes in a hypermarché; all accept plastic.

The big names are: Auchan, Champion, Géant-Casino, Interprix, Carrefour, Leclerc, and the fading Rallye. Certain chains are featured in certain parts of the country or become more prominent or get a reputation for a certain type of customer.

Note: To buy fruits, veggies, or anything that has to be weighed in a hypermarché, place your choice in the plastic bags that are provided, just like in America. Go to a nearby weighing station that has a clerk. There may be a line. The clerk will weigh your purchases, staple the bag closed, and mark the price on each item. They do not weigh your goods at the checkout lane as in America.

JOKER A highly discounted type of train ticket, which even applies to Eurostar trains. See chapter 2 for train information. The ticket is very restricted, but if you can plan ahead you'll save a heap.

LAGUIOLE Type of deluxe knife, far more chic and *branché* (with it) than a Swiss army knife. It comes in pocketknife format as well as a carving format; there's even the new Lady Laguiole. They also make a corkscrew that is very chic.

Laguiole is not a brand name or a trademark, it's simply a type of a knife. That's one of the reasons why there are so many variations available and why new ones keep coming along. Even Philippe Starck has created one. Some of the knives are made in the town of Thiers and some in Laguiole. Aaron got one for Christmas when he was 14 and still thinks it's the bee's knees. *Choute*, man.

LAMPES BERGER Think of a chic oil lamp and you've got the idea, only this version doesn't burn oil, it burns scent. It wipes out odors caused by smokers, pets, humidity, and so on. Every French home has one or more. There are scads of styles and scads of scents. The firm has its own flagship store in Paris, but Galeries Lafayette carries a huge selection. Genevieve Lethu has her own designs in each of her shops all over France. Fancy design and home furnishings stores in resort towns also carry some versions.

The lamp itself costs anywhere from $40 to $100, depending on style. There are 17 different scents. I use Océane. Since it's illegal to bring the fluid on the plane, reorder yours in the United States (☎ 800/321-0020).

LAVENDER   The patron flower of Provence grows in abundance in the Luberon region, where it is harvested the first week in August. Tourists are regularly harvested of their souvenir budget in every town in the south of France—actually, lavender is sold in TTs (tourist traps) all over France—where the most common form is a cellophane-wrapped string of three, four, or five lavender-filled cotton sachets. A four-unit package commonly costs about 45 F ($8) in any TT in Paris and 25 F ($4.50) (or less) in any TT in Cannes or Nice.

The scent of lavender is said to have soothing properties and is thought to help induce sleep.

LE FIGARO   One of France's leading daily newspapers publishes a Saturday edition as big as the Sunday *New York Times* that includes a magazine, a TV section, a women's magazine (*Madame Figaro*), and many supplements. Because the paper is Paris based, readers in provinces will also subscribe to a local regional newspaper.

Le Figaro has excellent consumer information reporting on travel, fashion, antiques, and so on. If you can squeak by in French, you will enjoy the information.

MAKEUP & BEAUTY   Rumor has it that American women began to wear makeup after World War I when the boys who served in France came home exclaiming *ooh la la*. While we're all familiar with the French luxury cosmetic lines (since most of them are also sold in the United States), there is a trend toward being *drôle* in France. Part of being drôle means giving up expensive Bordeaux wines, drinking cheap wine from obscure vineyards in Provence, and quitting the big names in makeup and beauty to go for pharmacy and dimestore brands.

My single favorite product is what I call the Blue Tears. The proper name is Gouttes Bleu, and it is not sold in the United States because there's something in them that the FDA does not like. Note that the drops almost always have an expiration date on them. I usually buy the cheapest ones I can find in a plastic squeeze bottle, but Innoxa makes a brand with a longer shelf life that comes in a small glass bottle. One drop in each eye and good morning, America.

Here's a short list of the products you'll find in my makeup case, toiletries bag, and carry-on:

Annick Goutal A cult designer brand owned by the same people who own Baccarat crystal. They make a full and fabulous line of perfume and scent products. I travel with small bars of the Hadrien scented soap, which I appropriate from my hotel rooms at those Concorde hotels that use this line for amenities.

Bourjois It's made in the same factories that make Chanel makeup. However, it is not identical to Chanel. It's similar in some of the colors, but some of the items are coarser in texture.

Innoxa Makeup brand sold in dime stores and pharmacies; inexpensive and fun. I use their lipstick pencils. They also make the infamous blue eye drops (see above).

Perlier This line is easy to find in the United States; I often buy mine at TJ Maxx! While I've always liked its honey bath products, I've gone bonkers for its Île de Vanille bath line—the foaming bath is one of my current faves.

MARCHÉ A French market is almost always a fruit and vegetable market at which regional foodstuff (such as honey, jam, olive oil) are also sold. A supermarket is never called a *marché*.

MARCHÉS AUX PUCES A flea market. There may be some vendors selling cooked foods, crepes, or soft drinks, but there are no fruit and veggie stands.

MAXI CHOCOLAT   A giant *pain au chocolat* (see below), easily measuring 5 by 7 inches, if not more.

MICHELIN   A tire company that got the brilliant idea to promote driving around the countryside by writing books about nice places to stop to eat. Its system of awarding stars to the best chefs has become such an important commentary that the announcement of each new annual edition is a major news story. Stars range from one to three, and there are fewer than two dozen three-star chefs. When chefs are mentioned along with the number of stars they have earned, these stars are only from Michelin. No one else's really count. (Gault Millaut gives toques; they do count.)

MIMOSA   Small, yellow polka dots of sugar, about the size of a Saccharine tablet, used to sweeten coffee or tea in the south of France. Usually served by spoon from a sugar bowl. May also be served mixed with candied violets. I just bought a jar of them, marketed by Fauchon, in a grocery store in Paris for $10. Great gift item!

MINITEL   French information service proving that the information highway is not just in cyberspace but may be in your hotel room, too. Minitel addresses are listed in phone books, on ads and billboards, even on business cards, so that you can go on-line (for a fee) to receive more information. Theater, train, airline tickets, and so on, can be booked on-line.

Some hotels provide guest rooms with a Minitel; the phone book in your room provides clear instructions (with pictures) on how to use the system. Your hotel concierge can also check Minitel for you.

Note: Because making reservations using Minitel is so easy, people often book for trains and planes but don't show. You may be trying to get a seat on a train, but your hotel concierge will say such a seat is not available because he is using Minitel. If you go directly to the train station, or airline counter, you may find that seats do exist. Never trust Minitel for the last word on actual availability. Virtual reality, *oui*. Actual, *non*.

MUSIC   You can't hop in your big rent-a-car and drive around France without the right kind of cassettes, can you? I put several friends (all my age, please note) to work on what tapes and CDs to buy in France. Here's the list they came up with: Edith Piaf, Johnny Hallyday, Sylvie Vartan, Françoise Hardy, Serge Gainsbourg, Marie Laforêt, and Jean Ferrat. Almost every city in France has a branch of FNAC, the book and record chain.

If you've spent a few grand on the trip, do it right with a tape or two. You have not lived until you and your honey are driving the back roads of France and suddenly you hear "Da Do Run Run" in French. You just might have to pull the car over, turn up the sound, and dance in the street.

NOUGAT   Candy made from caramelized honey with local nuts and/or dried fruits added. Each region of France and each maker has a slightly different variety based on what types of nuts, seeds, or fruits are grown locally. The candy is often sold from stalls at markets or roadside stands in the south of France. Many makers also sell their own honey.

OLIVE OIL   The best kind is extra-virgin. You may also be given a choice between one that is *douce* (sweet) or regular. Americans often prefer the sweet one. You may buy yours directly from the *moulin* (mill), and it's cheaper if you bring your own container. High-quality extra-virgin olive oil is expensive; expect to pay about 50 F ($8.50) per liter.

Olive oil products and olives, including olives in airtight resealable plastic bags, are also sold in mills or stores that specialize in Provençal souvenirs. One of my favorite mills advertises that if you buy a dozen bars of soap, you get one free. But it's not a baker's dozen—the free bar is not full-sized!

Olive oil is serious stuff in Mediterranean regions. The winner of last year's gold medal was Maurice Lottier of Menton. The silver went to Louis Brocardi of Grasse.

PAIN AU CHOCOLAT   These are envelopes of light and flaky croissant dough filled with melted chocolate.

PANIER   Now then, a *panier* is technically a basket, but when you go to a store and want one of those plastic shopping baskets for your things, it is a panier.

The big grocery stores now also have shopping carts (*chariots*) for which you must pay 10 F ($1.70); you get your money back only when you return the cart to the line and click it back in place. You forfeit your money if you leave the cart in the parking lot.

PARADOX   Also sometimes referred to as the French Paradox, this is the noted phenomenon that French people eat a lot of rich foods and drink wine but don't die of heart attacks at any greater rate than anyone else. Supposedly this is because the tannin, or something or another, in red wine cuts through the cholesterol or the fat cells or something. Can't drink? *Pas de problem.* There are Paradox pills. Honest.

PARAPHARMACIES   These stores are the latest trend in Paris and are also spreading to the provinces. They are large discount drugstores that sell an enormous selection of drugstore-brand makeup and skin care, health, diet, and beauty products at 20% off. Many have fidelity cards as well.

PARKING   Lots are marked with the letter *P.* Most have an electronic message board out front that tells you if the lot is full (*complet*) or exactly how many spaces are available. Rather ingenious.

In traditional parking lots, you take a ticket as you enter. You usually pay for the ticket before you get in your car to leave; few lots in France have drive-out tellers as in the United States. If there is a long line at the *caisse* (cashier), see if there is a machine on a nearby wall that allows you to insert your ticket, pay for it, and have it canceled. You show the canceled ticket as you leave.

Street parking is paid for with a similar method. Park your car. Find the machine attached to a nearby wall and buy a ticket for the amount of time you estimate you will need. Return to your car with the ticket and attach it inside your car on the driver's side of the windshield. Then lock the car. Parking is expensive in France.

If a French presidential election approaches, jokers run wild. It is tradition for the incoming president to excuse all parking fines and tickets. Locals, who park just about anyplace under normal circumstances, have a wild time.

I have also decided that the code in the license plate tells the police you have a rental car and you are much more likely to be ticketed. I actually paid one of my parking tickets just to be able to tell you how to do so, should you feel compelled to pay your ticket.

To pay a ticket:

- Go to a tobacco shop (*tabac*) and present the ticket.
- Pay the fine to the salesperson, who will give you two sets of stamps.
- Fix half the stamps to one page of the ticket and half the stamps to the other page.
- Mail the part that is addressed to be mailed and keep the other part as proof that you have paid the ticket.

PASTIS Frankly, this liqueur is the most disgusting thing I've swallowed in a long time, but there's a resurgence in interest in this local French drink—considered a spring and summer drink by some—and there's even an "in" brand. Ask for Henri Bardouin.

PERFUME Perfume accidentally came to France via the glove industry. It seems that in the Middle Ages, M'lady always kept her hands in kid gloves, but the tanning process produced fine kid gloves that smelled yucky. In order to make life bearable for

Madame, the glove makers (conveniently located in the town of Grasse, near Cannes) created floral essences that would blot out that nasty waxy yellow buildup. Before you knew it, the perfume industry was born. Grasse remains the industrial center of the industry, although the best buys in terms of discount and duty-free stores are in Paris.

Since people have written books on this subject, I'll just pass on a few tidbits you might not know.

- Why does French perfume of the same brand smell different in Europe than in the United States, or why do two different bottles of the same scent wear differently on you? Because French perfume has a different chemical composition than the U.S. version; it is made with potato alcohol. Supposedly this produces a cleaner version of the scent that wears better.

- If you can't afford true perfume, which is which after that? Perfume is very pricey because of the ingredients and because of all the money they have to pay Shalom Harlow to be in the ads. All the derivatives move away from the original scent in a matter of generations. So, *parfum* is the most concentrated, then comes *eau de parfum*, then *eau de toilette*, then *voile de toilette*. Prices decrease in the same order.

- Are there any bargains out there? Well, 100ml of a fragrance does not cost much more than 50ml, a marketing ploy that makes it smart for you to buy the larger bottle and get twice as much for less than twice the price.

- Is the concept of layering valid? To the true believer.

- Where should you buy your perfume in France? The duty-free store at the airport is one of your worst choices, friends. Very best is any of the many big-time discounters in Paris who offer 25% to 30% off list price regardless of how much you buy. Then, if you qualify for *détaxe*, you get another 15% taken off.

- Figure airport discounts at 13% to 15%, so even in the south of France, where there aren't too many discounters, if you find someone who will give you 20% off (not counting détaxe) you'll do better than at the airport.

PILLS The French seem to think there's a magic pill for just about everything. It's common practice to self-prescribe homeopathic remedies galore. Also check out pills for getting a suntan, pills to prevent wrinkles (Catherine Deneuve takes them!), pills to banish cellulite, and so on. The pills Deneuve takes are called Oenobiol capsules. They are sold in every pharmacy. However, Oenobiol makes a variety of pills for a variety of beauty flaws, so read the package carefully.

POCHETTE Pocket square worn in man's jacket. Hermès makes them.

POISSON D'AVRIL For years I have wondered why they sell chocolate fish in the spring in France. First I thought it was a beach gimmick or maybe a religious thing. No, it's just Poisson d'Avril, April Fish, the French equivalent of April Fool's Day.

POMMEAU You know that metal hose spritzer thing attached to the taps in the bathtubs in France that you hate? It's technically called a *pommeau.* Pascale-Agnes calls it *la pomme de la douche.* Richard says you can also call it *la douche du main.*

PONT The French word for bridge, but I'm neither singing nor dancing about Avignon. Oh no, what we're talking about is the tendency toward a long weekend. What Americans call the 4-day holiday weekend is known as the *pont* to French, and it can affect restaurant and store openings, especially in May. If the holiday falls on a Wednesday and people take off until Monday, it's not a pont but a *viaduct!*

POTERIÉ Although hand-painted ceramics are an art form in France and the world over, local shops that sell *poterié,* especially in the south of France,

How to Wash Your Hair, French Style

If you are staying in a hotel that does not have the kind of shower you are used to, and the *pomme de la douche* does not attach to the wall or to a bracket so it can be stabilized, you may be wondering how the French wash their hair. I thought you would never ask. You may thank my sister-in-law for teaching me this.

First, you are seated in the bathtub with enough hot water to keep you comfortable. You have finished bathing or relaxing or whatever you do in the tub. Judy taught me to do this sitting cross-legged in the bath. If you can fit, it will give you a stronger back and better angle for the task.

Now, you turn on the spritzer and adjust the water temperature to your hand (how civilized, these French!). Only after you've gotten the water just right, you bend your neck forward, raise the pommeau above your head, and drench yourself, use your free hand to move your hair around to make sure it gets good and wet. Once your hair is wet enough, you turn off the pommeau and replace it on top of the taps.

Next, apply shampoo, suds up, and wash. When finished, turn on the spritzer, lean forward at the neck so the flood doesn't go in your eyes and mouth, and rinse.

On the other hand, PA was horrified after seeing the above instructions. She says you should put on your terry-cloth bathrobe, stand or kneel outside the tub, and lean over the tub while you wet your hair. Then you take off your robe, get into the tub, suds up, and wash. Next you step out of the tub, put the robe back on, and lean over the tub and rinse your hair. I tried it and was not amused.

usually sell simple, monochromatic earthenware that is glazed either brown, blue, green, or ochre—the colors of the south of France. Painted poterié is called *faience*.

POUCE DU MERCREDI *Pouce* (not to be confused with puces) means "thumb," but this is the name of a promotion run by Air InterEurope, the domestic branch of Air France. This promotion, designated by a thumbs-up symbol (hence the name), means that any Wednesday you can call **Minitel** (☎ **36-15-AIRINTER**) and find out the offers of the day. Then you can hop on a plane to just about anywhere for 200 F ($33).

RED FRUITS You will frequently, especially in summer, be offered desserts, or even teas, *aux fruits rouges*, which is a composition of strawberries, raspberries, red currants, and blueberries. Those are the four red fruits, and they always come in that combination unless otherwise stipulated on the *carte*.

RESERVATIONS Sure you know to make a reservation for dinner, possibly even for lunch, but don't forget to make one for the train. Train fares are much less expensive if reservations are made in France rather than in the United States.

ROND POINT While you may know this as a particular spot in Paris, at the beginning of the Champs-Elysées, actually any roundabout (*rotary*) on any French road is a *rond point* and will be referred to as such in signs.

RUDE They're not rude; you don't speak French.

SANTON Close your eyes and picture a traditional Christmas créche, even the one you own at home. Okay, those little figures of the wise men, the sheep, the baby Jesus are what the French call *santons*. Now then, the French craftsmen who make these have put a regional spin on the craft by adding local French characters from any village to the basic nativity bunch.

The tradition is basically from Provence, although santons are sold all over the south of France. Santons may be made of either clay or wood and are then brightly painted. Some are embellished with fabric or maybe even twigs or dried fruits. Price varies with size, quality of carving, and detail of painting. Most popular santons are only about 2 inches tall and cost 50 F to 90 F ($8.50 to $15) each. A basic créche may be sold as a set.

Note that aside from the traditional figurines in a créche, there is nothing religious about the rest of the figures—they are purely simple village folk, from the woman who comes to market with her cauliflower in hand, to the glazier who uses a trumpet to attract customers.

Marcel Carbonel is perhaps the most famous craftsman; his workshop is in Marseille (see chapter 12). There is a small paperback guide to his creations that also serves as a common dictionary of the characters now thought to compose an entire collection. This book costs about 85 F ($14) and is in French and English; I bought mine in a tourist trap in Avignon, but it's sold in many tourist stores and in bookstores.

SAVON DE MARSEILLE   Traditional French soap, usually sold in a square cube measured by grams. When comparing prices, make sure you have learned the differences in size. In the United States, the 200g cube costs about $4. In France, the 400g size costs about 12 F ($2). The soap should be composed of 72% oil, which may be imprinted (in French) on the cube.

La Compagnie de Provence, located in Marseille (see chapter 12), is one of the national heroes of soap making. Others located in Provence include L'Occitane, 21 rue Grande, Manosque, and Savonnerie Marius Fabre, 148 av. Grans, Salon-de-Provence (which comes recommended by Alain Ducasse).

SERVICE COMPRIS   The service is included in the cost of a meal, as is the tax. Therefore, the price listed on the bill is the price you pay, totally inclusive. However, it is common, especially in fine restaurants or when service has been attentive or personal, to leave a few extra francs in cash on the table.

SOLDES   Sales. French stores tend to have only two sales a year. Traditional spring sales usually begin the last week in June and extend through the first week in July. Traditional winter sales are at the end of January, after Epiphany. Sales are usually advertised in newspapers, including the *International Herald Tribune*. Hard times have moved the seasons ahead, so that nowadays anything goes.

Some deluxe brands have special sale events once or twice a year, such as the Hermés sales in October and March when people line up for hours before the store opens.

SOULEIADO   Provence and the south of France are known for a specific type of cotton fabric that is printed in bright colors with swirls of paisley, flowers, and arabesques. The designs are created with wood blocks using the same style of fabric printing that has been done in India for centuries.

These fabrics entered France originally through the port of Marseille, hence their association with the south of France, where they became known as *tissus Indiennes* or even *tissus Nîmes*, Nîmes being another major textile center in the south (and the home of denim—de Nîmes).

While the fabric has been made locally for centuries, Charles Démery, a craftsman who began a fabric firm known as Souleiado, revived it in Provence in the late 1930s. Souleiado became popular in the United States in the 1980s through a firm called Pierre Deux, which at that time carried exclusive rights to sell Souleiado in America. Souleiado went bankrupt last year but was bought and reorganized. Pierre Deux stores in the United States now carry Les Olivades brand.

Of all the many firms making tissus Indiennes, Souleiado has the highest quality of screens and fabric and, by far, the highest prices. Details on shopping in the factory store can be found in chapter 12.

STAR   A word with many meanings in French and in Franglish: If it's a star in the sky its *l'etoile*; if it's the place in Paris where the Arc de Triomphe is located, it's *L'Etoile*; if it's a movie star, even a French one, he or she is a star. So *les stars* hang out in Cannes for the Film Festival. However, when a foodie is discussing a restaurant and he refers to a chef and his stars, he is referring to the chef's *Michelin Guide* ranking.

SVP   Abbreviation for *s'il vous plaît* (please), used frequently in print advertisements and directions.

TA MÉRE   This is the French colloquial expression that more or less equals "Yo' Mama" and is celebrated in not only slang but a series of joke books that are insults about your mother. This is an excellent way to get your teenager to read French. The books cost 45 F ($7.50).

TABAC   Tobacco shop where newspapers, magazines, cigarettes, gum, and the essentials of life are sold, including stamps and phone cards. Also where you pay parking tickets.

TAMTAM   This French version of a pager receives messages 24 hours a day.

TAPENADE   Specialty food item from the south of France, where olives are the mainstay of life. Tapenade is essentially a spread made from mashed-up olives with a few spices, some olive oil, and other ingredients. The combination of spices used and the texture of the mashing make for the variety of styles.

Olives have quite a piquant taste, and tapenade is very full bodied, possibly more than you might imagine. Each maker prepares his or her tapenade a little bit differently, so there's room to taste your way across the south of France. The blend may also be quite spicy—some makers chop up an anchovy or two into the mix.

I cut mine with a tomato product called *sauce tomate au basilic,* which is sold at the same stores and stands that sell tapenade. Tastes great on top of a bagel with cream cheese (*le bagel Provençal*).

You can buy tapenade in jars in most markets in the south of France. Surprisingly, Brand X from the guy at the market in Nice is no more or less expensive than the version Roger Vergé sells in his boutique in Mougins. The going price for a small jar is usually 20 F.

TÉLÉCARTE An electronic phone card that not only makes calling home, or calling anywhere, an affordable breeze but leaves you with a collectible that you can sell or trade.

You can buy phone cards at any tobacco shop or news kiosk. The smallest denomination is 40 F for 50 units. This will go surprisingly far, especially if you are calling within France. If you are calling the United States or will be consistently using your phone card, buy one as soon as you arrive in France and buy a larger denomination of units. The more units to the card, the more savings.

While you can still find telephones that use a *piéce* (coin), they are more popular in the boonies than in big cities. The days of needing a coin or of not being able to figure out how to use the phone are over. *Voilà, ma chère:*

- Locate a modern-looking telephone booth or one that has a horizontal slot in it for the phone card.
- Lift the phone off the receiver and insert the phone card.
- Read the electronic message, which will give you instructions in French. Don't read French? Not to worry. Anyone can figure these out. For example, "please wait" is written "*patience, svp.*" Easy as *un, deux, trois!* And you didn't know you spoke French.
- The units will click away electronically and visually. When you are down to the last few units, a beeping noise will ensue. Time to say *au revoir.*

TGV *Train à Grande Vitesse,* if you insist on knowing. As far as I'm concerned, it's Trains-R-Great-4-Vous. The TGV is one of the oldest high-speed train networks in the world and its trains go

True Télécarte Confession

I called my husband from a pay phone in France once. To save money, I asked him to call me back. I gave him the number, which is clearly printed on the phone.

So I stood there in the phone booth, where it was hot as blazes. I stood and I waited. I waited forever. People came to use the phone booth, and I do not speak enough French to explain I was expecting a phone call. I mimed, and I avoided eye contact.

Finally, I looked at the computer part of the telephone that keeps track of your units and gives you directions. Although the phone was not ringing, and had never rung, the message said I had a call. I picked up the receiver and, *voilà*, my husband!

up to about 200 miles per hour. Also, more and more TGV track is laid each year, so you can get to more and more regions of France quickly.

THALASSOTHERAPIE   The French, who are great believers in spa treatments for improving or maintaining health, have recently gone bonkers over thalassotherapie, which is spa treatments related to seawater. Major spas are located on the French Atlantic coast, although Prince Rainer in Monte Carlo has recently opened a spa there to capitalize on the trend and to make his life easier—now he doesn't have to travel out of town to get treatments.

A key part of the treatments is soaking in seawater or seaweed-enhanced bathwater, the theory being that seaweed will rebalance the impurities in your body. For proper treatment, your soak should be at body temperature, to encourage osmosis. This is rather cool for a bath—don't be shocked if you're asked to pay $40 to sit in a cold bath of smelly brown water for a mere 15 minutes. A nice hot bath is traditionally 103° to 106°, not a lowly 98.6°.

While I have yet to test any of the world-class spas offering the treatment in France, I did test the technique on a ship in France. I found it expensive and uncomfortable. It was also incredibly annoying to be interrupted by the technician who tried to sell me the products to take home with me, all while I was paying $112 for 10 baths.

My friend Alec tested the same products in the same shipboard spa. He cheated on the temperature and had a steaming hot bath, told the attendant to leave him in privacy, and swore it was heaven—worth every sou he paid.

The $30 I invested in a 500ml bottle of *bain moussant aux algues* (algae bubble bath) by Thalamanche—one of the leading suppliers of thalosotherapy products in France—was the best money I've ever spent on myself. One capful of this green liquid in my hot tub (sorry, I cheat) and I can smell the sea, feel the sea in my skin, and float my cares away.

I bought mine in St. Malo. A variety of brands of thalassotherapie products are sold throughout France, especially in spa areas. Alec likes the Phytomer brand sold in its new boutique in St. Malo. Phytomer has better distribution in Paris than Thalamanche and can be bought in most department stores there, but Alec agrees that Thalamanche is the best in France.

TIMBRE   French word for stamp. Pronouncing it (*tem*-bre) is only half the battle. Knowing that you peel the paper off the backside and don't lick it is the other half.

TIRE-BOUCHON   A corkscrew. You'd be surprised how many styles there are until you visit the museum. Are you snickering? You're obviously not French. Corkscrews are a serious collectible.

TRAVERSIN   How adorable: Your traditional French bed has a bolster and you and your loved one are about to count sheep (*mouton*) and count your blessings for having found such a cute little French inn. You need to know that the bolster does not move and is not adjustable. Call for pillows before you try to make it through the night.

USINE   For the longest time, I thought it was a bear. Don't ask me why. Turns out a *usine* is a factory. *Magasins d'usine* are factory outlet shops.

As in every other part of the world, there are real factory shops and fake factory shops. Watch out for some of those factory-direct perfume shops in the south of France. Even some of the real factory shops, such as the Souleiado shop in Tarascon, offer no bargains.

There is a new trend in France toward American-style outlet malls. Check out the city of Troyes, about an hour from Paris, for Boutiques des Fabricants. Troyes has become the outlet capital of France since the early 1990s; Style du Vie Cheval de Troyes is another outlet mall there. Patricia Wells tells me that the brands are mostly French ones that Americans probably wouldn't find that interesting. Pascale-Agnes agrees; in fact, she couldn't find anything she wanted, and she's French.

Centre Mac Arthur Glenn, another American-style, American-managed outlet mall with French and American names (including Ralph Lauren and Nike), is in Pont-Ste-Marie.

Paris is dotted with factory-direct stores that sell old stock, much of it from big names such as Cacharel, Sonia Rykiel, and Fabrice Karel. Note the use of the word *stock* in the names of such shops.

Just as in the United States, the outlets with the best bargains are the ones either inside the actual factory or nearby. These tend to be in out-of-the-way places that are not average tourist stops. Not all of them are great (or cheap) though.

Neither Pascale-Agnes nor I are impressed with the Cacharel outlet in the factory in Nîmes. We like the Paris outlet shop better. For the lowdown on the Souleiado factory shop, see chapter 12.

VO Movies with the original voice (VO) have subtitles in French. You can see any American or British flick in a French theater and not only understand the whole thing, but teach yourself French while reading the subtitles. VO movies are most common in Paris, in the big movie theaters along the Champs-Elysées, but they play elsewhere as well.

WINE If you say no to wine, you say no to France. If you think I'm going to go beyond that, you're nuts. There are books and books and books about all this. Study them; subscribe to the mags.

In the United States, call ☎ **800/522-WINE** for a free booklet on French wine and wineries that are open to visitors. Or you can try the Web site at www.frenchwinesfood.com.

AN ALPHABETICAL GUIDE TO INTERNATIONAL BOUTIQUES & CHAINS

Here is a sampling of some of the big names in French retail. Some are well-known designers; others are multiples (chain stores) with numerous branch stores all over France:

AGATHA Tiny shops found all over France that sell whimsical costume jewelry at moderate prices. Some stores are found in the United States.

AGNÉS B Upscale casual wear for men and women, often sold in separate shops. Hip but not too outré.

AUTOUR DU MONDE French version of Banana Republic. Carries casual travel and weekend wear and some gadgets.

BLANC BLEU BCBG (*bon chic, bon genre;* preppy) looks with a nautical edge and a Ralph Lauren feel.

CAMIEU Cheap version of Sweden's H&M for inexpensive fashions; not as well made as Pimkie but worth a look.

CARRÉ BLANC Chain of linen stores for bed and tabletop that also has bridal registration. Good source for duvet covers, which are hard to find in abundance in the United States.

CERRUTI 1881 Clothing lines designed by Nino Cerruti. Men's and women's are usually sold in separate boutiques. These classic, tailored designs are sold wherever people are rich.

CHACOCK Status design firm known for bright colors, ethnic inspiration, lots of knits for winter, and floating cotton for summer. It also has sensational looks for the south of France, where dash and flair really count. Prices are equal to American designer bridge lines.

CHIPIE Blue jeans and casual clothes with French chic.

COMTESSE DU BARRY Large chain of gourmet food stores carrying packaged goods with its house label.

DESCAMPS Bed linen, bathrobes, great baby gifts, and a wonderful line of scented rocks. Its freestanding stores were closed in the United States, but it's alive and quite well all over France.

ELECTRE Chain of boutiques selling cheap to moderately priced copies of hot fashions for young women. Also offers suits for working women with dash.

FLORIANE Chain of expensive, but adorable, kiddie clothes. Young and hip meets traditional.

FNAC Chain of book and record stores that sells CDs, tapes, and all forms of communications. Great place to meet young people. Slightly better prices than regular music shops. Huge selections.

GENEVIÈVE LETHU Provençal designer with hundreds of tabletop boutiques all over France and a few outside of France. The colors are great; the style is vibrant and contemporary while still being a little traditional. Often creates ingenious products, such as the wicker water-bottle cover (39 F/$6.50).

HABITAT/THE CONRAN SHOP These are two totally different firms, although each was begun by Sir Terrence Conran, and they sell very similar goods: items with country flair and clean contemporary lines for the home. As impossible as this seems, the designs are at the same time very French and very English. Habitat is a major multiple located throughout France. The Conran Shop is only in Paris (117 rue du Bac, 7e).

HERBIER DE PROVENCE International chain selling a packaged version of Provençal charm. Most noted for its French version of aromatherapy products and its lotions and potions made with French herbs. It sells Marseille soap in cubes as well as some foodstuff.

INÈS DE LA FRESSANGE Former muse of Karl Lagerfeld turned designer and boutique-owner with shops here and there in the bigger French cities. She's made a small push into continental Europe, but a few stores have also closed, so she is consolidating and trying to survive. The avenue Montaigne shop in Paris is great fun; otherwise, the stores are nice to look at, creative in the field of accessories, and overpriced in the realm of BCBG (preppy).

IRENE VAN RYB There are just a handful of these boutiques, which sell high-fashion, tailored, expensive women's clothing; sort of the Calvin Klein of France.

LACOSTE The world's most knocked-off alligator is alive and well and living in France in major department stores, as well as in freestanding boutiques. Here's the catch: The goods are often less expensive in the United States. But there are styles in France that are not exported to the United States.

MARINA RINALDI Italian brand of large-size fashions from Max Mara; sold throughout France in freestanding stores and in Max Mara boutiques. The leading line in European plus-size fashion.

MONOPRIX Chain of dime stores owned by Galeries Lafayette; a great place to shop for

affordable everything. Many of them also have grocery stores attached. The house private label is called
Miss Helen. While there is a branch of Monoprix in
almost every French city, be sure to check out the
ones in fancy suburbs and good neighborhoods—
they have the best supply of chic for choc. Monoprix
now owns Prisunic, which was the competition.

PIMKIE   Cheapie teenage fashions with cutting-
edge style; a really great place to get the hottest looks
for not much money. There's one in every town.

REDOUTE   Major catalog company, sort of like
JCPenney; has now also opened its own retail shops.

REPETTO   Traditional ballet house known for first
introducing stylish ballet slippers into mainstream
fashion. It now makes slippers (and mocs) in a variety of colors and skins. Products are sold in its own
shops and in big department stores.

SEPHORA   Chain of stores that sell all makeup
and fragrance brands, as well as some hair accessories, its own line of bath products, and every other
beauty treatment you can imagine.

TEHEN   Young, hip, somewhat body-conscious
clothes, but in keeping with sophisticated looks for
a woman over 30. Or 40. Great stuff.

TROIS SUISSES   Major catalog company. Basically
cheap clothes, but it does have guest designers making seasonal offerings. It even offers Vivienne
Westwood.

UN DIMANCHE À VENISE   Don't you just love
the name? Chain of shoe stores with moderate to
high prices but lots of style.

Chapter Six

· · · · · · ·

SHOPPING PARIS

WELCOME TO PARIS

· ·

When you leaf through French magazines, you'll notice that in ads, the addresses for branch stores are written as "Paris" and "Provinces." Not Provence, that's provinces. You see, even to the French, it's very simple: There's Paris, and there's the rest of France. Even to the French, if you're not in Paris, you're in the provinces.

There may be no place like home, but, trust me, there's also no place like Paris. This fact will become particularly clear if you tour the countryside of France and then conclude your visit with a few days in Paris.

Paris is indeed the City of Light. It is the beginning and the end of a certain kind of light. For a shopper, Paris means serious shopping. There is no comparison between the energy—yes, even shopping energy—that vibrates off the streets of Paris and what goes on in the countryside. Maybe that's my point: Paris is about energy, while the countryside is about the luxuries of time, space, sunflowers, wine, slow meals, and slow shopping.

Note that this edition is written in alternate years with *Born to Shop Paris,* so you might want to coordinate addresses given in this chapter with those in your latest edition of *Born to Shop Paris,* and call stores or ask your hotel concierge for help if need be. Not too many stores have closed, but many have opened up new branches, so a more convenient opportunity may lurk around the corner.

And yes, you're right, there's lots of new stuff. Le Drugstore has closed on the Left Bank to make room for M. Armani; new stores are up and down the avenue des Champs-Elysées from **The Gap** to **Louis Vuitton** (how's that for going from the ridiculous to the sublime, or vice versa?); the Left Bank continues to attract more and more big names (even non-French names such as Canadian makeup guru **MAC**) and everything is hot, hot, hot. **Monoprix** bought up **Prisunic**—how's that for hot, hot, hot?

Concept stores are getting bigger and bigger, too. Note that first **Chanel** opened its own fancy jewelry store and now has just opened its own makeup and fragrance store, on rue Royale. Meanwhile, having nothing much to do with Chanel, Karl Lagerfeld has opened a teeny-weeny gallery on the Left Bank that sells his photography and his men's scent Jako. It also sells some very esoteric clothes downstairs and, hmmm, academically interesting, it's called **KL Gallery.**

Americans are doing Paris more than ever. Sunday hours are opening up. Terrence Conran is planning on feeding the French in a newly opened restaurant. What will they think of next?

Ooh la la, did I tell you about **H&M?** They've invaded France, with a large store on rue Rivoli and smaller branches here and there—ignore the small ones and head right for the big one. If you don't know H&M, shame on you—this Swedish firm has had a store in London for eons and is famous throughout the world for hot, kicky clothes for dirt cheap prices.

Meanwhile, you've probably read about **Colette,** which the French think is the hottest thing since bottled water. In fact, the store has a bar that specializes in bottled waters. I'd like to tell you that this store is a must-do, but truth is, it's very American and it only makes me laugh. If you insist on seeing what the French think is fabulous, and a lot of expensive American brands, pop in—the store is around the corner from the Hotel Meurice.

But trust me, there's a lot more in Paris that you just have to see and be part of. So put down this book and hail a taxi, *allons-y!*

BUT FIRST

. . . .

If you are in the planning stages of your trip, if you can put that taxi on hold for *un moment,* let's talk about getting organized and getting to Paris. Plans need to be made. You see, it makes more sense to leave France through Paris than to arrive through Paris. Of course, you don't need to come to Paris at all, but if you are planning to include Paris on your trip and aren't certain of the details, hear me out.

Paris represents intense shopping. It's only after you've been through France and done the country bit that you'll know what you still need for your at-home use or for your own psychic rewards. It's also silly to shop in Paris and fill your suitcases with items you will have to schlepp in and out of a series of hotels.

Also note that if you don't know Paris well, the amount of shopping services available can be downright overwhelming, so rather than get a headache, heart palpitations, or make a shopping boo-boo, seek Paris as a last resort—in all senses of the word.

I was never so glad to see Paris in my life as I was when we arrived after a 3-week drive across France a few years ago. Even though we only had 24 hours in Paris—and it was raining—Paris was more meaningful to me than ever because I knew what I needed from the city emotionally. I always try to stay in Paris for more than a day, but sometimes it's just not possible. I am an understanding woman.

Paris by Arrondissement

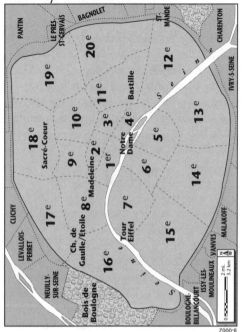

On this big trip we took, my actual needs, such as wrinkle cream, gifts, and souvenirs, had already been met quite well in the countryside. What I needed, and got, in my 24 hours was the thrill of being in the midst of it all. There's no thrill in the world like a day in Paris.

Paris is different from all of France, and while you can buy many of the same things in other parts of France, there's only one Paris and that's why it's Paris.

PARIS ON THE RUN

If you are going to be in Paris for an extended visit, I suggest you buy *Born to Shop Paris*. The book you are holding has been created specifically for people who will be in Paris with only a day or two, or possibly just a few hours, to shop. (It happens, even in the best of families.)

This chapter is built to give you an overview of Paris—the latest addresses for your favorite shops, the newest places in town that may have opened since you were here last (or since my Paris edition was printed), some ideas on how to best use the small amount of time you have in town, and some of the best shops worth seeking out in specific categories of goods. You're a shoe freak? I've got shoes for you.

This chapter is limited to very simple basics without a lot of room for descriptions or explanations. Some of the previous chapters in this book have background material you may need on who some of the players are.

THE LAY OF THE LAND

. . . .

Part of your job in selecting a hotel for a short stay is to study the lay of the land and get nestled into an *arrondissement* (neighborhood) that will serve as many of your needs as possible. Also make sure you have good Métro connections, as that will be your best way of getting around—and shopping around. Just learn the basic lay of the land per your own addresses and interests.

There is good shopping near most of the major tourist sights and museums, so you can combine culture with shopping. The only tourist neighborhood that is really out in left field, so to speak, is Montmartre. Your shopping in this hilltop artist community is limited to TTs (tourist traps), street vendors, caricature artists, and the city's leading discount store, **Tati,** which is not for the average tourist or shopper.

Come to think of it, there isn't too much shopping immediately around the Eiffel Tower, either. But you can see the Eiffel Tower from many shopping hot spots, and that's what counts.

GETTING AROUND

. . . .

Paris is a great city for walking. You can spend your days staring at the architecture, the stores, and the people. If you want a quicker method of transportation, the Métro connects every part of town. Buy a *carnet,* a book of 10 tickets, to save money and time.

The most essential thing for getting around is a map: Get a free map—along with a Métro map—from the concierge desk of any hotel. The big department stores also give them away.

Please note that it is against the law for a taxi sedan to carry five adults. Therefore, if you are a group of four people and one of you does not drive a taxi, you may find yourself fighting with taxis or having to call a special taxi. **TaxisG7** (☎ **01-41-27-66-67**) has vans. For airport runs, they will give you a flat rate charge. They like you to call an hour in advance and make a reservation, which costs 50 F ($8.50)—if you're not there for the pickup, you lose the 50 F, otherwise it is counted toward your fare. Your hotel concierge can book for you.

Avis has chauffeur service, not just rental cars! Call ☎ **01-45-54-33-65** in Paris or arrange it all through your travel agent before you leave home.

SLEEPING IN PARIS

. . . .

HÔTEL DE CRILLON
10 place de la Concorde, 8e (Métro: Concorde)

There isn't a more French status hotel in all of Paris; if you can afford these luxury digs—*voilà!* Intimate in scale, the hotel has the big picture of Paris—you overlook place de la Concorde and sit at the base of the Champs-Elysées; 1 block away is La Madeleine. More importantly, you are only meters from the best shopping districts of Paris, and you can walk just about everywhere. (What you save on taxis you can spend on the room rate.) There's also a Métro stop right in front of the hotel. I have never felt so giddy in my life as the evening I went out for my newspaper at dusk, rounded the corner, and saw the pink light on La Madeleine.

Yes, the Crillon does have a few promotional rates and U.S. dollar prices. It also has some interesting package deals, which often include a variety of luxuries that are nice for anything from a honeymoon to a New Year's Eve you won't forget. There's one package that, at $600 per night, may at first seem expensive. Considering that it includes dinner in the hotel's restaurant, Les Ambassadeurs, prepared by the multistarred and famous new chef, well, it turns out to be a very good value.

The Crillon also offers another shopping package, which includes all sorts of gifts and things, and I've heard from people that it is a sensational value. The Crillon Shopping deal begins in November and goes through the end of March, so you really get in Christmas plus the sale seasons and into pre-Easter shopping. With the package you get your room, an American breakfast, Taittinger champagne, 3 hours of chauffeur-driven car, and a list of shops that will welcome you properly. This means they give you a VIP gift when you come to visit. You get some of the gifts only if you buy something; other stores give you the gift regardless. I know a couple who said they booked the trip and then gave the freebie gifts as their Christmas gifts to business friends and made out like bandits.

For reservations in the United States, call **Leading Hotels** at ☎ **800/223-6800,** or call Hôtels Concorde at ☎ 800/888-4747. The hotel's local phone is ☎ 01-42-65-24-24; fax 01-44-71-15-02.

Four-Star Finds

HÔTEL DU LOUVRE
Place André Malraux, 1er (Métro: Palais Royal)

Although it's not the fanciest place in town, this hotel feels very French and offers many special qualities. The prices are reasonable, and the location can't be beat. What more could you ask for than a hotel that is across the street from the Louvre and 1 block from Monoprix and the Palais Royal? Some rooms overlook the Garnier Opera.

Get a rate guaranteed in U.S. dollars (prices change with the seasons; rooms run about $200 per night when you get a dollar deal) by calling ☎ 800/888-4747. The local phone is ☎ 01-44-58-38-38; fax 01-44-58-38-01.

CONCORDE SAINT-LAZARE
108 rue Saint-Lazare, 8e (Métro: St. Lazare)

First things first: See that I have the word *Concorde* in the name of this hotel? This is very important because there's more than one St. Lazare Hotel in Paris and unless you want to be screaming at taxi drivers and having a total breakdown, you will use the Concorde part when you arrive in Paris and will want to be taken here.

That aside, I almost hate to tell you about this hotel because it's my new secret find and I am terrified it will be overrun and I won't be able to get a room. I cried on my way here, terrified that I had goofed by trying this part of town. Turns out I had tears of joy when I saw the hotel and the landmark lobby, which is more like a set from a movie.

The hotel lobby is drop-dead gorgeous, historical, and protected by French law, and it's also in a well-priced hotel with the best location for shoppers. It's particularly great for people in town for just a day or two, because everything you really need is within 5 minutes of this hotel.

If you've come with nonshopping members of the family, note that this is the historical "Quartier de L'Europe" area of Paris where all the Impressionists painted and there are books and walking tours to the side streets of your very hotel.

If you are a shopper (if?), note that you are next door to a branch of **Euro Sante Beaute,** my favorite *parapharmacie* chain in France, and half a block from a new mall (**Passage du Havre**) that has a branch of everything and leads to the big department stores. Beyond the Passage (this could be the title of a novel) stand all the great department stores in Paris.

There are all sorts of good rates, but expect to pay about 1,400 F ($233) per night. Call **Concorde Hotels** in the United States at ☎ **800-888-4747.** The local phone is 01-40-08-44-44; fax 01-42-93-01-20; www.concordestlazare-paris.com.

NORMANDY HOTEL
7 rue de l'Echelle/256 rue St. Honoré, 1er (Métro: Louvre)

I have not stayed in this hotel and I know that it is not in the same family as the two listed above; however, it has a great location and prices that are a little lower, so you might want to inspect it or phone and see what's going on. I found the hotel by accident: It's a block from the Louvre and from Monoprix and also near the Hotel du Louvre. The local phone is ☎ 01-42-60-30-21; fax 01-42-60-45-81; e-mail: normandy.hotel@hol.fr.

HÔTEL TERMINUS NORD
12 bd. de Denain, 10e (Métro: Gare du Nord)

If your brief visit to Paris is punctuated by train travel, you might be delighted with this fabulous find: a very chic hotel located directly across the street from the Gare du Nord, which is the station for Eurostar. This hotel does not look like much from the street; the lobby looks promising but you may be nervous. Trust me on this, the hotel is a gem. It's been decorated in the gorgeous French country chic of one of the country's best designers and is part of the Libertel/Westin-Demeure chain. Also, the prices are around $175 to $200 a night, making it a wonderful find. I wish I knew a hotel like this in every town!

To book in the United States, call ☎ 800/**WESTIN-1.** The local phone is ☎ 01-42-80-20-00.

LE BIG QUESTION

. . . .

Recently a friend called: He was planning a Valentine's Day trip to Paris with his wife. He wanted to know how to choose between The Ritz, The Bristol, the Meurice and the Plaza Athenee. I thought this was a valid point—when you're booking a room like this, where is the real value? How do the hotels compare and what do you get for more or less the same amount? And is it the same amount? Are there any deals that will help you decide? I booked myself into the big three to give this report. Note, the going rack rate for all these hotels is about $500 a night. That doesn't mean you can't get a deal, however! Depending on season or promotional rates, you may be able to get one of these rooms for as little as $335 to $400 a night. Also note that I sent my friends to The Crillon, where they got a dollar rate through Concorde Hotels of $428 per night.

Hôtel Ritz
Place Vendome, 1er (Métro: Tuilleries or Opéra)

I wanted to hate The Ritz. I wanted to say there was no reason to stay here, to book here, to dream here, to think twice. I wanted to say The Ritz is for people who don't know who they are, so they hide behind a hotel with a reputation as big as The Ritz. But now that I've been there, I can't say a word of that. In fact, I think the only people who book here are the ones who know themselves, and Paris, quite well and realize that you can do without many things in life, but if you are a Ritz person, The Ritz is not one of them.

I learned a million things about life, and hotels, while I stayed at The Ritz. Mostly I learned that the person who stays here only wants to stay in the Vendome part of the hotel (ask when you book) and wants to appreciate the details. My hot water bottle was filled and placed into my bed; a letter was delivered on a silver tray, waiting on my pillow with a rose.

In terms of price, The Ritz is very expensive but can be competitive with the other hotels in this group. In the off-season, you can possibly negotiate a better deal. Call **Leading Hotels of the World** for reservations in the United States. The local phone is ☎ **01-43-16-30-30.**

THE BRISTOL
112 rue du Faubourg St. Honoré, 8e (Métro: Matignon)

Most insiders agree that The Bristol is the best hotel in Paris. It's quiet, not flashy, and beautifully run in a way that doesn't actually seem French: Everything in this hotel works and nothing seems to go wrong. It is not for the person who needs or craves the limelight of The Ritz; it's for the quiet wealthy who don't like to be recognized. It's also a great business hotel.

In terms of location, the hotel takes some getting used to. It is on the city's fancy shopping street, but at the far end, closer to Champs-Elysées. The good news is that you can walk either way, and the bad news is that if you're used to being in the first arrondissement (1er) or the more middle sections of the eighth arrondissement (8e), this does take some getting used to.

Important details to note: The chef trained with Ducasse and is considered the best hotel chef in Paris; adjacent to the hotel is **Anne Semonin,** a skin guru who does the best jet lag treatment in the world, so ask the hotel to book an appointment for your arrival. Hotel amenities are by Hermès and Anne Semonin and the down duvet is worth the price of the room.

For U.S. reservations book through Leading Hotels of the World. The local phone is ☎ 01-53-43-43-00.

THE MEURICE
228 rue de Rivoli, 1er (Métro: Tuilleries)

The Meurice has been my regular hotel in Paris for over a decade, and I only moved to the Crillon when things got a little shabby. Now the hotel has just undergone an enormous renovation to welcome it to The Audley Group, which also owns The Dorchester in London. The idea is to upgrade Meurice to that level. The front door has been moved to rue du Rivoli and much has been changed. I stayed here during the renovations because there was a great dollar deal of $335 a night during the works. Obviously rates will rise, but to lure customers back, there will be promotional deals. Check them out.

Meurice has the best location in town for me, a one-star chef, and a gorgeous room for breakfast (similar to the gorgeous room in the Crillon). Call Leading Hotels of the World in the United States. The local phone is ☎ 01-44-58-10-50.

WINTER BREAKS & SHOPPING DEALS
· ·

As you saw, The Crillon has one of the most extraordinary shopping packages in the business, but it is not the only hotel to have a shopping package or a winter deal. Just about every hotel in Paris drops its prices, especially between December 15 and January 15; many have great deals until the end of March (unless Easter falls in March).

For a luxury room with a great reputation, a good location, and a fine dollar deal, check out some of these finds.

LE PARC
55-57 av. Raymond-Poincare, 16e (Métro: Victor Hugo)

One of the fanciest hotels in Paris, and the home of Alain Ducasse's Paris eats, this hotel is in the 16e for easy shopping in luxury areas. Winter rates are $250 to $270 per night, and that includes breakfast. This is the deal of the century! Note the chain also has other properties that are almost as nice, so if this one is full ask about the others. For reservations in the United States, call **Westin Hotels** at ☎ **800-WESTIN-1.** The local phone is 01-44-05-66-66.

HOTEL ROYAL MONCEAU
37 av. Hoche, 8e (Métro: Courcelles)

From December 15 until January 15 of each winter season, the rates go down to about $300 per night, which may make this a nice luxury bargain. The hotel was built in 1928, has a gorgeous pool, a chef who trained with Alain Ducasse, and a location at the top of the Champs-Elysées. The local phone is ☎ **01-42-99-88-00.**

PARIS HILTON
18 av. Suffren, 15e (Métro: Bir Hakeim)

This hotel is not in the heart of any Paris shopping district, but it's not totally inconvenient either and they often have good Hilton breaks. My girlfriend Dominique stayed here with her car and said the location was great for getting in and out and around. In the United States, book through ☎ **800-HILTONS.** The local phone is 01-42-73-92-00.

SHOPPING HOURS
· ·

You're in the big city now, so forget everything you learned about provincial shopping hours. Most stores in Paris are open during the lunch hour; all big stores are open on Monday mornings. Shopping hours are usually 10am to 7pm. Some big stores stay open until 9pm or even 10pm.

The big department stores tend to open at 9:30am, while the dime stores (**Monoprix** and **Prisunic**) open at 8:30am. Gourmet Lafayette is open until 9pm as are some of the other dime stores. The **Prisunic** on the Champs-Elysées is open until 10pm in winter and midnight in summer.

SUNDAY SHOPPING

Sundays aren't dead in Paris. They never really were because of the flea market and antique business, but now more and more districts have stores fighting government regulations against Sunday openings. In fact, it's my bet that in short order Sunday shopping will be legal.

Currently, to be open on Sunday an area must be designated a tourist zone—both the Marais and the Champs-Elysées are so-called. Richard Branson started it all by opening his Virgin store and paying the fines; now almost all stores on the Champs-Elysées are open on *dimanche*. Thank you, Richard.

Flea markets and antique "villages" are also open on Sunday. The mall in the Louvre is hopping. On a Sunday I love to do the rue Cler and then the Village Suisse, both of which are near the Paris Hilton.

According to French law, stores that don't pay fines and aren't in tourist areas may open five Sundays a year. These events are usually held in the fall to build up to Christmas. Some stores do an opening on Easter Sunday or Mother's Day. All such openings are called *oeuveture exceptionelle*.

SHOPPING STRATEGIES

Sometimes it takes a plan to save money or some time. Also, there's every chance that once the European Union switches to the euro, the dollar will go down in value, so you'll be forced to look for value and smart strategies.

- If spending 1,200 F ($200) takes some doing on your part, but you want to take advantage of the tax refund (*détaxe*) in France, plan ahead of time where you think you are most likely to spend that kind of money and get the refund. Then allow time for the paperwork. I usually buy my perfume and makeup once a year in one power spree to get the tax back. You can also do all your shopping within one department store so you can add together your purchases to reach the 1,200 F total. Don't buy a little here and a little there if you think you can save money with a strategy.

- Check for stores that will let you collect receipts over a period of time, so that you can get the refund once you hit the 1,200 F magic mark. As long as the spread is no more than 6 months, this is legal. It's especially convenient if you are traveling throughout France and may buy a little something here and a little something there. Chanel taught me this trick, Sephora is happy to comply, and most big firms will help out.

- Note that real life in Paris is expensive. You'll do best if you splurge on one fabulous something or limit yourself to small gifts, food items, and souvenirs in the $5 to $10 range. I met a man who buys his wife a single Hermès scarf once a year when he goes to Paris on business. That's smart shopping. Best buys in France are luxury goods that will last forever (and possibly gain in value) or cheapie fun things and edibles.

- Stores begin to open around 9:30am, so start with one that opens at that time and keep on going nonstop. I usually begin at Catherine (7 rue Castiglione, 1er; Métro: Concorde), which is a tiny perfume shop best visited at 9:30, before it gets crowded. The store offers a 45% discount (30% regular store discount plus 15% détaxe refund), making it one of the best duty-free shops in town. If you don't qualify for the détaxe refund, you still get the flat 30% discount on all goods except Chanel and Christian Dior, which are offered at a 20% discount. If you show your copy of this edition of *Born to Shop France*, you will receive a 25% discount on Chanel and Christian Dior as well. Catherine offers customers détaxe after they have spent 1,600 F gross (amount spent before flat discount is taken).

- If you are planning to shop in any of the big department stores, try to get there around 10am or earlier, when they open. By noon, they will be very crowded.

- When you shop in small stores, remember your French manners; see chapter 4.

- Consider making one big haul of the same item as gifts for everyone; with luck you'll buy enough to qualify for détaxe. I've been buying candle gifts the last year or two, stocking up at L'Occitane, Diptyqe, or Marriage Frere, listed in financial progression. Marriage Frere's candle is almost $50 a pop, but it's great. Diptype sells for about $40 in the United States and about $30 in France. Yesssss!

- Wear comfortable shoes and a handbag that either fits across your body or can be worn under your coat. Paris is not any more dangerous than any other big city, but with jumping on and off the Métro and bustling around, you want to make sure you aren't an easy target.

- As you plan your day, know where you want to end up for lunch. If your time is limited, your shopping will be much more successful if planned properly. Even if you just want fast food, know which neighborhood you plan to hit at lunchtime and the type of meal that will best fulfill your fantasies. Also plan a proper tea or coffee break for around 4pm. You may also want to work in a drop-off point to get rid of your packages.

- The big sales are held in mid-June and mid-January. There is a page in *Le Figaro* newspaper called "Le Carnet du Jour," which lists the major happenings of the day. On this page each of the

big-time designers takes out an ad to announce
his or her big sale dates—even Hermès. Flea markets or special shopping events can be found in
the listings part of the page.

- Use credit cards whenever possible to get a better rate of exchange.

- Keep receipts to declare your goods when you
return home. Don't try to run anything past U.S.
Customs officers; nothing screams out like a new
handbag or a pair of *ooh la la* shoes.

- Allow at least a half-hour at the Paris airport for
reclaiming your tax refund if you are leaving the
European Union from Paris. If you are going on
to another country in the EU, no sweat—you only
claim your refund as you depart the EU for good.
If it's the height of the summer season, allow an
hour.

SHOPPING HOT SPOTS

Since you're on a tear, I thought I'd list the best neighborhoods for indulging. You may not even need
specifics—just go on a prowl and see what you turn
up.

The Best-Known Tony Shopping Street

Of course it's the rue du Faubourg St. Honoré. Most
of the stars in international design have shops here.
This is a strolling and window-shopping street with
a few affordable stores and many of the world's fanciest art galleries, antique shops, and designer
flagships.

Choose from **Gianni Versace** (Italian), **Joan &
David** (American), **Jaeger** (British), and big names
such as **Yves Saint Laurent Rive Gauche,** which happens to have a new story to tell—this line is now
designed for YSL by an American in Paris. While
new stores keep opening up here and the area is
important for its image, this might not be on your
must-do list unless you are really into big-time

labels. Perhaps all you can afford to do on this street of dreams is eat a burger. If so, check out Café Bleu, inside the Lanvin men's store (no. 15).

Do note, however, that this street connects magnificently to other, more realistic, shopping spots. It's only 2 blocks from a shopper's department store heaven (see below), 1 block from place Vendome (more fancier-than-thou shops), 2 blocks from Opéra, and just down the street from a marvelous and relatively inexpensive shopping street, the rue St. Honoré, which is an extension of the rue du Faubourg St. Honoré. Once you've shopped them both, you won't get them confused.

Indeed, I'm big on the area adjacent to the rue du Faubourg St. Honoré, including the rue Royale, which leads to place de la Madeleine, rue St. Honoré, rue de Castiglione, and to a nugget of great stores with great addresses that aren't directly on the Faubourg. I also eat my lunch in this part of town almost every day—at **Angelina,** a tea room on the rue Rivoli; **Hôtel Lotti,** which offers a fixed-price full menu for about $25 per person; or **Pizzeria Venus,** on the rue St. Honoré (No. 326). I eat a lot of pizza in Paris. Across the street from my pizzeria is **Colette,** a newish American style store that is *the* place to be seen, to drink water, and to nosh. If you prefer the uptown scene, there's the bar at the **Hôtel Meurice,** or the fine dining at **Hôtel Costes,** each a block from here; both located to be part of the scene and make your day a perfect one.

The Fanciest Shopping Street

Get a look at avenue Montaigne; shop this 2- to 3-block stretch and see it all. On the way, you'll pass every big name from **Bulgari** (no. 27) to **Ungaro** (no. 2). Hmmm, make that **Valentino** (no. 17) and **Vuitton** (no. 54), with Christian **Dior** (no. 30), **Nina Ricci** (no. 39), and **Perfumes Caron** thrown in for good fun. Eat an affordable but ever-so-chic lunch at the cafe in **Joseph** (no. 14). **Inès de la Fresange** is the girl next door. If you're flush with francs and want something to remember for the rest of your life, have lunch in the courtyard at the Hotel Plaza Athénée (no. 25), where you'll dine on custom-made **Porthault** linen replete with red geraniums. There's more shopping, of course. Yes, even **Chanel** (no. 42). By the way, I call this the *good* Chanel because the help here is friendly and helpful, not like at the Cambon store. Note that there's a new Vuitton on the Champs-Elysées and much is changed in Paris, but **Calvin Klein** came to Montaigne (if the Montaigne can't come to Mohammed) and that Dior has totally redone the store so that it is stunning and much more fun to shop.

Best Born Again Shopping Street

I used to detest the Champs-Elysées, but I am finally impressed—it was the new **Louis Vuitton/ Marc Jacobs** stuff that did it for me. I think The Gap outside of the United States is just funny, but there's a big new **Gap** store at Rond Point and there's much stuff in between, including a marvy **Prisunic**, a Disney Store (puh-lease!), a new **FNAC** to compete with Richard Branson's **Virgin Megastore**, a new branch of **Laduree** that will knock your socks off, and ever so much more. **Sephora** has become a local icon for perfume and beauty cures.

The Best of the Left Bank

Wait a minute Mr. Postman! *Zut alors* and *mon Dieu!* The funky Left Bank is changing as you read. Paris's premier fun-style shopping neighborhood has sold out, and gobs of big-name designers are moving in. Get there before all is lost.

This is the part of town where you used to just wander and find all sorts of wonderful things. Now that's a little bit harder, but the back streets are still sublime. Various nooks and crannies of the neighborhood are devoted to shoes or fabric houses or antique shops. There's even a 1-block stretch (on rue St. Placide) of discount shops across from the department store Bon Marché; it's for the strong of heart.

For a lunch break, you can splurge on one of the famous (expensive) cafes on boulevard St. Germain, although the Brasserie Lipp gives the good tables to the celebs and Yves Saint Laurent. Les Deux Magots was a Hemingway hangout and Café de Flore is almost as famous.

The best little streets are rue Dragon, rue Cherche Midi, rue de Seine, rue de Buci, and the tiny place de Furstemburg. To see, and feel, the spirit of the Left Bank, you must leave the boulevard St. Germain!

The Best of the Louvre

The back end of the Louvre stretches along the rue de Rivoli for several blocks. Inside there may be art treasures, but outside—stores. In fact, there are even stores underneath. Check out **Carrousel du Louvre,** an American-style shopping mall attached to the Louvre. It has a food court on the mezzanine level, and it is attached to the Louvre through a gallery lined with museum gift shops and a row of stores, including **The Body Shop, Esprit, Lalique, Courreges,** and **Virgin Megastore.** Everything is open on Sunday, so if you need a shopping fix when Paris seems closed, this is the place.

Across the street is a building filled with antique dealers, **Le Louvre des Antiquaires.** One block over is the Palais Royal, which has a hidden garden filled with arcades of tiny, wonderful shops. This is one of my favorite spots in all of Paris. Don't miss **Shiseido,** if only to gawk: No, it's not a Japanese store, it's a gorgeous makeup and perfume shop.

Meanwhile, the 2-block parade along rue de Rivoli across from the museum is door-to-door tourist traps, selling every imaginable sweatshirt, T-shirt, ashtray, and lighter, plus a few perfume and scarf shops. One block away, discreetly tucked behind that gold statue of Joan of Arc, is a branch of **Monoprix.**

Don't miss the opportunity to eat lunch at Café Marly, which faces the courtyard of the Louvre. Lunch runs about $15 per person.

Best Museum Shop

Hard to pick, especially since most of the museums banded together to form their own buying and selling operation. Still, get over to the Hotel de la Monnaie, not a hotel at all but the French mint. There they have super jewelry gift items inspired by money. The museum is located at 11 quai de Conti, 6e, and the boutique is at 2 rue Guénégaud, 6e. Open all day on Monday through Friday, they close for lunch on Saturday from 1pm until 2pm. To see more, try the Web site at www.monnaiedeparis.fr.

The Best Department Store Street

This could be department store heaven or hell, depending on what time of year it is and how you feel about crowds. The two most famous department stores in Paris, **Galeries Lafayette** and **Au Printemps,** are side by side on the boulevard Haussman.

The stores are both divided into several buildings, so it can get confusing. Have patience; you're about to have the time of your life. Also note that across the street from the French biggies is British retail giant Marks & Spencer, where many French yuppies prefer to shop. Meanwhile, next door to Galeries Lafayette there's a branch of **Monoprix** with a fabulous supermarket upstairs, **Gourmet Lafayette.** This is not a very good Monoprix, but Gourmet Lafayette is true heaven.

On the curb in front of all these stores there are stalls and hawkers selling promotional merchandise from inside the stores. Buy a crepe and munch and stare.

For lunch, get a picnic from Gourmet Lafayette, or head for **Ladurée** (16 rue Royale), a famous tea room, for a light lunch or snacks. Ladurée is around the corner from the big department stores and halfway to rue St. Honoré.

The Best Weird Place You Won't Find on Your Own

Le Viaduct des Arts   An old viaduct has been transformed into a mini shopping mall, with stores located in the archways! It's in the 12th arrondissement, and it runs along the avenue Daumesnil between Bastille and Gare de Lyon. Take the Métro to Daumesnil.

The Best of the Marais

Hidden away in an almost medieval part of Paris, the Marais features a large square surrounded by an arcade of stores and a series of small back streets. This area is home to a lot of the funky designer shops that are the backbone of Paris style. Small multidesigner shops feature the latest from people like Helmut Lang. Come for tea and a stroll—especially if you believe in magic.

Outside the Marais, but only 2 blocks away, is the Village St. Paul (rue St. Paul), a small antique district between the Marais and the Seine. The 50 stores here are open on Sunday; many of the stores in the Marais are also open on Sunday.

In the other direction from the river, back into the depths of the small streets, is the Picasso Museum. As you walk there, you'll pass more and more tiny shops featuring the latest ideas from the cutting edge of Paris style.

The Best Street Markets

Rue de Buci, 6e (Métro: St. Germain)

Every day of the week except Monday—don't miss it for the world.

Rue Cler, 7e (Métro: Latour Marbourg)

Sunday mornings; for real foodies and gourmands.

The Best Flea Markets

MARCHÉ AUX PUCES
St. Ouen (Métro: Porte de Clingancourt)

The most famous flea market in Paris is actually a city of almost a dozen different flea markets, each with its own name and type of goods. Located about a half-hour from the center of Paris, it's open Saturday, Sunday, and Monday only.

PUCES DE VANVES
14e (Métro: Porte de Vanves)

Closer to central Paris and more of a tag sale sort of a thing, this Saturday and Sunday market is the real insider's place to get a bargain. On Sunday, there's also a fruit and food market one street over.

BASIC PARIS RESOURCES
FROM A TO Z

. . . .

The Big Names (French & Italian)

AZZEDINE ALAIA
7 rue de Moussy, 4e (Métro: St. Paul)

GIORGIO ARMANI
6 place Vendome, 1er (Métro: Tuileries)

ARMANI EMPORIO
150 bd. des St. Germain du Prés, 6e (Métro: St. Germain des Prés)

BACCARAT
11 place de la Madeleine, 8e (Métro: Madeleine)

BALMAIN
44 rue François, 8e (Métro: Franklin Roosevelt)

BERNARDAUD
9 rue Royale, 8e (Métro: Concorde)

HUGO BOSS
374 rue St. Honoré, 8e (Métro: Concorde)

MARIELLA BURANI
412 rue St. Honoré, 8e (Métro: Concorde)

CACHAREL
34 rue Tronchet, 8e (Métro: Madeleine)

PIERRE CARDIN
29 rue du Faubourg St. Honoré, 8e (Métro: Concorde)

CARTIER
13 rue de la Paix, 2e (Métro: Opéra)

49 rue Francois 1er, 8e (Métro: Franklin Roosevelt)

41 rue de Rennes, 6e (Métro: St. Germain des Prés)

CÉLINE
38 av. Montaigne, 8e (Métro: Franklin Roosevelt)

24 rue Francois 1er, 8e (Métro: Franklin Roosevelt)

CERRUTI 1881
15 place de la Madeleine, 8e (Métro: Madeleine)

NINO CERRUTI JEANS
27 rue Royale, 8e (Métro: Madeleine)

CHANEL
30 rue Cambon, 1er (Métro: Concorde)

42 av. Montaigne, 8e (Métro: Franklin Roosevelt)

CHLOE
54 rue du Faubourg St. Honoré, 8e (Métro: Concorde)

ANDRE COURREGES
7 rue de Turbigo, 1er (Métro: Etienne Marcel)

CHRISTIAN DIOR
30 av. Montaigne, 8e (Métro: Alma Marceau)

16 rue de l'Abbaye, 6e (Métro: Saint Germain des Prés)

FAÇONNABLE
9 rue du Faubourg St. Honoré, 8e(Métro: Concorde)

LOUIS FÉRAUD
88 rue du Faubourg St. Honoré, 8e (Métro: Concorde)

SALVATORE FERRAGAMO
45 av. Montaigne, 8e (Métro: Alma Marceau)

50 rue du Faubourg St. Honoré, 8e (Métro: Concorde)

GIANFRANCO FERRE
23 rue du Faubourg St. Honoré, 8e (Métro: Concorde)

JEAN PAUL GAULTIER
6 rue Vivienne, 1er (Métro: Palais Royal)

GENNY
51 av. Montaigne, 8e (Métro: Alma Marceau)

GIVENCHY
29–31 av. Georges V, 8e (Métro: Georges V)

GUCCI
2 rue du Faubourg St. Honoré, 8e (Métro: Concorde)

HERMÈS
24 rue du Faubourg St. Honoré, 8e (Métro: Concorde)

KENZO
Place de la Madeleine, 8e (Métro: Madeleine)

Place des Victoires, 2e (Métro: Palais Royal)

MICHEL KLEIN
6 rue du Pré aux Clercs, 7e (Métro: Bac)

KRIZIA
48 av. Montaigne, 8e (Métro: Alma Marceau)

LACOSTE
372 rue St. Honoré, 1er (Métro: Concorde)

CHRISTIAN LACROIX
26 av. Montaigne, 8e (Métro: Alma Marceau)

73 rue du Faubourg St. Honoré, 8e (Métro: Concorde)

LALIQUE
11 rue Royale, 8e (Métro: Concorde)

GUY LAROCHE
22 rue de la Tremoille, 8e (Métro: Franklin Roosevelt)

HERVÉ LEGER
29 rue du Faubourg St. Honoré, 8e (Métro: Concorde)

LOLITA LEMPCKA
14 rue du Faubourg St. Honoré, 8e (Métro: Concorde)

LÉONARD
36 av. Pierre, 1er de Serbie, 16e (Métro: Iéna)

LOEWE
46 av. Montaigne, 8e (Métro: Alma-Marceauc)

MAX MARA
265 rue St. Honoré, 1er (Métro: Concorde)

THIERRY MUGLER
49 av. Montaigne, 8e (Métro: Alma Marceau)

MUIMUI
10 rue Cherche Midi, 6e (Métro: Sévres Babylone)

JEAN PATOU
7 rue St. Florentin, 8e (Métro: Concorde)

PRADA
5 rue de Grenelle, 7e (Métro: Sévres Babylone)

NINA RICCI
39 av. Montaigne, 8e (Métro: Alma Marceau)

SONIA RYKIEL
70 rue du Faubourg St. Honoré, 8e (Métro: Concorde)

175 bd. St Germain, 6e (Métro: St. Germain)

Yves Saint Laurent
32 & 38 rue du Faubourg St. Honoré, 8e (Métro: Concorde)

Yves Saint Laurent Variation
9 rue Grenelle, 7e (Métro: Bac)

Chantal Thomass
1 rue Vivienne, 2e (Métro: Palais Royal)

Emanuel Ungaro
2 av. Montaigne, 8e (Métro: Alma Marceau)

Valentino
17 av. Montaigne, 8e (Métro: Alma Marceau)

Gianni Versace
62 rue du Faubourg St. Honoré (Métro: Concorde)

Louis Vuitton
58 av. Montaigne, 8e (Métro: Alma-Marceau)

78 bis av. Marceau, 8e (Métro: Etoile)

6 place St. Germain des Prés, 6e (Métro: St. Germain)

101 av. des Champs-Elysées, 8e (Métro: Victor Hugo)

Other Big Names

Akris
54 rue du Faubourg St. Honoré (Métro: Concorde)

Laura Ashley
261 rue St. Honoré, 1er (Métro: Concorde)

Episode
277 rue St. Honoré, 1er (Métro: Concorde)

Escada
51 av. Montaigne, 8e (Métro: Alma Marceau)

14 rue de la Paix, 2e (Métro: Opéra)

JOSEPH
44 rue Etienne Marcel, 2e (Métro: Etienne Marcel)

14 av. Montaigne, 8e (Métro: Franklin Roosevelt)

RALPH LAUREN
2 place de la Madeleine, 8e (Métro: Madeleine)

JOYCE MA
Jardins du Palais Royal, 1er (Métro: Palais Royal)

ISSEY MIYAKE
3 place des Vosges, 3e (Métro: St. Paul)

JIL SANDER
52 av. Montaigne, 8e (Métro: Alma Marceau)

Chocolate & Foodstuff

DEBAUVE & GALLAIS
30 rue de St. Pères, 7e (Métro: St. Germain)

33 rue Vivienne, 2e (Métro: Palais Royal)

One of the Louis kings gave these guys a royal warrant, and they've been chocolating since 1800. Check out the chocolate postcard for $6; great gift item.

NICOLAS
189 rue St. Honoré, 1er (Métro: Palais Royal)

This is a chain of wine shops with stores all over Paris and all over France. I happen to use this branch because it's part of my regular shopping prowl. Not only do they have a good selection at affordable prices, they also print up a list of prices so you can comparison shop.

MARRIAGE FRÈRES
260 rue du Faubourg St. Honoré, 8e (Métro: Ch.-de-Gaulle Etoile)

Do not think from this address that this is near the good shopping part of the Faubourg. Marriage Freres is near l'Etoile, in the 16e, in an area that's still part of the fancy Paris shopping, but it's not in the prime shopping district. I ended up taking a cab when I realized I was lost in space. There are other branches!

This famed tea room also sells its product, and the product is more than hundreds of varieties of tea! There's also information on tea, teapots, tea scented candles and much more. Watch out—this place is mobbed on weekends.

Hediard
126 rue du Bac, 7e (Métro: Bac)

There are a handful of shops in this famed gourmet family—I choose this one because I also want you to stroll the rue du Bac, the source of all French foodstuff, from mustards to pastry to chocolates. They also have a newly renovated shop at place de la Madeleine (no. 21), where most fine French food-stuff shops are located.

La Maison du Miel
24 rue Vignon, 9e (Métro: Madeleine)

Around the corner from the big department stores, near many of the temples to French fine food, and in the path of almost all shoppers, this tiny shop is a photo-op as well as a step back in history. All they sell is honey, honey. Note that they open at 9:30am, so you can pop in on your way to les grands magasins.

Department Stores

They are called *les grands magasins* by the French, a term you need to know because it is often listed in the resource list in magazine ads. The two most famous ones, Galeries Lafayette and Au Printemps, have stores all over France—although nothing can compete with their flagship stores in Paris.

Those in a hurry may find that visiting one or even two department stores is the answer to all their prayers. These stores are huge: They carry a little of everything, they are great on a rainy day, and they offer a flat 10% discount to foreigners (pick up the free discount vouchers at your hotel or at the store) plus a *détaxe* refund when you qualify.

Both stores have information desks where someone always speaks your language. They might not offer an intimate French moment, but they can be convenient. Also note that the two biggies are in a war of renovations and innovations and are modernizing each day.

AU PRINTEMPS
64 bd. Haussmann 9e (Métro: Havre-Caumartin)

This store has two parts; Printemps Maison is my favorite. The street level offers perfume and makeup, but the rest of the store is devoted to home style and tabletop. The other store is a full department store with everything and anything the entire family could want or need.

BHV
52 rue du Rivoli, 4e (Métro: Hôtel de Ville)

This is an average department store with the most famous basement in Paris: hardware and gadgets galore. Much fun.

BON MARCHÉ
5 rue de Babylone, 6e (Métro: Sévres-Babylone)

This is getting to be my favorite department store in Paris. There's a grocery store (across the street), a flea market (upstairs from the grocery store), and everything in the world you could need inside the mother store. It's also in a great Left Bank location, and they open at 9:30am every day (closed on Sunday).

GALERIES LAFAYETTE
40 bd. Haussmann, 9e (Métro: Chaussée-d' Antin)

There are actually four stores that make up the whole and a slew of street vendors out front and in the streets between the parts of the store. You'll either love Galeries Lafayette or leave it. Certainly you can't fault the place for drama—do look at that ceiling—or the fact that they have the widest selection of every possible French maker right under their many rooftops.

Be sure to stop under the dome on the street level of the main store—it's where the newest French fragrances are always launched.

Design & Tabletop

Some neighborhoods are pockets of designer showrooms; check out the design resources on the Left Bank. Paris stands for high style and unfailing perfection. Check out chains such as **Genevieve Lethu, Conran,** and **Habitat,** and stores such as **Printemps Maison** and **Galeries Lafayette.** The basement (SS level) in Galeries Lafayette is crammed with more glories than the mind can absorb.

Maison de Famille began on the Left Bank but now has a store on the Right Bank (10 place des la Madeleine, 8e) and is branching out to other towns with their very chic, country-style tabletop and gifts.

Souleiado
78 rue de Seine, 6e (Métro: St. Germain)

This is the most famous name in country French fabrics and design. In addition to stores all over France, there's a rather nice Souleiado tucked into the Left Bank. It's not cheap, but it's less in France than in the United States.

Muriel Grateau
Jardins du Palais Royal, 1er (Métro: Palais Royal)

Once the darling of ready-to-wear, Ms. Grateau now does linens and tabletop and is the most chic label on anyone's table in Paris.

DIPTYQUE
34 bd. Saint Germain, 5e (Métro: St. Michel)

Since I imagine scent for the home falls into this category, I've gone with a specialty listing that you need, partly because looking at the address doesn't begin to tell you that it's not where you think it is or want it to be. Note the store is in the 5th and you get out of the Métro at St. Michel! This is not the regular shopping part of St. Germain. Still, it's worth a special trip because you can get all the gifts—great soaps, candles, and scents—you may ever need and treat yourself as well. Prices are about 30% more in the United States and they do have mail order. Closed on Monday.

ESTEBAN
48 rue de Rennes, 6e (Métro: Saint Germain des Prés)

While we're on the subject of home scent, this gentleman has made his rep on it. There's even scented vacuum cleaner powder. The line is sold in most department stores and specialty stores, or you can visit the free-standing store devoted to candles, drawer lining, incense burners, and much more. Good place for gifts. Not sold in the United States that I know of.

Discount & Resale

Stock means what it says. It's leftover stock sold at a discount at assorted stock shops, many run by designers. They are packed together in neighborhoods. Check out either the rue Alesia, 14e, for names like Sonia Rykiel and Cacharel, or the rue St. Placide, where there are jobbers who sell stock.

ANNA LOWE
104 rue du Faubourg St. Honoré, 8e (Métro:Concorde)

Right near The Bristol's end of town, this famous resource has moved and has its usual selection of name merchandise at prices lower than retail. Last time I was there, there wasn't too much to brag about, but over the years this has been a fabulous source and it's convenient enough to dash in to check out. The Web site is at www.Sollers.fr/AnnaLowe.

RÉCIPROQUE
123 rue de la Pompe (Métro: Pompe)

Queen of the Parisian resale shops, with several stores in a row selling men's and women's clothing and household items. It's in to cluck over how high the prices have gotten.

CATHERINE BARRIL
14 rue de la Tour, 16e (Métro: Passy)

Right off the rue Passy, all the easier for Madame to stop by for a slightly used Chanel suit.

LA CLÉ DES MARQUES
20 place du Marché Saint Honoré, 1er (Métro: Tuileries)

Last season's big names, everything from Dior to Valentino.

TATI
140 rue de Rennes, 6e (Métro: Rennes)

13 place de la Republique, 10e (Métro: République)

Several shops on boulevard Rochechouart, 18e (Métro: Anvers)

The mother ship—a string of many storefronts—is the best known, but it's in the middle of nowhere. The Left Bank shop only begins to give you the flavor of what Tati has become: famous. Make that *infamous.*

Tati dumps unwanted junk on the marketplace, but every now and then it lets go of a gem. Models and big names have been known to pick through the bins. If you can take it, you may have fun. Only for those with true grit and time to spare. Their pink and white gingham shopping bag is a statement in reverse chic. I was once thrown off the property of The Ritz Hotel for toting a Tati shopping bag. Really.

French Passages

GALERIE VIVIENNE
Rue Vivienne, 2e (Métro: Palais Royal)

GALERIE VELO-DUDAT
2 rue Bouloi, 1er (Métro: Louvre)

PASSAGE ROYALE
Rue Royale, 8e (Métro: Concorde)

Shoes & Bags

ROBERT CLERGERIE
5 rue du Cherche Midi, 6e (Métro: Sévres Babylone)

PATRICK COX
62 rue Tiquetonne (Métro: Etienne Marcel)

DELVAUX
18 rue Royale, 8e (Métro: Concorde)

MAUD FRIZON
83 rue des Saints-Pères, 6e (Métro: Sévres-Babylone)

STEPHAN KELIAN
13 bis rue de Grenelle, 7e (Métro: Sévres Babylone)

CHRISTIAN LABOUTIN
19 rue Jean-Jacques Rousseau, 2e (Métro: Palais Royal)

DIDIER LAMARTHE
219 rue St. Honoré, 1er (Métro: Concorde)

DIEGO DELLA VALLE
52 rue du Faubourg St. Honoré, 8e (Métro: Concorde)

ROGER VIVIER
24 rue Grenelle, 7e (Métro: Bac)

Lingerie

Nothing could be more French than fine lingerie. The department stores have excellent selections; I often buy at Monoprix because it is cheaper than department stores. But there are a number of French chains in Paris and the provinces that are sort of like Victoria's Secret. I must also confess that while I paid $100 for a brassiere and two pairs of bikini panties (I consider this outrageously expensive), this is the best bra I've ever owned and I look great in it (not out of it).

SABBIA ROSE
73 rue des St. Pères, 6e (Métro: Sèvres Babylone)

Expensive beyond belief ($600 for a pair of silk drawers), this is the most coveted address in a man's little black book. Madonna gave me this address.

LA PERLA
20 rue du Faubourg St. Honoré, 8e (Métro: Concorde)

Italian line of luxuries, which includes not only underwear but bathing suits and made-to-measure items for the hard to fit.

WOLFORD
66 rue de Rennes, 6e (Métro: Saint Germain des Prés)

This is an expensive brand of pantyhose and lingerie/body items, but the quality is high and they last forever and prices are better than in the United States. Check out "Starcknaked," a stretch thing designed by Philippe Starck for Wolford.

Malls

LE VILLAGE ROYAL
25 rue Royale, 8e (Métro: Madeleine)

This is an itty-bitty mall—done village style, à la Beverly Hills—located right in the heart of Paris's luxury shopping district. Stores are affordable and include Et Vous, a fashionable line for work or weekend.

LES TROIS QUARTIERS
23 bd. de la Madeline, 8e (Métro: Madeleine)

This is an American-style mall with a large perfume shop (Silver Moon) and branches of many French designer shops, including **Chacock** and **Tehen,** as well as **Dorothée Bis, Kookai, Agatha,** and even **The Body Shop.** The prime shopping location makes it all worthwhile. It's 1 block from Le Village Royal.

CARROUSEL DU LOUVRE
100 rue Rivoli, 1er (Métro: Palais Royal)

It's not just the shopping that's fun—it's the whole thing: You're under the Louvre, you've got access to museum gift shops (lots of 'em), there's a great food court (mezzanine level), and some branches of name-brand stores. Despite its American flavor, I like it here.

MARCHÉ SAINT GERMAIN
14 rue Lobineau, 6e (Métro: Odéon)

This new American-style mall predicts the unfortunate nature of the developing Left Bank—The Gap takes up half the mall; English multiples fill the rest. An important piece of Paris was destroyed to build this little folly. It could be the end of civilization.

FORUM LES HALLES
Les Halles, 3e (Métro: Les Halles)

Site of the former food markets, now a giant mall without any charm whatsoever. It's near the Centre Georges Pompidou and two fun streets to stroll for French fashion designer shops, rue Etienne Marcel and place des Victoires. As for the mall itself, I think you can take a pass.

PLAZA PASSY
53 rue Passy, 16e (Métro: Passy)

A small American-style mall with the Gap and French yuppie hangouts. I love the grocery store. Honest! Big toy store if you need items for the kids.

PASSAGE DU HAVRE
109 rue St. Lazare, 8e (Métro: St. Lazare)

Located at the back end of the boulevard Haussmann, so you can move right on to the major department stores, this American-style mall has one of every French multiple you can imagine and is a super find for those in a big rush. There's a large branch of **Sephora** at the far end of the mall as well as branches of everything from **L'Occitane** to **Nature Company** to all the cheap clothing lines, and jewelry. There are some fast-food places as well as a tiny branch of **H&M**, which does a terrible disservice to H&M,

Markets & Fairs

Paris has a wide assortment of regular street markets for fruits, veggies, and other foods. Every district of Paris has its own markets, which are open a different day of the week. If it's Tuesday, this must be Raspail, or something like that. The markets do differ with some of the neighborhoods; to get a true taste of Paris, you might want to try several. The best shopping is at 7am. Bargains begin around noon because the stall holders pack up by 1pm.

Street markets are usually closed on Monday morning, but open Tuesday through Saturday, from 7am to 1pm, and if there is an afternoon market, 4 to 7pm. On Sunday, business ceases at 1pm. There are Monday markets; check specifically for them in Le Figaro.

There are also a number of regular flea markets for weekend shopping fun.

In addition to the regular flea markets, Paris has a number of special shopping events offered once, or sometimes twice, a year. In a few cases they are every other year—such as the biggest, fanciest antique fair in France. Tony antique events charge a fee to weed out the riffraff; the higher the fee at the door, the fancier the dealers inside.

Since there is so much going on at any given time, ask your hotel concierge about specific events and check those freebie magazines you get at your hotel, as well as French newspapers and even the *Herald Tribune.*

Antique fairs are held for a week to 10 days almost every month from February through May. The admission is usually about 25 F ($4.20); 40 F ($6.70) for the big-ticket events. The regular flea markets are free.

Menswear

Men's clothing in Paris is expensive, partly because it has to be (after all, this is Paris) and partly because the moderately priced stuff is imported. Both American and British looks lead the pack. Gap is big as is Ralph Lauren; Levi's are a fashion must-have. Le Brit is also influential; check out London firms from Paul Smith to Burberrys. Don't be shocked to learn that many snooty French business-men buy their business suits from Marks & Spencer.

Most French women's-wear designers have men's lines or even men's shops, such as Sonia Rykiel Homme, Rodier Homme, and Christian Dior Monsieur. Nothing is more important to the wardrobe than an Hermès tie (bought at a duty-free shop, we hope). Air France has the best prices in the air (450 F/$75).

HENRY COTTONS
52 rue Etienne Marcel, 1er (Métro: Etienne Marcel)

This is actually an Italian chain that does a preppy look very similar to Ralph Lauren, but with a European fit. Fabulous store right off place des Victoires. Very BCBG (preppy).

DANIEL HECHTER
66 rue François 1er, 8e (Métro: Franklin Roosevelt)

Preppy but with a designer twist.

CHARVET
28 place Vendôme, 1er (Métro: Opéra)

The leading French maker of shirts and custom tailoring. While they also make women's things, this is one of the last holdouts of the old regime. Status galore.

Perfume & Makeup

If you don't have your own regular duty-free store for perfume, makeup, and beauty treatments, try mine: **Catherine**, 7 rue Castilgione. It's a small shop with personal service; they give the best discounts in town.

If you don't want discount but you do want selection, try **Sephora**, which carries a little of everything. I happen to like Sephora, but it is expensive and offers no discounts, although it does have an automatic and electronic tax refund when you spend 1,200 F ($200) and qualify for détaxe. Try its Web site for a quick lesson in how fab they are: www.sephora.com. An updated price list is available on the Web so you can know exactly what to expect or how to compare at bargain sources.

MAKEUP FOREVER
5 rue de la Boétie, 8e (Métro: St. Augustin)

Major hangout for supermodels, teens, and les girls. They do carry foreign brands, making it less than a totally French experience, but the house brand is famous, as are the women who shop here. Right off the Champs-Elysées; the house brand is also sold in **Sephora** stores.

STUDIO SHU UEMURA
176 bd. St. Germain (Métro: St. Germain)

Japanese makeup artist Uemura is the best in the world for color. The place also has a complete testing bar where you can play for days.

LES SALONS SHISEIDO
Jardin du Palais Royal, 1er (Métro: Palais Royal)

No, this isn't a Japanese beauty parlor—it's the most gorgeous, stunning, special little find in the world, complete with Serge Lutens's own perfumes, about $100 per bottle. They give fabulous freebie samples of everything when you buy; there's also a treatment line.

L'ARTISAN PARFUMEUR
24 bd. Raspail, 6e (Métro: Rennes)

One of those fancy-dan almost private label perfume houses—they will create a signature scent for you—with an almost cult following at its 30 shops in France, plus a few others here and there, including New York. There's a bath line as well as five different fragrances for the home.

ANNICK GOUTAL
14 rue de Castiglione, 1er (Métro: Concorde)

Look at the mosaic sidewalk, then float into this tiny shop with golden bottles and bars of soap that are a scent-sational souvenir. Hadrien is my favorite scent in soap; I've been using Eau Sud as a summer perfume since it was launched.

LES PARFUMS DE ROSINE
Jardin de la Palais Royal, 1er (Métro: Palais Royal)

Remember that arcade of shops in the garden of the Palais Royal I told you about? This is one of the shops—a tiny space filled with pinks and golds and the house scent, made of rose and violet. There are two newer scents, as well as soaps and lotions. Getting some international press as a cult find.

SANTA MARIA NOVELLA
3 rue des Canettes, 6e (Métro: Mabillon)

Can't make it to Florence? Not to worry. The famous pharmacy with goo made by nuns has a small Paris branch.

Skin Care

The French are into what they call *soins* (cures). Each mother teaches her daughter, and so on. I buy most of my cures at the parapharmacie and I've tried 'em all. Sephora also has a good selection. But nothing prepared me for Anne Semonin, a private little spa place in The Bristol, which now does my skin and my jet lag cures, even when I'm not staying at The Bristol.

The skin products are mixed just for your skin and they are sold (and mixed) at Barneys and Neiman-Marcus in the United States at very high prices. Try Paris, 108 rue du Faubourg St. Honoré, 8e, ☎ 01-42-66-24-22.

Souvenirs

If you're into kitsch (as I am), you will adore the tourist traps (TTs) lining the rue Rivoli across the street from the Louvre. There's also a bevy of similar TTs half a block from Notre Dame. You can find anything from toothbrushes with names on them (in French) to tiny snow domes with the Eiffel Tower (also with your name on them). They have a book of names at the cashier's desk, so don't panic if you can't find the name you need.

I think foodstuff makes fabulous souvenirs—they're usually inexpensive and take a true taste of the country home to your family or friends.

Looking for something classier? All the museums in France have a united merchandising program and now offer excellent gifts and souvenirs in their museum shops. Just about every museum in Paris, and all of France, has a museum gift shop—even places like the Museum de la Poste and the French Mint.

Teen Heaven

Teens love shopping in Paris partly because there's lots to do and see away from their parents. Vintage clothing shops abound; record stores allow them a place to hang out; and street fashion is hot, hot, hot. Make that *chaud*.

H&M
120 rue de Rivoli, 1er (Métro: Hôtel de Ville)

H&M is a Swedish firm, known for their young, kicky clothes at very low prices—so low that every teen in Europe clamors for the stuff. I happen to buy a lot here too. There's men's, women's, kids, underwear, and beauty. The branch stores in Paris are dreadful, and you will think I'm nuts if you don't go to the main store on the rue de Rivoli, 1 block from the department store BHV.

MORGAN
165 rue de Rennes, 6e (Métro: Sévres Babylone)

The latest darling of continental chic, hot not only in Paris. This is must-have fashion at moderate prices, also sold in department stores.

AU VRAI CHIC PARISIEN
47 rue du Four, 6e (Métro: Mabillon)

8–10 rue Montmartre, 3e (Métro: Les Halles)

I just like the name. Cheap versions of hot looks; it's a chain. The rue Montmartre is not in the Montmartre section.

PROMOD
67 rue de Sévres, 6e (Métro: Sévres Babylone)

There's tons of these stores in Paris and all over France, so the above address is just one of many. This is a chain of shops with trendy clothes, a cross between The Gap and maybe the Limited Express but not as trendy as Morgan or H&M. Let's call it middle-aged trendy? Weekend clothes and resort looks for the south of France are the spring and summer specialty.

ZARA
44 Champs-Elysées, 8e (Métro: Franklin Roosevelt)

128 rue de Rivoli, 1er (Métro: Tuileries)

This is actually a Spanish designer who has gone global and has tons of stores all over France. The look is cutting-edge chic, but Zara copies everyone from Armani to, uh, Zara. Prices are low. Even grown-ups can shop here. If they don't mind shooooort skirts. Looks are more geared toward business clothes and suits and nice dresses, not too much weird stuff.

Paris Shopper's Stroll & Tour

1. If breakfast is included at your hotel, of course you'll eat there. If not, and if you can stand to splurge, let's head for the dining room of the **Hôtel de Crillon,** where the continental breakfast is a little pricey (120 F/$20); but if you consider that you're dining more or less in a museum, it begins to amortize the costs. Besides, 120 F is the going rate for a continental breakfast in any grand hotel.

   This is a working breakfast: Please note the custom-made dishes that were created to match the mosaics on the floor. The walls and ceiling of the room also deserve notice, ranking with The Ritz in London and the Louis XV in Monte Carlo as one of the fanciest dining rooms in Europe. Also be sure to indulge in the jam cart, an idea I haven't seen elsewhere. Your job since this is a working meal? Soak up all the details of Paris glamour so you can relive them later in your life. Breathe deeply.

2. By 9:30 you are finished with breakfast and off to **Catherine,** located across the street from the Meurice, but you have to go outside and enter at 7 the rue de Castiglione. Catherine is a duty-free parfumerie where they will give you an extra discount on Chanel if you are a Born to Shop reader. Note that they give you the refund instantly, a rare practice in France. Ask them to hold your packages for you, so you don't have to lug them around all day.

3. Depart Catherine via the rue de Rivoli and walk uptown, toward the Louvre and away from the place Concorde. You will now pass several blocks of tourist traps; shop as you pass by. This is also a good time to buy postcards, which are sold for less money if you buy in bulk; usually 12 for 10 F ($1.70) is the best you can do.

4. When you get to the **Musée des Arts Decoratifs,** cross rue de Rivoli to pop into the two-part gift shop. One side offers a marvelous selection of

books on style and design (in many languages) and some expensive arty postcards and great stuff. The other side is a more traditional gift shop with reproductions of items from the collection.

5. Stay on that side of the street, exit the museum, and walk just a few hundred meters to the entrance of the **Carrousel du Louvre.** Here you can get a crepe or a coffee at the food court on the mezzanine level or take the escalator down one more level to the shopping mall. Don't spend too much time here, but browse. Everything is well designed, nonkitschy, and often affordable.

6. Back on the rue du Rivoli, cross the street and walk 1 short block to the Palais Royal. It takes a little doing, but look behind the Comédie Française until you find the entrance to **Les Jardins du Palais Royal.** At first they look like gardens with a modern art presentation, but actually there are some of the best stores in Paris tucked into the arcades along the garden. Explore both sides and give yourself enough time to walk under the trees in the garden itself. This is a moment that only comes to some once in a lifetime.

7. Exit the gardens and slowly enter the real world, walking along **rue St. Honoré.** In the first few blocks it will be sort of real-people Paris. As you get closer to the **rue de Castiglione,** where you started this morning, the street changes to a more designer-oriented shopping street. By the time you get to the **rue Royale,** the street changes its name to **Faubourg St. Honoré** and is the fanciest shopping street in Paris. Shop or simply stare at everything. Work your way up one side and back down the other side.

8. Shop or stroll; whenever you are ready for lunch, return to the rue Royale and **Ladurée,** the tea room and luncheon spot that is very upper-middle class French and just the place for you to eat a light lunch, rest your weary feet, and

stare at the patrons. You can get a quiche and salad or something a little heavier, but be sure to leave room for dessert.

9. Depart rue Royale and head for the **place de la Madeleine,** which is in the next block. Continue on 1 more block, and the street changes its name to the rue Tronchet. Never mind, follow it to **boulevard Haussmann,** which is where all the big French department stores are located. Turn right onto boulevard Haussmann. You'll see all the big stores immediately.

10. Before I let you loose in les grands magasins, I'm sending you to **Monoprix** and then up the escalator in the Monoprix lobby to **Gourmet Lafayette (GL).** As for me, I probably need no more to keep me happy. I do most of my shopping in these two stores and usually take back a picnic from the grocery store for my dinner.

You can wander into the various parts of GL and the two Au Printemps stores to get a look at everything in the world you haven't yet seen. Quit when you can take it no longer. Or return to Monoprix; they're now open until 9pm almost every night. You can truly shop till you drop. Our plan today is simple: After shopping Printemps Maison, you will spy the alleylike pedestrian street between the two branches of Printemps. In this alley, there's a back way into the Passage du Havre, a mall that has one of every store you need in France, including Sephora. Look for the signs to FNAC, the record and CD discounter. After you shop FNAC, pop into the mall.

Chapter Seven

· · · · · · · · ·

SHOPPING CHAMPAGNE

WELCOME TO CHAMPAGNE

· ·

Champagne is a French *departement* and the name of a very particular drink. By law, if the grapes for this sparkling wine aren't grown in this region of France, the bubbly ain't champagne. So welcome to a destination that really sparkles.

Bordeaux is way too big a category for me to fully grasp, so instead I will focus on the more manageable region of Champagne, where you'll have a ball while you test and taste. Take back your Château Petrus; give me the Roderer Cristal. Okay, so I'll settle for the Dom Perignon. Welcome to the magic flute.

Champagne is not a boring subject, especially in these days as we turn into the next century. There's been much controversy over what champagne to drink for special New Year's Eve celebrations and there's been lots of hype, which is thankfully dying down now. There have also been some new brands. Even our old buddy Alain Ducasse has just inaugurated his own champagne!

While you certainly associate the Champagne district with the grapes and shopping for bubbly, and maybe with one of the best cathedrals in the world, you might also want to know that this district has become one of the most famous discount shopping areas in France. The town of Troyes (say *trois,* like the number three in French) used to be a textile city but the mills are mostly outlet stores now.

Locals take day trips from Paris and there are also tourist overnights and fancy tours that take you to Troyes for the shopping and then to Eperney for the tasting.

If you look at a map of this district, you'll see that it is an unusual shape; while grapes are everywhere, the most famous sipping cities are to the northern part of the region and there's more shopping than sipping in the southern part. But you won't go thirsty, believe me!

So welcome to a very special part of France, a part of France that can be enjoyed as a day trip, an overnight trip, a weekend away, or a week's exploration. Welcome to a visit that will stay in your memory bank forever after.

CHARM ALERT

. . . .

Before you get all excited about Reims, the capital of the Champagne region, or in wondering how many bottles of bubbly are on the wall, let me warn you that if you are thinking romantic, if you are thinking beautiful, you might want to sit down now and try to cope before you are off, running, and daydreaming.

Reims is not adorable. It was bombed in World War I (though not the vineyards!), and while it has a very nice Gothic cathedral (also not bombed), there is not a lot of quaint charm to win your heart and head. That understood, Reims is a terrific place to have some fun, tour a few caves, buy your champagne, and eat gourmet meals.

Reims offers the perfect day trip or weekend away because there are many options. You can tour at your own pace, and you can travel with or without a car. Ian Cook, my Born to Shop British correspondent, and I planned this without a car but soon rented one because we had much more freedom with wheels. The real joy of the region is to get up and go, go, go.

GETTING TO REIMS FROM PARIS

· ·

Although most of the big champagne houses are within the city limits of either Reims or Epernay, Reims is on the main train line and Epernay, which is technically closer to Paris, is not.

Catch the train at the Gare de l'Est in Paris; it's a 90-minute trip. I got our train tickets ahead of time through **Rail Europe** in the United States (☎ **800/ 438-7245**).

If you are driving, this is very easy—just head out past Disneyland Paris on the A4, pay a few tolls (they take credit cards), and pick your exit depending on the houses you wish to visit.

When Ian and I did this trip, we started south and therefore got off at Exit 21, Epernay, and took the N3, following the signs to Epernay, passing many signs marked Route du Champagne. This is the slow way, but it's scenic.

The last time I went to Reims, I went with three other friends who didn't want to take the train and wanted to be able to drink, so we hired a van with a driver. This turned into a very interesting day because the driver was from Paris and while he was a great guy, he didn't know the back roads that well. Even though we had directions and a map for the Route du Champagne, well, he got lost and it really screwed up our day.

I mention this not to complain but to pass on the basic tip: If he got lost, you can get lost, so be prepared to be either flexible or stick to main roads. Also, don't use a simple tourist handout for a map; use the very detailed and excellent Michelin road map.

GETTING TO REIMS FROM THE UNITED KINGDOM & BELGIUM

Because of its northerly location, Reims is easy to get to from the United Kingdom and Belgium; many Brits like to take their cars over on Le Shuttle and then drive to Reims and load up on champagne before returning to the United Kingdom.

GETTING AROUND REIMS

The train station is alongside downtown Reims; you can walk just about everywhere in the downtown area, but the cathedral is across town. There are taxis waiting for you at the train station and some drivers will make a deal for a day of sightseeing.

Ian and I asked one driver his price to go from Reims to Ay, where Bolly is located: 400 F ($67) each way. We rented a car for 24 hours and dropped it off in Paris for 435 F ($73), so seriously consider renting a car, either in Paris or when you arrive in Reims. Most of the rental prices include 300km (126 miles) per day, which is enough to let you drive around and still get back to Paris.

Reims is 26km from Epernay. The main road between them is the N51, a national road. The best way to do it is to drive. If you can't drink and drive, get a chauffeur and a good map.

SLEEPING IN REIMS

Most of the famous kitchens in Reims also have rooms, because people like to linger over a gourmet dinner or they want to drink.

LES CRAYERES
64 bd. Henry Vasnier, Reims

This is not only the number-one choice for all discriminating visitors, but *Travel Weekly* recently named it one of the top five country hotels in the world. Although the formal name of this restaurant and hotel is Les Crayeres, most people call it Boyer, in honor of the famous chef who owns the icon, so don't get confused if people send you to Boyer.

Located across the street from the Pommery château and almost in the heart of town, this manor house is in a small park and comes complete with so many luxuries you'll have to pinch yourself to make sure it's real.

There are only 16 deluxe rooms in this mansard-roof mansion. They cost about $200 per night and they are almost as delicious as dinner. Your host and hostess are Gerard and Elayne Boyer. Book in the United States through **Relais & Châteaux** (☎ **212/ 856-0115**). The local phone number is 03-26-82-80-80; fax 03-26-82-65-52.

L'ASSIETTE CHAMPENOISE
40 av. Paul Vaillant Couturier, Tinqueux

Don't freak over the address: This is a suburb of Reims, and you are minutes (2km/1.2 miles) from downtown. You are seconds from Carrefour and a string of local stores that feature champagne and discounts and even a bowling alley.

Again, your host is a famous chef, so you come here for the kitchen and for the fact that the property is very modern and has an enclosed swimming pool. Rooms begin around $100 (☎ **03-26-84-64-64**; fax 03-26-04-15-69).

ROYAL CHAMPAGNE
Champillon-Epernay

This property is for those who prefer to be closer to Eperany, more out on the Route du Champagne. It is a **Relais & Château** property created from a former post house. There are 27 rooms; rates begin

Reims

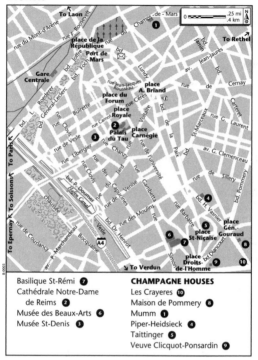

Basilique St-Rémi ⑦	**CHAMPAGNE HOUSES**
Cathédrale Notre-Dame	Les Crayeres ⑩
de Reims ②	Maison de Pommery ⑧
Musée des Beaux-Arts ⑥	Mumm ①
Musée St-Denis ③	Piper-Heidsieck ④
	Taittinger ⑤
	Veuve Clicquot-Ponsardin ⑨

around $125 per night. For reservations in the United States, call ☎ **212/856-0115.** The local phone is 03-26-52-87-11; fax 03-26-52-89-69.

DINING IN REIMS

. . . .

It's not surprising that there are scads of Michelin-starred chefs in the area, so you'll have no trouble eating well. You haven't been to Reims if you don't eat at least one meal with Gerard Boyer, who is open for lunch and dinner, so even day-trippers have no excuse. While my heart still belongs to Alain Ducasse, Gerard Boyer is gaining, as am I when I eat this kind of food.

LES CRAYERES (BOYER)
64 bd. Henry Vasnier, Reims

Everything about Les Crayeres (more commonly known as Boyer) is perfection, from the moment you enter the driveway. Sip champagne in the glass-enclosed lanai while you order your meal, then move into the formal dining rooms—which smelled of burning hickory wood the winter I visited—and give in to the sensuality of a fine table with finer food.

I came away with an autographed menu (Gerard Boyer is a star and don't you ever forget it), a memory of one of the best meals I'd ever eaten, and at least 2 kilos of chocolate soufflé around my hips. There are a variety of set menus, so you can afford this once-in-a-lifetime treat. Do call ahead for reservations, especially in season (☎ **03-26-82-80-80;** fax 03-26-82-65-52).

L'ASSIETTE CHAMPENOISE
40 av. Paul Vaillant Couturier, Tinquex

I did a lot of research before booking our 2-day trip to Reims, and Jean-Pierre Lallement came up time and again as the second-best chef in the area, after Gerard Boyer. Ian says our meals here were on equal par with Boyer's. I had such stars in my eyes from all the food and all the champagne that I could barely judge.

The surroundings are not formal; the restaurant, located in a suburb just outside Reims, lacks the overall impact of Les Crayeres, but the food is just great. The Menu du Marché is 300 F ($50); the Menu du Champagne is 485 F ($81), or 585 F ($85) if you choose a *grande cuvée* (☎ **03-26-84-64-64;** fax 03-26-04-15-69).

SHOPPING CHAMPAGNE IN REIMS

. . . .

Since most people go to Reims partly to see the incredible cathedral, it's important to know that you can gawk, worship, and then go shopping all in the same space. There are a handful of excellent wine shops that sell many, many brands and offer great gifts.

Almost all of them sell chocolate champagne corks, which I think are a super gift. I'm also big on small bottles of champagne for the folks back home, so they can taste a range, and I love the fact that a few houses (Moet in particular) make six-packs of small champagne bottles.

LA VINOCAVE
45 place Drouet d'Erion, Reims

This store is toward the end of the pedestrian shopping street that leads from the Reims train station toward the downtown area and the cathedral. You'll recognize the store by the 3-foot-tall bottles of champagne standing outside. Inside, the large selection includes both big-name and little-known makers, and the helpful staff speaks English.

LA BOUTIQUE NOMINÉE
Place du Parvis, Reims

I think this is the best of show, although I don't feel good about Reims until I've been to all the stores. This one is across the street from the cathedral at the front door end, which is called *devant la Cathédrale* in case you have to ask for it. The store is large and well organized; it has plenty of gift items and even has hard booze in the rear.

They have a gift set of two champagne flutes filled with chocolate corks that I think is adorable, about $12. Postcards are 3 F (50¢), but they're nice ones. Best is the huge selection of demibottles. The shop is open Monday through Saturday from 10am to 7pm and stays open for lunch.

CHAMPAGNE SELECTION
Face à la Cathedrale
Sorry, but that's the only address they give; if you want to call for directions, the telephone is ☎ 03-26-77-95-65. Actually this is such a specialty

place that you probably won't even need it, but I adore it and consider this one of the great finds of my life.

This tiny shop is two stores from La Boutique Nominée (the previous listing) and is also in front of the cathedral. They make custom champagne corks, so you can get ones that announce the baby or celebrate a big birthday. You can provide a photo of the celebrant to be imprinted on the metal top that goes over the cork. The minimum order is 250 pieces and it costs about $100. They can personalize a bottle in 2 minutes. Other novelties are available as well.

LE VINTAGE
1 cours Anatole France, Reims

Located directly across from the rear of the cathedral, this store has a huge selection of champagne, including small-sized bottles of the *grandes marques*, which make great gifts. I never knew there were so many choices. I paid 80 F ($13) for a half-bottle of Bolly to bring home.

ABOUT THOSE COOKIES
. . . .

You can buy Biscuits de Reims in any grocery store in France, but if you want the real thing from the real source, check out **Fossier**, 25 cours Jean-Baptiste-Langlet. The point of the biscuit is that you don't get drunk and they get dunked. Fossier is the most famous brand and the *rose* is preferred.

SHOPPING HOURS
. . . .

Most stores are open from 9am to noon and 2 to 7pm. The *hypermarchés* are open nonstop until 9pm. (Although, frankly, they don't have that much good champagne and their prices aren't much lower than regular retail.) Some stores open at 10am and then stay open during the lunch hours. Monday mornings are slow.

MARKETS & FAIRS

There are markets open in Reims from 6am to 1pm every day except Sunday. On the first Sunday of every month, except August, there is a flea market from 8am until 7pm at the Parc des Expositions.

Galerie Jamin (6 rue Jamin) is open Monday and Friday from 2pm until 7pm; Saturday and Sunday, from 10am until 7pm.

TOURING THE CHAMPAGNE HOUSES

About Addresses

Many of the champagne houses have two (or more) addresses, since they have a showroom and an actual château out in the fields, where the grapes are grown. Most often, the château is used for private functions or can be visited only by appointment.

A few of the big houses own several brands, so the addresses are the same. Don't worry.

Call before you drive any great distance, as there may be a closer address for what you want to see, taste, or buy.

Sipping Hours

Most champagne houses follow the same hours as local retail shops: They open about 9:30am and close for lunch around noon. Many close at 11:30am so the final groups are out by noon. One or two actually close at 11am for the same reason.

After lunch, everyone reopens, usually at 2pm. Champagne houses close for the day at various times—some close at 3:30pm, some close at 7pm. Anything in between is also possible. Hours may also vary with the season.

Believe it or not, most champagne houses are open on Sunday! However, some houses are closed on Monday and Tuesday.

Money Matters

Many châteaux have elaborate visitors centers and tours (even train rides); most of them charge an admission fee for the show, usually about 20 F ($3.30) per head. The price includes a glass of champagne at the end of the tour. If you don't want the tour or the tasting and just want to buy, you can usually be admitted directly to the shop without paying for the tour.

You can also buy champagne at many stores in town or even at Carrefour, the *hypermarché* right outside of town at the junction of RN31 and BP7. Carrefour may be slightly cheaper, but only by about $1 per bottle. We went, hoping to find God, but we were disappointed: The selection was not very good, and the savings weren't worth the trouble.

Do not expect factory outlet prices at the factory. In fact, prices will only be slightly less than in Paris and may be similar to prices at home. In some cases, prices will be better at home. Forget about airport duty-free prices in the United States or France, you'll do better on the street.

Rendez-Vous, SVP

It is better to have an appointment for a tour; at some houses you will be seen only with a private appointment. Many of the houses advertise, especially in French food, wine, and cooking magazines. They also have roadside signs. Please note that just as in Bordeaux, there are a lot of mixed messages out there and conflicting sources of information.

If there is a house you'd like to visit, but someone tells you, "Oh, no, they are not open to the public," call or fax yourself. Also note that there is a difference between the showroom and the château, so there may be a difference in how happy one or the other is to see you.

Brace yourself for a wide discrepancy in style at the various houses. At Bolly, the selection was terrible and the attitude was worse. At Pommery, they were prepared for princes and kings and treated me as if I was both. The selection is bountiful, well displayed, and easily accessed.

Also brace yourself for cultural differences and know your French manners. There's a huge difference in style between the big commercial houses and the tiny, family houses. There are also many medium houses in between. I discovered one such house and wanted to return to Reims to buy directly from the house. When I called for an appointment, it was easy and well done. When I called to tell the house we were late, which I thought was incredibly polite, they denied that I had an appointment and didn't know what I was talking about or with whom I had booked.

Another house tried to trade me over to a sister firm, one that I had no interest in. Don't be so polite that you end up wasting your time.

Matters of Taste

It only took a few hours in Champagne for me to begin to suffer from the Belgian Chocolate Syndrome, which I acquired doing research and which left me sick at the very sight of chocolate (I have since recovered).

If you go on a few tours, have a few tastings, and have lunch with Gerard Boyer, you will learn the good stuff from the average stuff. My palate began to rebel at the taste of the very average nonvintage champagne that is served at the end of a tour. Yuck, I kept thinking. Don't laugh, it can happen to you.

Better Brands

Why does each house make several kinds of champagne, and are the more expensive cuvées worth it? You might not be able to afford the difference, but the difference in taste between nonvintage and vintage grande cuvée is enormous. You can pay $30 for a bottle of champagne or $65 for a bottle of champagne, but you will be able to taste the difference. Nonvintage champagne is for those who aren't willing to spend the money to learn that there is a difference.

Note that prices on important vintages and brands can be less in America than in France, especially if you luck into a year-end promotional event. Know your stuff before you commit to a big-ticket item in France. The shopping in Reims is really for brands or vintages you can't get in America.

The Magic Flutes

CHAMPAGNE BILLECART-SALMON
Château: 40 rue Carnot, Mareuil-sur-Ay
☎ 03-26-52-60-22

CHAMPAGNE BOLLINGER
16 rue Jules Lobet, Ay
☎ 03-26-53-33-88

CHAMPAGNE KRUG
5 rue Coquebert, Reims
☎ 03-26-84-44-20

Château: Le Clos du Mesnil, Mesnil-sur-Oger
☎ 03-26-57-51-77

CHAMPAGNE LOUIS ROEDERER
21 bd. Lundy, Reims

CHAMPAGNE MOET ET CHANDON
18–20 av. de Champagne, Reims
☎ 03-26-54-71-11

Château: Abbaye d'Hautvillers, Rue Cumières, Hautvillers
☎ 03-26-59-42-67

CHAMPAGNE MUMM
34 rue du Champs de Mars, Reims
☎ 03-26-49-59-70

Château: Moulin de Verzenay, Verzenay
☎ 03-26-49-59-69

MAISON PERRIER-JOUET
26 av. de Champagne, Epernay
☎ 03-26-53-38-00

MAISON PHILIPPONNAT
Château: Le Clos de Goisses 13 rue de Pont, Mareuil-sur-Ay
☎ 03-26-52-60-43

CHAMPAGNE PIPER-HEIDSIECK
51 bd. Henry Vasnier, Reims
☎ 03-26-84-43-44

POL ROGER
1 rue Henri Le Large, Epernay
☎ 03-26-55-41-95

CHAMPAGNE POMMERY
5 place du Général Gourand, Reims
☎ 03-26-61-62-63

CHAMPAGNE RUINART
4 rue des Crayères, Reims
☎ 03-26-85-40-29

CHAMPAGNE TAITTINGER
9 place St. Nicaise, Reims
☎ 03-26-85-45-35

Château: Château de la Marquetterie, Pierry
☎ 03-29-54-04-53

CHAMPAGNE VEUVE CLICQUOT PONSARDIN
1 place des Droits de l'Homme, Reims
☎ 03-26-89-54-41

The Little-Known Houses

Of course, a champagne need not be world famous to be good. Without a big advertising budget, a house may remain little known. Part of the glory of champagne shopping in Reims is that you can uncover your own finds and fall in love.

There are thousands of little champagne houses; you can drive around and taste for years. I bought just a few specialty bottles that were suggested by the wine stores in Reims or by experts. Most of these brands are carried in the stores in downtown Reims; few bottles are exported to the United States.

Please note that most of the wines I tested were vintage, top-of-the-line cuvée. It does make a difference. A nonvintage wine from the same house will not be the same. I have mentioned by name the bottle that I found so special, just to steer you toward the right taste, although you may find other vintages more appropriate when you shop:

CHAMPAGNE PHILLIPONNAT
Clos des Goisses 1986
13 rue de Pont, Mareuil-sur-Ay
☎ 03-26-52-60-43

CHAMPAGNE PLOYEZ-JACQUEMART
n.v.
Ludes, Rilly-la-Montagne
☎ 03-26-61-11-87

CHAMPAGNE SALON
Les Mesnil 1983
Mesnil-sure-Oger
☎ 03-26-57-51-65

CHAMPAGNE ALAIN THEINOT
Grande Cuvée 1985
14 rue des Moissons, Reims
☎ 03-26-47-41-25

CHAMPAGNE VILMART
n.v.
4 rue de la République, Rilly-la-Montagne
☎ 03-26-03-40-01

Boyer's Babies

I asked three-star chef Gerard Boyer, the biggest star in Reims, for his personal list of small houses. Herewith these choices with the name of the house and its location. Gerard Boyer says you can use his name as a reference.

- Christian Busin, Verzenay
- Diebolt-Vallois, Cramant
- Pierre Gimonnet, Cuis
- Lasalle, Chigny-les-Roses
- Lilbert, Cramant
- Monmarthé, Ludes

And Now, M. Ducasse

Alain Ducasse, who has probably served more champagne than any other chef, has decided to launch his own brand along with Paul Drouet. The brand, called Champagne Alain Ducasse, is expected to have worldwide distribution by the time you read this.

"It's a very simple, pure champagne," says Ducasse. "I chose the taste, it's what I wanted."

The champagne is nonvintage. Ducasse suggests you age it for 2 to 3 years, tops. You can also buy it at his restaurants and gift shops.

WELCOME TO TROYES

. . . .

Most of the people I know come here about once a year for the big factory outlets, which they say have improved each year and are now worth visiting, although they all caution that French outlets are not as sophisticated as American outlets.

I also hear from my buddies inside La Maison France, which is the French Government Tourist Office, that tours from Paris can easily be arranged, so check with them in either a U.S. office or in Paris.

But I was welcoming you to Troyes, not giving out disclaimers or lessons on American outlet malls. *Excusez-moi.* The Troyes I welcome you to, the one I've seen in my research and in issues of *Gault Millaut* magazine, is adorable, very half timbered and cute and divine, not at all like Reims.

Aside from the mills, the outlets, and the grapes, there's a fine Museum of Modern Art, marvelous architecture and, of course, plenty of cute places in which to stay and eat. There are not as many American tourists, so there's a lot of that sense of discovery. So just get in the car and go, starting with the cute and then working your way north.

The Outlets

To read about my trip to a French outlet village, see chapter 8. You'll learn about the outlets I went to in Lille, which happen to be the first factory outlets opened in France.

Marques Avenue is in Troyes; the Web site is www.marisy.fr/marques_avenue. This is the largest and most famous outlet, with the big designer names, though there are two other outlets nearby.

The outlets are about 1½ hours from Paris, south toward Dijon. If you do not go on an organized tour, you will need a car. To get there, head south on the A5, get off at Exit 21. For directions or specifics, call the outlet center at ☎ **03-25-82-00-72.** Or call the Tourist Office in Troyes, 03-25-73-00-36.

Note that the outlets are in suburbs of Troyes.

MARQUES AVENUE
114 bd. de Dijon, Saint-Julien

MACARTHUR GLEN
Zone Nord, voie du Bois, Pont-Sainte-Marie

TEXTILE CENTER
11 rue Robert-Keller, Pont-Sainte-Marie

Fairs & Markets

There's market every day at Baltard.

Sleeping in Troyes

CHAMPS DES OISEAUX
20 rue Linard-Gonthier, Troyes

This is a tiny, cute little inn near the cathedral with rooms under $100. The local phone is ☎ 03-25-80-58-50.

ROYALE HOTEL
22 bd. Carnot, Troyes

This three-star, family run hotel is in the old-fashioned traditional style. They have a restaurant on hand and charming decor. The local phone is ☎ **03-25-73-19-99**; fax 03-25-73-47-85.

Eating in Troyes

LE CLOS JUILLET
22 bd. du 14 Juillet, Troyes

Most foodies agree that not only is this the best table in town, but it's reason enough to visit Troyes. For reservations, call ☎ **03-25-73-31-32.** It's closed Sunday for dinner and on Monday.

Chapter Eight

. . . .

SHOPPING THE TEXTILE CITIES: LYON & LILLE

FRENCH TEXTILE CITIES

. . . .

France has been famous for the quality of its textiles for centuries. The northern, more industrial part of France still houses factories—some are still working factories and some have been turned into our favorite kind of store, factory outlets. Of course, many factories have closed, but that is the way of the modern world.

Lyon, which is south of Paris, has long been the silk center of France and is where Hermès makes its scarves (sorry, no outlet at its factory!). As science and technology have advanced, Lyon has become a center for cottons, knits, and especially bathing suits and lingerie. Several international textile trade fairs are held in Lyon each year.

Lille is cotton land, where most of the textiles for bed linen are made. I went to the Porthault factory and zillions of nearby outlet stores. Not familiar with Porthault? This old French firm is considered by many to make the best and most luxurious linens in the world. If you buy in one of its tony retail stores, you will pay more than $1,000 for a king-sized sheet. I bought sheets for $100 each. Twin size, so I bought two. Tee hee: laughing all the way to the outlet store. Join me?

Aside from the manufacturing aspects of these cities, each is laden with charm, even Lille. Lille is sort of the Manchester, England, of France, and French people love to insult it. Take it from me, Lille is a great find! And when you find out about the antiques fair they have had every September since the 1200s, you will be singing my praises as well as this city center's.

Allons-y! Let's get out of Paris and into the big cities and textile centers; into the fiber and soul of manufacturing France.

PICK ONE

· ·

If you are in the difficult situation of having to pick one of these cities, I don't envy you. They're rather different yet have some similarities in subtext, so I can't give you a firm nudge toward one or the other. Take these facts into consideration if you are forced to choose:

- Lille is closer to Paris and then only a half hour from Brussels, so you almost get two for the price of one. It seems a shame to visit Lille and not go on to Brussels.
- Lille actually requires more than a day if you plan to also shop outlets and then go on to Brussels.
- Lille has more northern weather, similar to London.
- Lille's best shopping is in outlets that do require a car.
- Lille and Lyon are both good dining towns, but Lyon is one of the most famous in France. Lyon has a local wine tradition as well.
- In terms of downtown shopping areas, Lyon has more to it than Lille.
- In terms of luxury hotels, Lyon has more, although the best hotels are on the edge of, or completely outside of, town.

- Lille is a little funkier than Lyon; Lyon is more sophisticated. Neither city is Chicago.

DAY TRIPS FROM PARIS

Both Lyon and Lille are close enough to Paris so that they can be visited as day trips. If that's all the time you can spare, so be it. Use the opportunity to get to know the city—at least a little taste of it—and then vow to return. You do an injustice to yourself and each of these destinations if you only visit on a day-trip basis.

Please note that if you plan to go to the Porthault factory store, it is impossible to get any real sense of Lille as well. You need more than 1 day, so spend at least 1 night.

Both cities have TGV train service, and more information about trains is located in each city's listing. If you do not keep a car in Paris, I suggest you might want to take the train to each city, especially if you are doing this as a day trip.

Note: Lille and Lyon are important to each other and to France. There is direct TGV service between these two cities with seven round-trips each day making the 3-hour journey.

WEEKEND AWAY

A Paris-Lille-Lyon-Paris week would give you a look at French shopping at its best. Lyon and Lille make great weekends away from Paris.

Several car and hotel programs offer 2-night stays as part of their packages. Some of the better luxury hotels (usually in the countryside) require a minimum 2-night stay, especially during the season. But wait: Both Lille and Lyon participate in a weekend program that offers hotel nights on a twofer basis—you get 2 nights for the price of one! And these hotels are right in town.

PARIS TRAIN STATIONS

Paris has a number of train stations built to serve rail lines heading to various destinations. For Lyon you want Gare d'Lyon and for Lille, Gare du Nord. Both Lyon and Lille have two train stations.

- TGV trains depart from and arrive at specific train stations that are equipped with those tracks. You may be using different stations depending on the type of train you are on.
- In some cities, you will have a choice of which train station you arrive at; sometimes one choice is closer to town than another. One facility may be better equipped to deal with luggage than another, so if this is not a day trip and you have luggage with you, ask for specifics.

LYON

Welcome to Lyon

Originally, I thought I could do Lyon as a day trip. I don't mean that I felt that I could get to know a city in a day. I thought with TGV service at a mere 2 hours, I could go, do a little looking around, have lunch at one of the famed multistar tables, sample Bernachon's chocolates, and call it a day trip.

In the end, I stayed for 3 days and started babbling about moving there. I came back as soon as possible, for one of those French 4-day bridge weekends. Lyon has a lot more to offer than you think.

So welcome to Lyon, the perfect place to go for a day, a week, or maybe a lifetime. Welcome to Lyon, one of France's biggest towns, offering industry and commerce as well as daily food markets, a picturesque Old Town, a serious food and wine tradition, and all sorts of shopping. Shopping for chocolates? Did someone say let's spend the day eating chocolate? *Pas de problème.*

Much fabric manufacturing takes place in and around Lyon— and yes, where there are factories, there have to be outlet shops. And jobbers too. Step into my day tour.

This is also a cultural kind of a place, with a gorgeous rehabbed opera house downtown. There are plenty of designer clothes to buy as well as resale shops to survey. Most of the French majors have stores here so you can also revisit your favorite chains, and even my beloved **Euro Sante Beaute,** the *parapharmacie*, has a branch in Lyon. Welcome to Lyon, a city that has just about everything you want, a town of many colors and many flavors guaranteed to appeal to all tastes.

Location, Location, Location

Let's talk about the big picture first. Yes, Lyon is a mere 2 hours from Paris by TGV train, and you may think of it as a fancy suburb of Paris. When you check your map, however, you'll note that Lyon is in the heart of the Beaujolais country. It's on the way to Geneva, and it is also on the way to the south of France. When you're driving around the area, you'll see signs for the Alps and the famous ski resorts.

For those who don't drive, I point out this midpoint location because I've used Lyon as a stopping-off visit on the long train trip to the Riviera. I thought the idea of 7 hours on a train to Cannes was way too much, more a burden than a pleasure, so I stopped en route to Cannes. Not only did I enjoy Lyon but found the train ride to Cannes was easier.

Lay of the Land

Lyon is huge and is divided by the convergence of two rivers, La Saône and Le Rhône. The city is divided into *quartiers*; there are also *arrondissements*, just like in Paris, but we will pretty much ignore them.

Lyon

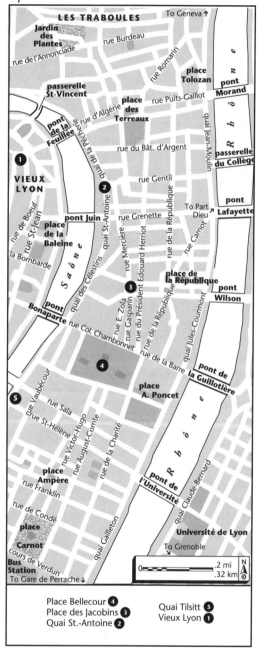

LES TRABOULES

To Geneva ↑

Jardin des Plantes

rue Burdeau

rue de l'Annonciade

rue Romarin

passerelle St-Vincent

place Tolozan

pont Morand

rue Puits-Gaillot

place des Terreaux

rue d'Algérie

rue de la Pêcherie

pont de la Feuillée

quai de la Pêcherie

rue du Bât. d'Argent

quai Jean-Moulin

passerelle du Collège

❶ VIEUX LYON

quai St-Antoine

rue Gentil

❷

pont Lafayette

To Part Dieu →

pont Juin

rue Grenette

rue de la République

place de la Baleine

rue St-Jean

rue de Bœuf

quai des Célestins

rue Mercière

place de la République

pont Wilson

la Bombarde

Saône

rue Carnot

❸

rue E. Zola

rue Gasparin

rue du Président Edouard Herriot

rue de la République

quai Jules-Courmont

pont Bonaparte

rue Col. Chambonnet

rue de la Barre

pont de la Guillotière

❹

place A. Poncet

Rhône

❺

rue Vaubécour

rue Sala

rue St-Hélène

rue Victor-Hugo

rue August-Comte

rue de la Charité

place Ampère

rue Franklin

quai Claude-Bernard

pont de l'Université

rue de Condé

place Carnot

quai Gailleton

Université de Lyon

cours de Verdun

Bus Station

To Gare de Perrache ↓

To Grenoble

0   .2 mi   .32 km

N

There are good parts on both sides of the two rivers, and the heart of the city actually lies on a small peninsula between them.

Please note, it is possible for a tourist, especially a day tripper, to not even realize how big Lyon is and to only visit one part of the town, missing a great deal of what's available. Sticking to one part of town simplifies things if you are on a day trip, but it doesn't give you a good overview of what's available or much of an understanding of Lyon.

In terms of the basic lay of the land, the Part Dieu train station, where you will probably arrive if you take the TGV from Paris, is on the farthest bank of the Rhône. The heart of the city is on the peninsula between the two rivers, and Vieux Lyon (Old Town) is on the far side of the Saône. Presqu'ile is the island in between where most of the shopping and tourist sights are located.

Getting There from Paris

TGV trains are classified by numerical categories and are priced by the category. If you have a train pass, the categories don't matter. Peak travel trains are N2 trains, and they cost more than N1 trains. Travel time varies from 2 hours, 1 minute, to 2 hours, 8 minutes.

If you look at a printout of the train schedule, do not get confused between the train number and the train departure time. TGV train number 643 does not leave at 6:43am (it leaves at 7:35am). There are some 22 round-trip TGV trains per day. Trains have first- and second-class service. There is a cafeteria and a telephone.

You must have a reservation on TGV trains. Your reservation printout includes the car number and your seat number.

It makes sense to arrive and depart from Part Dieu Station given the chance, even when heading south, because Part Dieu is a modern station that is mostly flat and has handcarts and access for serious passenger traffic. Perrache Station is older, has no handcarts, and is not built for getting around easily. However, trains that originate in Lyon for the south of France usually leave from this station rather than from Part Dieu.

Die-hard shoppers may also want to note that Part Dieu is a commercial center as well (a giant shopping mall), with branch stores of just about every French multiple. Therefore, it's technically possible to have your day trip to Lyon at the train station and just pop out to dine in one of the famous restaurants and make a quick tour to **Bernachon** before heading back to Paris. Of course, that's cheating.

Getting Around

For a day trip, you'll probably want to cab it. Since I stayed for several days, I used a combination of cabs, Métro, and old-fashioned foot power. The city is far too big, and the train stations too far away, to be able to consider this a mere stroll-and-shop kind of town.

The Métro is great, but it is not extensive enough to completely serve you, especially if your time is limited. The train goes underground and aboveground, depending on the route, so it can be very exciting. It's a new, modern train with clean stations and easy-to-use directions that are posted everywhere. Try to use the train at least once during the day. It's part of the fun of being in Lyon. There is a Ticket Liberté for 28 F ($4.70) a day that allows you unlimited access to the Métro; you can buy one at the tourist office. A single ticket, bought at any Métro station, costs 10 F ($1.70).

Wear comfortable shoes when you explore Lyon, especially the Old Town; you will be doing a lot of walking, and there are some hills and stairs.

I admit that in some of my explorations of the town, when I was really in the farther patches of tourist land, it was not easy to find a cab or even a taxi rank. Therefore, you may want to call **Allo Taxi** (☎ **04-78-28-23-23**). It has daily 24-hour service, and some 300 radio taxis.

Weekend En Ville

Lyon is one of several major French cities participating in a weekend promotion coordinated through SCNF, the French trains. You can get a discount TGV ticket as well as 2 hotel nights for the price of 1 at zillions of participating hotels, including most of the best hotels (though I don't think the Relais & Châteaux properties are included). For more information, use Minitel 3615SNCF or call ☎ **08-36-35-35-35**—both of these are toll lines. Breakfast, tax, and so on, is included in the hotel promotion and each participating city has free brochures at the tourist office. To go on-line for information about Lyon, try www.Mairie-Lyon.fr.

Sleeping in Lyon

Lyon has a large convention business, so be certain you know where your hotel is located. For example, Hilton customers may be thrilled that Hilton has just opened in Lyon, but shoppers will note that this hotel is next to the convention center and not near anything of much charm.

GRAND HÔTEL CONCORDE
11 rue Grolée, Lyon 2e

This is my regular hotel in Lyon, mostly because of the location and the fact that it is a Concorde Hotel, so I can book it easily. This is a grand-style hotel; the lobby has been modernized and the rooms have been renovated, but thankfully there are still old-fashioned wide corridors, high ceilings, and enormous French doors leading to balconies overlooking the Saône. (*Note:* River-view rooms are more expensive.)

As for shoppers, you can't get a much better location. You are right in the core of the city and can walk to just about everyplace in town. There is a Métro stop a block away.

When it comes to prices, you will be even happier: The U.S. dollar rate of $110 (out of season; $135 in season) includes a big buffet breakfast. This hotel participates in the Bon Weekend program so you can get 2 hotel nights for the price of 1.

While this may not be a five-star, fancy-dancy, drop-dead chic hotel, it has an excellent location and great rates. For reservations in the United States, call ☎ **800/888-4747**. The local number is ☎ 04-72-40-45-45; fax 04-78-37-52-55.

LA TOUR ROSE
22 rue du Boeuf, Lyon 5e

This is the most famous hotel in town and possibly the best. It's small, intimate, old-fashioned, and located on an eensy-weensy street in Old Town. The chef is famous, and the hotel is a fantasy come true. Unfortunately, it only has a dozen rooms, so book early. The local phone is ☎ **04-78-37-25-90**; fax 04-78-42-26-02.

SOFITEL
20 quai Gailleton, Lyon 2e

This is a modern hotel, also on the quai side so you get the river view. It is in a fine shopping location with a few stores in the hotel, including a small branch of Franck et Fils, a fashion boutique in Paris. The local phone is ☎ **04-72-41-20-20**.

VILLA FLORENTINE
25-27 Montee St. Barthelémy, Lyon 5e

This Relais & Châteaux property is on the edge of the Old Town overlooking the city. It has great views and a great kitchen—come for a meal and a look if you aren't staying here. The local phone is ☎ **04-72-56-56-56**.

Lyon's Best & Worst Buys

FOOD Lyon and food are synonymous, not only to the French, but to food lovers everywhere. Many make the pilgrimage to Lyon just to eat and/or buy food.

You can certainly eat chocolate all day, although I will admit outright that after visiting a few chocolate shops, my eyes began to cross, my stomach went into knots, and I had not-so-fond memories of the time I ate my way across all the chocolatiers in Brussels and was sick for 3 days. Indeed, I found the most heavenly chocolate was in a pastry form, not a candy form. Still, I brought candy bars from Bernachon as gifts to many friends.

SECONDS, OVERRUNS & ODD LOTS Lyon is surrounded by fabric mills and clothing manufacturers. I was delighted to bump into two different jobbers just by accident. Each specialized in unloading cheap clothing. I extended my wardrobe threefold for a mere 200 F ($33). Also, there's a very good branch of **Tati** in Lyon so you can get more of this sort of thing, if you're strong enough. Note that Lyon manufacturers are particularly big on underwear and bathing suits, so these are good items to find at jobbers.

SILKS I'd like to tell you that I was impressed with the silks or that they are the thing to buy in Lyon. I found the silk shops in Old Town very touristy, and the silk factory in the silk district was downright embarrassing. I must have been in town during cocoon season.

And since I know you want to know, here's the skinny on Hermès. Yes, the factory is in Lyon. Yes, you can arrange to tour it if you have a VIP group or arrange it ahead of time. No, there is not a shop. Employees buy Hermès at any store with an employee discount. They don't need a factory store.

Although the style of silk screening that Hermès made famous is of a type that originated in Lyon and at one time was thought of as a city-wide style, there are no other silk makers in Lyon that make anything near what Hermès does. In some of the tourist guides, I saw ads for various touristy silk factories in Lyon. The scarves pictured appeared to be in the Hermès school of design. In person they were laughable.

PUPPETS & MARIONETTES If I see another Guignol marionette I may puke.

Shopping Hours

Stores usually open at 9:30am and stay open until 7 or 7:30pm. In the big shopping mall, Commercial Centre Part Dieu, the stores are open from 10am to 7pm, 6 days a week.

Thankfully, you're in the big city now, so not that many stores close for lunch. Even though part of your day trip is to eat at one of the famous Lyonnaise restaurants, it's nice to know that many stores are open when you want them to be. You can also have pizza for lunch (I often do) and spend more time exploring the city.

Just about everything is closed on Sunday, except for a few neighborhood food stores. But there is a big business in antiques here, especially on Sunday. There's both an antique village, with fancy stuff, and the best flea market I've ever been to in France. There's a small crafts market in the Old Town, which segues into a small *brocante,* neither worth going out of your way to discover.

The food market along the river is especially good on both Saturday and Sunday; don't miss it.

Some stores are closed on Monday mornings and some are closed all day on Monday. Most of the large stores, and all 200 stores in the Parte-Dieu shopping mall, are open on Monday.

Markets & Fairs

There's a very nice, although rather simple, fresh food market that stretches along the quay side of the Saône at Quai St. Antoine. The market is best over the weekends but is open every day. While the colors are beautiful, and some of the regional produce is unique and special to survey or even sample, this market is thin on weekdays and doesn't have as much energy as I would like. Weekends are heavenly!

Foodies like to visit the market in the early hours with hopes of spying one of the area's famous chefs. There is also an indoor market on Quai Tilsitt.

The regular Sunday brocante is held on the canal, called **Puces de Canal**—not only is this in the middle of nowhere, but you may be frightened on first approach. Please don't fret; it's fab. The market is very funky, with an indoor part and an outdoor part and lots of tag-sale types of vendors and tables. It's a local market superb for buyers and market sophisticates. If you speak no French and like your markets sugar coated, this might not be for you.

Cite des Antiquaires is very clean, neat, and upmarket. The architecture is a little strange and the design of the building may lead you to think it is closed when, indeed, it is not. It has clean bathrooms and good selection, although most of it is fancy. There's a wonderful rooftop cafe and a few dealers who sell sensational kitchenware.

Shopping Neighborhoods in Lyon

Lyon is enormous. My shopping neighborhoods have been organized according to what makes sense to me and may mean little to a French person. Study your map as you read this to get a better understanding of the lay of the land, and which parts of town you want to visit if you are on a limited schedule. I have included just the main shopping parts of town—no out-of-the-way finds.

DOWNTOWN PRESQU'ÎLE Presqu'île is the name of the peninsula that juts between the two rivers. It is home to the central part of Lyon and much

Getting Around the Fleas

I was staying downtown and had no car; there weren't even any taxis at the taxi stand at 9:30am Sunday morning. My hotel called a taxi, which took me to the Canal Flea Market. Once I saw that I was totally isolated, I asked the driver to come back for me in an hour. Instead, he suggested that he wait for me and we set a fixed price of 200 F ($33) for the whole adventure. Since the meter read 100 F ($17) just to get there, I thought this was quite fair. Be advised, all negotiations were done in French.

Saturday and Sunday are the best days for old papers and books along the Quai des Bookinistes, on the left bank of the Saône, 1er, where about 20 book and ephemera dealers open their stalls. A few of these dealers are open during the week, but most of the action is on weekends.

There is a crafts fair on Sunday from 8am until 1pm on Quai Romain Rolland, 5e. I found it sort of your average high school bazaar kind of thing. There is, however, an adjacent flea market, and you're right across the bridge from the fruit, flower, and veggie markets so all in all, do 'em and enjoy the day out.

There's another brocante in Vaise, a suburb of Lyon, on Sunday.

Every June (usually the third weekend) there is a giant antique salon, the Brocante du Vieux Lyon. On the first Thursday of October, the antique shops on rue Auguste Comte hold open house until 11pm.

The nouveau Beaujolais is released at midnight of the third Wednesday in November. While people all over France get together at midnight to drink and celebrate, the goings-on are particularly festive in Lyon.

of the main shopping district in terms of department stores, boutiques, branches of French multiples, and so on. Although different parts of this peninsula have different names, the heart of it, where the main shopping is located, is what I call "downtown."

On your map, this is basically the area to the right of the Place Bellecour (if your back is to Part-Dieu and you are facing the Saône) and the Place de la Bourse.

This area is rather mainly in a grid, and the streets are all packed with stores. The main shopping street is rue de la République, but don't overlook rue du President Edouard Herriot or any of the streets that radiate outward from the place des Jacobins. The Grande Hotel Concorde is located in this neighborhood.

The rue de la République is a pedestrian street in part of the downtown. It begins at the place Bellecour, where it has more of the student and real-people shops (FNAC has a branch here) and heads away from the heart of town, with the department stores sprinkled along the way. **Prisunic** is smack dab toward the end of the main shopping part, about 3 blocks from the center.

There are more real-people shops (and some jobbers) on the rue Victor Hugo, which has fewer of the French names and multiples as on rue de la République, but more teenagers.

Rue du President Herriot has many big names, ranging from **Hermès** to branch stores of **Alain Figaret** (no. 104) and **Chacock** (no. 100), two better-known French yuppie brands. **Laura Ashley** is also on hand (no. 98).

Tati is a little difficult to find; it's tucked back near Rue Herriot, but closer to the Prisunic end of things rather than the Bellecour end.

Please don't forget the rue de Brest, which is closer to the Saône side of things. Here you'll find a number of tabletop and design shops and tons of cheap clothing stores. Don't miss **Genevieve Lethu** (no. 6) for colorful, affordable tabletop.

DELUXE DOWNTOWN Obviously there's a lot of shopping in this small downtown area. The fanciest stores and the most deluxe French names are primarily located on the rue Gasparin and the rue Émile Zola, which are each only about a block long and run parallel to one another. They both begin at the place Bellecour and stretch toward the place des Jacobins.

UPTOWN ANTIQUES Leading away from the major park in the center of the Presqu'île (place Bellecour) lies the very small rue Auguste Comte, which is home to a handful of designer shops and many upscale antique and interior design shops.

VIEUX LYON The Old Town part of the city is on a hill overlooking the Saône. First you must cross the river, then wander around exploring and going up and down steps and deciding how high you want to go. Most of the shopping is lower rather than higher, thankfully. There are no big-name stores here (unless a branch of **L'Occitane** counts); this is boutique land. Note that stores don't open until 11am in this neighborhood and are closed on Monday.

CROIX ROUSSE I liked this part of town because it wasn't very touristy and I felt like a real traveler, but I got hopelessly lost and thought that everything I came to see was very overblown in various guidebooks. This is the part of town where the silk weavers used to hang out; supposedly the houses are built to allow maximum light. I found only one silk factory. It was a bust, and I think you can pass on it. It is on the same side of the river as the Old Town, but farther down. You can take the Métro.

FDR/THE 6TH Lyon does have arrondissements like Paris; I'll take the 6th. I only came to know the 6th because I had to have a taste at the famous chocolatier **Bernachon,** located on the cours Franklin Roosevelt (no. 42). How was I to know this street is a main thoroughfare in a rich little nook of Lyon where there are several designer boutiques as well as a branch of **Souleiado** (no. 54), just an éclair's throw away from Bernachon? You can take the Métro.

Note that cours Franklin Roosevelt changes its name to cours Vitton for no apparent reason. Therefore, the **Lacoste** shop, which is only a block from Souleiado, is located at 1 cours Vitton.

You may want to spend more than a day in Lyon just to take advantage of all the places to eat right in this little part of town. Bernachon has its own restaurant and tea room, called **Bernachon Passion** (also no. 42), located down from the shop. If you prefer food to go, try Bocuse & Bernachon, no. 46.

This neighborhood is not that far from where the Antiques Center is located; you can walk if you aren't carrying too many chocolate bars.

Finds

BAISER SAUVAGE
4 place des Jacobins, Lyon

30 rue de la République

Retailing concepts gone wild and wacky. This store (I think the name means savage kiss) began life selling underwear, but that brought in so many women that they expanded to serve the market and then knocked off Sephora, the makeup chain. So the rue République store is almost a department store with makeup on the ground floor and undies upstairs.

CASANOVA
56 cours Franklin Roosevelt, Lyon

This is an old-fashioned leather and saddle shop, the likes of which is not seen in this century. They sell luggage and handbags as well as everything you and your horse may need.

NATURE DÉCOUVERTES
58 rue de la République, Lyon

This is the French branch of The Nature Company. There is one in Paris, in the Carroussel du Louvre, so you do not need to jump on a train and come all the way to Lyon just for this store. However, if you have never seen one, it is a total joy, especially if you are familiar with the American cousin. There are lots of inexpensive gifts and great gadgets for kids; I'm partial to the frog clicker for $3.

Lyon Resources from A to Z

CHOCOLATES & FOODSTUFF

BERNACHON
42 cours Franklin Roosevelt, Lyon

This is the most famous chocolatier in town. To tell the truth, by the time I got here, none of the chocolate even looked good to me. I was already chocolated out. I was drawn to the chocolate éclairs however, and must say that I'd spend 9 hours in a plane just to do it again. Better than sex. Looking for a great gift for a fellow foodie? You can get 500 grams of cacao for about $10.

MALLEVAL
11 rue Émile Zola, Lyon

In Lyon since 1860; known as purveyors of gourmet foodstuff, wine, and champagne.

VOISIN
28 rue de la République, Lyon

A small chain of chocolate shops. Just to give you an idea of the going rate for local designer chocolates: 1 kilo (2 pounds) costs 267 F ($45); 750 grams (26$\frac{1}{2}$ ounces) costs 200 F ($33); 500 grams (about 1 pound) costs 135 F ($23); and 250 grams ($\frac{1}{2}$ pound) costs 95 F ($16). In short, for about $25 you can buy a pound of Lyon's famous chocolate. This is not the most famous chocolatier in town by any means, but it's a start.

DEPARTMENT STORES

AU PRINTEMPS
42 place de la République, Lyon

Right in the heart of downtown, next to the place du Jacobins, this is the department store you want where you want it. The only problem, it's in two buildings. I was lost in menswear for days.

GALERIES LAFAYETTE
6 place des Cordeliers, Lyon

Commercial Centre Part Dieu, Lyon

There are two GL stores: one a few blocks from the main shopping streets on the Presqu'île, the other inside the shopping mall at the train station. I haven't been to the mall location, but the downtown store is nice enough, with its basic offerings of designers, big-name perfume and makeup, and everything you may need for everyday.

PRISUNIC GRAND BAZAAR
31 rue de la République, Lyon

One of the strangest sights in French retailing: this storefront looks like a regular department store, which it must have been at one time, named Grand Bazaar. From the outside, it looks quite dramatic. Inside, it's rather ordinary, but it does have several levels, so it pays to poke around a bit. This is where I found Provençal-style contact paper in the housewares department!

TATI
17 rue de Brest, Lyon

Medium-sized store and somewhat more stuffed than your average Tati, I think because of the over-abundance of factories outside of town. If you don't mind shopping for junk from bins, you will have a ball. I bought a designer bathing suit for $10; the same suit was selling in a department store for $50.

DISCOUNTERS

AU BONHEUR DES DAMES
5 rue Dubois, Lyon

This is a resale shop (*dépôt-vente*) where designer clothes are sold. The shop is run by a lovely lady who does not speak English but will insist on chatting to you in French until you understand her perfectly. She told me it was a pity I was so tall and so big because she had lovely clothes but very little to fit me.

The goods weren't in the same class as what you find in resale shops in Cannes, but there were some good labels and I'm sure small women could have a ball.

EuroDif
43 rue de Grenette, Lyon

This is a jobber. They sell cheap clothing for prices that are low even in France. The best buys were women's teenage-style hot fashions and some accessories. EuroDif is a chain; there's also one in Nice on the avenue Jean Medecin.

Jaymes
35 rue de Brest, Lyon

Jaymes is a jobber selling big-name clothing from nearby French mills. The store is stocked with men's, women's, and children's clothing, and it is especially packed with fabulous and otherwise very expensive baby and toddler clothes from some of the best French brands.

Paradis???
1 place des Terreaux, Lyon

You simply can't miss this one for two reasons: It's near the gorgeous place des Terreaux, which you have to see anyway (think Rome) and it's a jobber with so much stuff crammed in that Loehmann's looks boring. Saturdays are filled with teenagers, so try it on a sane day and hope to get lucky. This place is a hoot and not for the weak at heart. Blue bloods stay away.

Lyon Shopper's Stroll & Tour

I'm keeping this fairly simple because you've already seen that there's lots happening in Lyon and you are going to have to pick and choose what works for you. I'm just going to point you in the right direction.

1. Leave Paris no later than 8am on the TGV.
2. Arrive in Lyon at 10am.
3. Taxi to Vieux Lyon and walk around the Old Town.
4. As you finish in Vieux Lyon, you'll end up approaching the river and must cross over. Choose whichever bridge is closest to where you end up, but use a map so you know how to segue into the downtown shopping. This is only a matter of a few blocks, so you have plenty of flexibility. Do be sure to look at the bridge, the view, and the glory of Lyon as you cross.
5. Once on the other side, you'll maybe need to browse the quai St. Antoine just to look at the food and flower market and to position yourself in the central downtown shopping district. Since the market runs along the same position as the Old Town but on the Presqu'île side of town, you're still in sync.
6. Your walk is determined by where you want to be in downtown and when and where you want to eat lunch. Lunch could be in any number of exotic or famous places. I'm picking Le Nord for our day trip because it's famous, because you can't be in Lyon and not do Bocuse, because it's convenient to all the shopping, and because it's a great fun place where the waiters will be nice to you even if you are alone. **Le Nord,** 18 rue Neuve, Lyon 2e, ☎ **04-78-28-24-54;** fax 04-78-28-76-58. After lunch, finish your shopping in the downtown area as chosen from the options above and your personal interests.
7. Taxi now to cours Franklin Roosevelt, which is on the other side of the Rhône. If you have time

to shop some more, you can begin at Souleiado and stroll for 2 blocks. If you're in a hurry for your train, simply stop by Bernachon (42 cours Franklin Roosevelt) for chocolate éclairs to go. If you're seriously dashing, have your taxi wait while you load up and then continue on to the train station for your triumphant return to Paris.

Steady the éclairs and the shopping bags and head for the train station. This time you want Gare Part-Dieu, which is only a sneeze from Bernachon. Once settled on the train, you'll have your tea, eat your éclair, and realize that you've celebrated 1 perfect day in Lyon.

LILLE

. . . .

Welcome to Lille

When I arrived at my hotel in Lille, I was handed a fax from my girlfriend who lives on the Riviera. It said only "What in the hell are you doing in Lille?" Indeed, this is a common reaction to Lille, especially among the French.

Tough luck for those who are missing out on a sensational shopping destination and a great city, to boot. Lille is famous as the heartland of French bed linen, the home of Porthault and Descamps, and the host of an enormous flea market street festival in September. It is also the capital city of northern France, recently turned around when the Eurostar picked Lille as its turnaround city (trains through the Chunnel all connect in Lille). They turn right to go to Paris or left to go to Brussels.

Lille has a kind of architecture you won't see in many other French cities: There's a lot in common with Brussels and more than a little chance for you to think about the cultural differences between the French and the Flemish. Traditionally speaking, because of the manufacturing, Lille and the north have been rich cities and locals have not been shy about showing off their wealth. The architecture here is embellished and even the middle class is into designer clothing. The beer is good, the food is flavorful, and the shopping is simply super.

Also note that culturally speaking, Lille is no backwater town. The recently renovated Palais des Beaux Arts (Decorative Arts museum) is stunning (and what an interesting gift shop!); the architecture of the new train station—built to accommodate the Eurostar—shows that Lille wants to have progressive as well as Flemish architecture. There is tons of energy and arts programs in theaters, operas, and even on the street.

Location, Location, Location

Lille is a mere 10 minutes from the Belgian border and a short distance from Calais. It's slightly northeast of Paris and directly north of Reims. It is equidistant to both Antwerp and Brussels.

Because of this location, and with the connections created by the Eurostar, Lille is one of the most international cities in Europe, with 100 million European citizens living within a 200-mile radius of the city. Lille is indeed the capital of northern France, the heart of Flanders, and yet it's virtually unknown to American tourists. Let's keep it our secret!

Lay of the Land

Like Lyon, Lille is also an enormous city with a great spread and many suburbs. If you're on a day trip you probably won't get to know these suburbs; if you have a car and get to outlets, you'll soon know many of the names of the nearby towns, especially Roubaix, where the big factory outlet mall (**Magasins d'Usine,** 228 av. Alfred Motte) is located.

The heart of Old Lille (Vieux Lille) is rather small, easily walked and enjoyed in a day trip. The center of the world is the Grand Place and the nearby Old Bourse is a must-see for its architecture. Don't miss the book market and its shortcut into the heart of the shopping district in the old city.

Because of the medieval nature of the city, it takes a little longer to get your bearings in the old part of Lille. I suggest repeated shopping forays and some patience with a map.

The old train station (pre-Eurostar) is named Gare Lille Flandres; it forms the end of the shopping and central downtown district at one side of town. The rue Faidherbe connects this train station and the Grand Place and the Bourse. Don't forget to take a nice hard look at the train station, as it happens to be an old friend of yours. It was moved, brick by brick, from Paris where it originally housed the Gare du Nord, the connecting link from Paris to Lille.

From the Grand Place, there are numerous streets that form the spokes of retail: the rue Neuve has the big chains (even **The Disney Store!**), while department stores (good branch of **Au Printemps**) are on rue Nationale. There is also a **Monoprix,** but it is slightly off center.

Take other spokes, such as rue de la Chaussée, toward the place du Lion d'Or to get deeper into the little medieval streets, see the luxury shops, and hit some of the linen stores.

Away from the center of town, but not that far from the original train station, is a doubleheader: a big new commercial mall (**Centre Euralille**) and the new train station, Gare Lille Europe (LE on train schedules), a big block past the mall. Because of the highway and main streets, it's not more than a stroll to the mall or the LE station.

Outside of town are the endless suburbs and connecting cities—more than 100 of them in the metro area. Shoppers will want to remember (even if they can't pronounce) Wazemmes, the site of the Sunday flea market. (You can get there on the Métro.)

Getting There

I originally thought getting to Lille would be a breeze; hop on the Eurostar to London but get off in Lille. Thankfully, before I employed this plan I learned that, while the Eurostar does stop in Lille, it takes on passengers but does not allow passengers to disembark!

Then I was presented with a very confusing train schedule with a variety of travel times, some marked LE, which could have been Greek to me. Now I know that LE means Lille Europe and designates the station. TGV and fast trains use both the LE station and Flanders station. Day trippers may want to use Lille Flandres station, since you can walk everywhere from this station.

While train schedules do change, day trippers may want to note that there's a 7:58am TGV from Paris Nord that goes nonstop to Lilles Flanders and arrives at 8:59am, getting you in town right as the stores begin to open.

The TGV train from Paris took exactly 1 hour and deposited me in LE, which could have been a space station on Mars for all I knew, since it was my first visit to this part of town. I had a lot of luggage and was totally lost; by the time I found a handcart, all the passengers had moved off, leaving me alone with no one to ask for directions. I finally managed to find the elevator and the taxi line, but it was not easy.

As it happened, I had a business appointment in Lille so I needed to be on time. My train went down on the tracks and was delayed 30 minutes (I'm told this is common). The phone on the train didn't work and no one on the train would let me use a cell phone (I think it was my bad French, not their bad manners). Once I got out of that hell they call a train station, I was confronted with an enormous line of people waiting for taxis and no standing taxis. Eeeek! Welcome to modern travel.

Getting Around

I would want a car for getting to outlets, though you can do the city center on foot. If you want to give up treks to Porthault and big-time outlets and just go to the outlet mall in Roubaix, you can take public transportation or make a deal with a taxi to drop you and pick you up a few hours (or weeks) later.

You can also take the train directly from Paris to Roubaix, then get a taxi to take you to the outlet mall and then go into town. If you do this, be sure you have the card of a radio taxi so you can telephone for a pickup at the outlet center.

There is a modern Métro system, although you probably won't be exploring to the extent of serious Métro hopping. You can take the Métro to the flea market on Sundays.

The tourist office has a rather unique program called Taxi Touristique, which you book right at the Tourist Office in the heart of downtown, place Rihour. This program has three different taxi routes that take you on a private tour of the city, prices ranging with the circuit from 160 F ($27) to 420 F ($70). Now, here's the great part: For an additional cost, you can add on to these tours. Surely you can add on a trip to some outlets!

Promotional Deals

Lille is another one of the cities that celebrates the Weekends En Ville promotion with TGV, and so on, and offers hotels on weekends at 2 nights for the price of 1.

Sleeping in Lille

HÔTEL ALLIANCE
17 quai di Wault, Lille

This hotel has been created from a 12th-century convent; the architecture is grand and the space comfortable enough. It is a four-star hotel with 83 rooms and 8 suites as well as a restaurant in the cloister. Weekend rates are about $75 per night with breakfast included. The local phone is ☎ **03-20-30-62-62;** fax 03-20-42-94-25.

HÔTEL CARLTON
3 rue de Paris, Lille

One of my first attractions to Lille was the knowledge that the best hotel in town is a Concorde
Hotel, has good rates, and is located a block from
the Grand Place and walking distance to all the shopping. This is a four-star hotel, small, but in the grande
dame tradition.

The best thing about the hotel is its location and
style. The next best thing is the computer system
they have for guests, the first I have seen like this in
France. You buy a card at the front desk and then
access the computer to send or check e-mail or surf
the Net. The front desk staff helped me and it was
great fun.

Rates vary with the time of year and the promotion. The Carlton is one of the hotels that participates in the two-for-one weekend deal. Expect to
pay from $125 per night on up. For dollar rates,
call Concorde in the United States at ☎ 800-
888-4747. The local phone is ☎ 03-20-13-33-13;
fax 03-20-51-48-17.

Shopping Style

Lille has few American tourists, and while it does
have a strong tourist and business visitor tradition,
its shopping style is very real-people oriented. The
outlets are mobbed (both locals and visitors) and
there's a strong tradition of ritual wherein locals
make the rounds at their off-price resources once a
month or whenever possible, since outlet shopping
is so hit and miss.

There are a few stores that only have branches
in northern France. My favorite find is **Spot;** shopping here is very much a blend of established
designer names (**Hermès, Lancel,** and so on), new-
to-me northern names, and French multiples and
outlet stores. A good bit of retail is hidden. If you
didn't know to ask where **Sephora** is, you wouldn't
find it (it's in the Euralille mall). But don't for a

minute think this town is so provincial that it doesn't have things like Sephora!

There's also a lot of British influence—more than in other parts of France—and most of the big British multiples have stores here. Sure, you can find **Marks & Spencer** in Nice and all over France, but other brands have stores here too, such as **Monsoon**.

Shopping Plans

If you do plan to get into some of the outlets, I suggest you have a plan of attack before you come to town and work with a map and a basic schedule. France has gone outlet crazy in recent years, so any French bookstore will sell you a copy of any number of guidebooks to outlets, be they regional guides or national.

My friend Judith met me in Lille with photocopied pages from a local guide; I had pages from *Le Guide Des Magasins d'Usine,* by Marie-Paule Dousset, and *Le Guide First Magasins d'Usine,* by Sylie Bontron. The Bontron book is older and I've had it for a few years. I don't know if it's been revised or updated or is even in print.

For my personal interest, the Porthault factory—about an hour's drive from downtown Lille—was my number-one priority. Because it is so off the beaten track from everything else, all my plans had to be coordinated around this trip. There is a lot of juggling and a good amount of driving, depending on how many outlets you are hitting, so make a basic plan and then be somewhat flexible.

I've also found that after a certain number of outlets, I begin to crack up. Make your plans based on your known tolerance for this kind of shopping.

Outlet Shopping

In the resources part of this chapter (see "Lille Resources from A to Z," below), I have listed the specifics of shopping at the outlets I personally visited. There are hundreds of outlets in the Lille area so you could spend a month here to shop them. If you are serious about this pursuit, get one of the outlet books mentioned above. I found that the opportunities I had more than wiped out my credit rating and my stash of French francs (you have to pay cash at Porthault).

In the end, despite the fact that I had pages of outlet addresses, there wasn't enough time, energy, or money to do much more than Porthault and the big outlet in Roubaix.

True outlet shoppers will remember that just as in the United States, the word and the notion of outlet shopping can be stretched. **Olivier Desforges,** a noted linen maker, has what it claims is an outlet in the basement of its boutique in Vieux Lille. Believe me, it was nothing to write home about or to even write a listing about for this book. There was also an outlet in the Roubaix mall, where prices were lower.

Packing Plans

When I told you about my hotel in Lille (Carlton), I didn't mention they packed up all my purchases for me! I bought so much in the outlets that I had no room in my luggage. I ended up getting an empty box from a factory, which I packed and then gave to the front desk of the Carlton. They taped it up and then did a string rope with a handle so I could take it as a piece of luggage with me on the train.

Don't go to a city like Lille on a shopping spree without an empty suitcase and some sort of shipping plan, especially if you go to the Braderie.

Markets & Fairs

Every year during the first weekend in September, the city hosts a giant flea market street fair called **The Braderie,** which is based on a medieval tradition whereby home owners allowed the servants 1 day a year to clean the house and sell off old junk. Now thousands of vendors line the streets, people eat mussels, drink beer, and shop way into the night. Naturally hotel rooms book up months in advance, so find out the dates and book early, or plan this as a day trip from Paris.

There's a small, daily antique and used-book market in the courtyard of the Old Bourse, and there's a Sunday flea market in the suburb of Wazemmes at place de la Nouvelle Aventure. *Important note:* To get to the Sunday flea market in Wazemmes, take the Métro from Ribour (downtown) in the Wazemmes direction, *but get off at Gambetta. Do not get off at Wazemmes.*

Because of Lille's location, there are many organized tours that go to markets (flea markets, art markets). People think nothing of a day trip to the United Kingdom, even to London, or a trip to Maastricht or Bruges or Brussels (great market town). There are even Christmas markets in Germany to think about with an all-day tour to the Christmas market in Cologne.

There are also some organized tours to outlets. Ask at the tourist office.

Shopping Hours

Regular stores open at either 9 or 9:30am and close for lunch and reopen at 2 or 2:30pm, or open at 10am and stay open all day, until 7 or 7:30pm. Factory hours are different and often specific to the factory; check before you drive out of the way. Stores are closed on Sunday. On Monday many stores are closed in the mornings but open at 2pm.

Money Matters

You can easily exchange French francs for Belgian francs until you switch over to euros; most stores will also take Belgian francs for payment.

Lille Shopping Neighborhoods

I found Lille difficult to grasp, especially in the core of the city, because it is not on a grid system and I have trouble with medieval streets that interconnect and possibly change names. You can pretty much wander, get lost, and be found and have a great shopping day. Just head for the Grand Place.

I've dissected the downtown shopping a little bit, in the hopes this will steer you on a clear path, although there's a lot to be said for the lost and found method.

GRAND PLACE   Like every Grand Place, this one has stores, cafes, banks, and everything else you want from a Grand Place. Don't miss a chance to shop **Spot.** There's also a branch of **FNAC** next door.

NATIONALE   This spoke from the Grand Place has **Printemps** and the bigger, commercial stores.

NEUVE   Another spoke, with many real-people stores such as **ProMod, Electre,** and **Pimkie.**

FAIDHERBE   This is the main street through the center of town with many big stores, including **Tati,** the discount department store. The street leads from the core of town directly to the Flanders train station.

RUE PARIS   This spoke from Grand Place runs next to Faidherbe and is the street where the Carlton Hotel is located, so it will help you get your bearings. Going away from town on rue Paris there's more shopping, including a local mall and a branch of **FNAC.** If you're just wandering this street past the Carlton Hotel (if your back is to the hotel, turn left) you'll pass the very unique **Le Journal,** which sells the newspaper (French) from the day your were born (no. 35). There's a branch of the fabric house **Toto,** which sells end cuts of designer fabrics (among other things), a few jobbers, and the mall with **C&A** and **FNAC.**

PLACE DU GENERAL DE GAULLE   This place adjoins the Grand Place and signifies the beginning of the fancy shopping district. Look for the **Lancel** shop. Yes, de Gaulle was born in Lille.

MEDIEVAL BACK STREETS   The streets run together here and don't really need names. This is a pedestrian-only area located behind the Grand Place in the streets from rue Esquermoise to the bd. Carnot (but doesn't include Carnot). You'll find **Marks & Spencer** back here, **C&A, Camaieu, Naf Naf, Zara**, many movie theaters, and real-people stuff. If this is too nebulous for you, head for **Zara** at 34 rue Bethune and then wander. At the back end of this district is the place de Lion d'Or, which separates the end of the designer chic and begins the funky.

FUNKY OLD TOWN   From the place du Lion d'Or, check out the rue du Monnaie for vintage shops and other nice shops (clothing, shoes, home design) owned by those who couldn't quite pay the higher rents a block away. Then cut back around the cathedral (Catheteral Notre Dame de la Treille) for more back streets with a few jobbers and some antique shops.

Snack & Shop

You'll have no trouble finding cafes or places to eat. There's always waffles and/or *frites* (French fries) sold in stands in the streets or in shopping areas, including the factory outlets at Roubaix.

LA ROBE DES CHAMPS
10 rue Faidherbe

Around the corner from the Carlton Hotel and therefore in the heart of most things, this adorable restaurant decorated in cute style serves baked potatoes as the meal. This is an English tradition but it's been Frenchified a tad. Great for a light meal.

LE COQ HARDI
44 Grand Place, Lille

Seems like every town I visit has a Coq Hardi, though I don't think it's a chain but rather a popular name. This is one of the many cafes on the Grand Place. My friend Judith chose it for us and I adored it here. I liked the prices (low), the food (excellent), the regional style cooking (love that smelly cheese tart), and the location in the heart of everything. Oh, I forgot to mention the beer.

L'HUITRIERE
Rue des Chats Bossus and rue Basse

This is a gourmet restaurant and a grocery store. The specialty of the house, as you can guess from the name, is oysters. Don't miss the decorative tiles outside or the decorative touches indoors. This is in the medieval part of town not far from the place de Lion d'Or.

MÉERT
27 rue Esquermoise, Lille

Traditional old-lady, old-fashioned tea room for waffles, pastries, chocolates, and so on. Established in 1761, it's still going strong.

PAUL
8 rue de Paris, Lille

This is a must-do, and since it's across the street from the Carlton Hotel and in the center of town, it should be an easy assignment. Have at least one meal in the flagship cafe of the bakery shop Paul. Paul also runs the cafe in the Palais des Beaux Arts, which is fine and nice, but don't miss the cute sit-down opportunity in town with wooden beams, tiles, charm, and good stuff to eat any time of the day. It's open daily from 6:30am until midnight.

My Visit to the Big Magasins d'Usine

228 rue Alfred Motte, Roubaix

My visit here did not start off great: It took forever to find a parking space and the industrial sprawl looked, uh, industrial. I perked up after testing both the French fries (excellent) and the waffles (not bad). There are several factory buildings turned into outlet centers, as is the style in the United States. The first one I entered had me laughing for a few seconds before falling into deep depression—not ready for prime time to an American shopper. This was a huge space subdivided into areas for off-loading junk, and it was depressing as well as distressing.

We came out of that building to the front of the outlet center and went into the free-standing **Texaffaire** outlet building. Texaffaire is the name of the outlets for Descamps and there are scads of them all over France, so I knew them already. Still, this was fantastic and I immediately cheered up. The spread included sheet fabric sold off the bolt by the meter, ranging from 35 F to 50 F ($5.80 to $8.50) per meter. This is per meter in length as the width is sheet width; it's very, very wide and therefore great fabric for making tablecloths!

Lille Resources from A to Z

ANTIQUES

The part of town with the most antique shops is right near the Cathedral Notre Dame de la Treille, although I did not go nuts for antiques in the stores. Better to wait for the Sunday flea market or The Braderie, each September.

There were other goodies as well, including sheets, towels, and washcloths. Things were brightening. Then we went into the big factory building, three floors of subdivided space housing just about every linen brand known to France as well as many clothing makers. Most outlets bore the name of the maker, so you knew what you were doing but some were tricky, just as in the States. Judith had to teach me that **Modaffair** was the outlet for **Pimkie.**

Just like in the States, not all outlets were outlets and not all had bargains or discounts. Many had current merchandise at in-store prices (Spot), and some had a mixture. The outlets with designer bed linen were best (Christian Lacroix), then came underwear, although American underwear is less expensive than French to begin with. The best outlet for designer sheets (in the non-Porthault category) was **Sous-Signé,** which had both Pierre Frey and Christian Lacroix.

A few outlets were fancy, like **Catamini,** the kids' line, but the prices were outrageously high.

CHEESE

LES BONS PATURAGES
54 rue Basse, Lille

Totally different in feel from Philippe (below), this is almost a cute store with a Disney feel to it and a lot of food, including cheeses.

PHILIPPE OLIVER
3 rue Curé St. Etienne, Lille

This small but well-known cheese shop also makes the regional specialty, *Flamiche au Maroilles,* which I call the smelly cheese tart. If you are a fan of strongly flavored (and scented) cheese, this is a winner. I took home two frozen ones, which I kept in my minibar until I could get back to Paris where the Crillon cooked them for me. Yum!

DEPARTMENT STORES

AU PRINTEMPS
45 rue Nationale, Lille

Excellent branch of Paris-based department store, large, well stocked, and chic. A pleasure to shop.

TATI
Rue Faidherbe, Lille

The usual Tati atmosphere, this one didn't touch my soul like the one in Lyon, but then, you have to be in the mood for Tati. There are two different stores next door to each other, so don't miss any of it, if you can cope.

Factory Outlets

PORTHAULT
19 rue Robespierre, Rieux en Cambresis

Be still my heart! I must confess to you that at the very beginning, when I first founded Born to Shop with a group of girlfriends, the book was totally different and we really wanted to concentrate on designer outlet stores. We made a wish list of places we wanted to find and the Porthault factory was our number-one choice. I tried to find it, but I guess I didn't try hard enough. It wasn't until one of the first outlet books was published that I knew our sense was right—there was an outlet store after all!

It took more than a dozen years, but I finally got there. Not only was it worth the wait, but it's worth a special trip to France. Before I elaborate, I warn you that this trip is not for everyone. I happen to adore Porthault prints and I think that Porthault is special and it means something to me. There are plenty of people who think this stuff is very old lady.

The factory is about an hour outside of Lille; it's not hard to get to but you should be used to driving in France. It is in the middle of nowhere and you may loose heart while driving since the factory itself is not marked. You should speak some French and have a phone card on you so that if you are lost, you can call the factory for directions. This is not a tourist attraction; there are few comforts of home. That means when (and if) you do find it, they have stand-up toilets.

However, this is about the most charming and authentic factory visit you may ever make. The woman who runs the factory store, Mme. Andree, is adorable, generous, and possessed of a great sense of humor, limitless patience and enthusiasm. She accepts only cash or a local check. She took my traveler's checks because they were in French francs.

What's available is very hit or miss; some of it is there because it's so ugly no one would want it. Some of it is simply old. Because so much of the Porthault style is classic, I don't usually care how old a print is. Prices are laughably low, running from 10% to 50% of the regular retail price.

Some examples of what I found: a baby set of three pieces for 120 F ($20); an adult bathrobe for 690 F ($115); and a set of three towels for 680 F ($113).

Here are basic directions: Head south from Lille on Autoroute du Nord, A1. Connect to N43, direction Cambrai. In Cambrai take N44 to the left for Reiux-en-Cambresis. The phone number is ☎ 03-27-82-22-33. Hours are Monday through Thursday, 10am to noon and 1 to 4:30pm. it's closed

Friday, Saturday, Sunday, and all month in August.

You will not notice that this is a factory or that it is Porthault, as the factory is unmarked. Look for the factory chimney and the ironwork at the gates. Drive into the tiny courtyard and park. At the reception desk ask to visit the shop. I'd call ahead and tell them when you are coming.

Lille Shopper's Stroll & Tour

1. Begin the tour at the tourist office, place Rihour, and cut across the Grand Place through the Vielle Bourse, looking at the architecture, passing through the book market and cutting through the courtyard to the place du Theatre.

2. Turn right and head along the rue Grande Chaussée, which is lined with designer stores (everyone, including **Hermès**) and shop your way right to the place du Lion d'Or.

3. Turn left on the rue de la Monnaie at the place du Lion d'Or and pass some of the smaller but fun stores such as **Ellen Desforges** (no. 28) for decorative and English table top and **Nostalgie,** 57 rue de la Monnaie, for vintage and resale. Don't buy too many clothes if you pop into **Yanka,** at no. 10, a candy shop known to locals for its chocolates.

4. Turn left and cut up toward placeaux Oignons and then head around the back end of the cathedral, taking in the small shops that range form **Les Ateliers de La Treille,** a men's discount shop (21 rue Masurel) to **Le Cedre Rouge,** the Pottery Barn–like French multiple.

5. Turn left at the corner of rue Basse, heading away from the cathedral for 1 shopping block and then turn right onto the tiny rue J. J. Rousseau, where you'll dart into **N de B Haute Mode,** a couture hatmaker, created by artiste Nathalie Sarazin, no. 6.

6. Returning to the main direction, instead of taking the spoke that is rue Basse (where you just

came from), go over one spoke to rue Esquermoise and head back, shopping all the way (*bien sur*) toward the Grand Place.

7. Now pass through the Grand Place and past place Charles de Gaulle to **Lancel** and then rue Neuve. Before you turn onto rue Neuve for more of the normal stores you have come to expect, be sure to visit **Le Furet du Nord** at 15 place General de Gaulle, the largest bookshop in the world.

8. Shop rue Neuve and the warren of streets back here, not missing rue Bethune with its **Zara** shop. Eventually, you'll end up right at the tourist office, place Rihour, where you started!

Chapter Nine

. . . .

SHOPPING THE RIVIERA: CANNES TO NICE TO CORSICA

WELCOME TO THE RIVIERA

. . . .

Welcome to the part of the world where lifestyles of the rich and famous have been an ordinary sport for more than 100 years. The Riviera isn't just a location—it's a state of mind. A few minutes among palm trees, blue seas, sparkling skies, mountain air, and topless beach bunnies and nothing else seems real.

The Riviera is where the concept of Beverly Hills was born. It's where glamour was born. It's where resorts and in season and even postcards were born. The idea of having a suntan came from Cannes. No, I'm not making any of this up. It was none other than Coco Chanel who made being tan the in thing.

If we didn't have the Riviera, Coco Chanel would have invented it. Indeed, it was Chanel and Picasso and Gerald Murphy (whose motto was "Living well is the best revenge") and Scott and Zelda Fitzgerald who resurrected the Riviera, reclaimed it from its posh Victorian past, and made it the playground of the Western world.

The duke and duchess of Windsor were regulars on the Riviera; they lived in Antibes. The Aga Khan was a regular. Grace Kelly, her serene highness, ruled.

The British, the Americans, the Russians, and even the Arabs have all held on to a piece of the dream and reworked the fantasy to meet their own needs. See those piers jutting out across the beaches and into the sea? They're for jet-setters who arrive by motorboat, and yes, during the International Film Festival in Cannes, they really do lay down the red carpet right on the pier.

The Riviera is all about red-carpet treatment, not only for stars and starlets, but for anyone who can pay the tab. And these days, the bill may be discounted enough to enable just about anyone to revel in the field of dreams.

On a recent trip to the Riviera, I came to the conclusion that the area is one of the few places in the world where you can still latch on to personal glamour. That is to say that you aren't following in the wake of the rich and famous as a wannabe, but that the magic happens to you too.

The Riviera works not because the rich and famous have walked that way, but because for the length of your stay, or for a few magical moments, you too can be rich and famous, if only in spirit.

After the spiritual part, you can go shopping.

Naturally enough, where there's money and glamour of this caliber, there's also good shopping. You might say this is where the born to shop were born. Hmmm. Styles and trends are often born on the streets, or beaches, here; just where do you think it was that topless sunbathing came into fashion? The lifestyle demands that an evening stroll becomes a fashion show on the catwalk of life. Everyone makes a public appearance in the south of France—that's part of the attraction. What's worn on the streets is as exciting as what's shown on the mannequins.

Unnaturally enough, some of what you see in those stores is even affordable. And, shock of all shocks, there are actually some bargains out there, down south, where they do not say *Bonjour ya'll.*

Whether you come for the film festival, the palm trees, the Arabian knights, the princes, the princesses,

The French Riviera

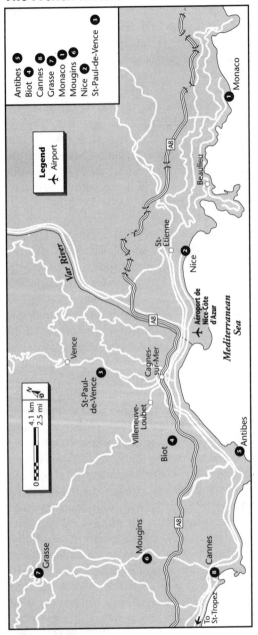

Legend

✈ Airport

Antibes ❺
Biot ❹
Cannes ❽
Grasse ❼
Monaco ❶
Mougins ❻
Nice ❷
St-Paul-de-Vence ❸

Monaco ❶

Beaulieu

A8

St-Étienne

Nice ❷

Var River

Aéroport de Nice-Côte d'Azur ✈

Mediterranean Sea

Vence

St-Paul-de-Vence ❸

Cagnes-sur-Mer

Villeneuve-Loubet

Biot ❹

Antibes ❺

Grasse ❼

Mougins ❻

A8

Cannes ❽

To St-Tropez

0 4.1 km
   2.5 mi

N

or the palaces; whether you come to stare or be stared at, as a star or an extra; you've come to one of the original places in the sun.

Slather yourself with suntan oil by day (yes, I'm afraid so, the French still believe in the tan) and wrinkle cream by night. Take off your top during the day and pull out Le Wonderbra by night. And don't forget to visit the spa, drink lots of healthy water, apply bust cream, and use your cellulite spray.

In between we are going to shop and eat and promenade—and be French. Okay, so we'll fake the last part. That's part of what the Riviera is all about, too.

ATTENTION SHOPPERS
· ·

If you're a regular to this part of the world, be it for conventions or festivals or annual vacations, you may be surprised to know that the last year or two have seen enormous changes in Cannes, especially in the retail scenery. Cannes is a town where sometimes stores open for a season (after Easter) and close by November, never to be heard from again. But Cannes is also the leading purveyor of luxury goods on the Riviera, outdistancing both Nice and Monte Carlo by miles. Cannes is also enjoying something very interesting in retail real estate right now: stores are fighting to open up freestanding storefront. The trend toward several designer lines being carried in one exclusive local boutique is dying out; more and more chains and designer hotshots have opened their own stores.

The fact that **Sephora**, **Zara** and **L'Occitane** have all just opened is reason enough for you to stand up and salute.

GETTING THERE

. . . .

By Plane

FROM THE UNITED STATES Nice–Côte d'Azur International Airport (NCE) is the second busiest airport in France, expanding so fast that by the turn of the century it will be the major transportation hub for not only the south of France and Provence, but for the entire Mediterranean.

I'm not sure if the Nice–Côte d'Azur International Airport was created to make my life better or just to boost Delta's bottom line, but if you are a south of France or Provence person, this airport was made for you and yours. Delta flies a daily nonstop to and from New York; Atlanta nonstop service is in the works. Delta and Nice are partners in welcoming us all to the Riviera.

There are other carriers to get to and from Nice airport, of course, but you'll find that this flight is so sublime that it's actually hard to book, especially on frequent flyer miles. It's an insider secret that everyone knows about; book early.

Delta has special winter promotions that do include Nice—one of the few places where the weather is still balmy even when Europe has its off-price season. I got some "Starving Artists Fares" coupons that made the round-trip ticket from New York to Nice a mere $399.

FROM PARIS You can travel to the Riviera through the Nice airport by booking connection through Paris, *bien sur.* This is easy but time consuming. It can also be costly if you want to come in or out of one city and in or out of the other. In fact, many people are not only shocked at how far the Riviera is from Paris, but at how high the airfare from Paris to Nice can be, especially if it's bought as a one-way journey. If you are writing a through ticket, however, the add-on is not as expensive, but you probably don't get to layover in Paris and you do have connecting times and terminals to keep you in line.

ONE-WAY TIX TRICKS

My friend Pascale-Agnes taught me this trick: Don't buy a one-way ticket. You buy the cheapest Air France round-trip ticket you can find (be sure to ask about various promotions and Saturday stays) and then you simply throw away the portion you don't need. Waste makes savings!

FROM NEARBY CITIES   If you want to fly into Nice and a connecting city is a must-do, depending on where you ware coming from, look into a variety of cities, since all connections are equal when you're just walking through airports and Paris is not the only possibility!

Note that as airlines deregulate in Europe, there are a bunch of start-up no-frills airlines, and many of them offer low fares that get lower during price wars. The British have the most low-cost flights from assorted London area airports to Nice. Note, however, that these flights do not originate from Heathrow, so if you are making a through connection, pay attention to the details! EasyJet is a British firm that does a lot of business in discount flights; they've just been attacked by British Air's new Go airline, another discount airline serving Nice.

Otherwise, consider these tricks: Amsterdam, Brussels, Milan, and Geneva! Because KLM and Northwest Airlines have a family relationship, you can often get into Amsterdam and then connect to a nonstop to Nice. Using Brussels as a hub, you can get to Nice on a variety of carriers; from Geneva you may want to pick up a rental car and simply drive into France—it's not that far away—or fly to Nice.

By Train

If you think you can avoid the high cost of a one-way plane ticket with a train ticket, hold the mustard Mr. Poupon. The train ticket may not be much cheaper, especially if you take an overnight train, which requires an additional fee for the *wagons-lit*. Also note, one-way fares are sometimes not half the price of round-trip fares; ask.

FROM PARIS   The beauty of taking a train from Paris to the south of France is that you can pretty much pinpoint your destination. You can also take an overnight train and sleep the whole way, so you don't have to complain about wasting a day of your precious trip on a 7-hour train ride. And, if you normally spend $400 a night on a hotel room, you will save money because the train compartment will be less expensive (about $25). You can also divide up the trip and do the area slowly, starting off in Lyon, moving to Avignon, then to Aix, and finally down to Cannes and/or Nice and even Monaco. All are on the main line.

   Note: A **TGV Mediterranee** is in works, currently bogged down in the usual real-world problems, but being laid across the Riviera so that by the turn of the century, the TGV train tracks will extend to Nice and possibly Monaco, then eventually to Turin. Also note that major cities on the line will open new train stations, so know where you're going and the specific station name!

   Not to be tacky about this, but until this service is on-line, I don't care what your travel agent or your friends or your train ticket says, there ain't no TGV service from Nice to Paris. If you hold a marked TGV ticket it means you take a regular train, which connects to the TGV train in Marseilles, where there is proper track.

GETTING AROUND THE SOUTH OF FRANCE
· ·
By Car

As you no doubt already know from the beginning of this book, I now drive in France—and got my start right here, at the Nice Airport. I continue to rent through Kemwel (see chapter 2) and I celebrate the day I got up the nerve and decided to try driving, because it has made me free.

Renting a car in Europe is tricky business and should always be done from the United States to save money. I find Kemwel's prices much, much lower than anyone else's, and their local agent, Citer, is just great. They have a desk right inside the Nice International Airport, smack dab in front of your face as you exit through Customs.

Avis continues to have the French train station concession, so if you don't want the car at the airport, you may want to investigate the Avis rail and road deals (see chapter 2). From a price point of view I must tell you that 4 days with Avis cost the same as 7 days with Kemwel, but sometimes these things are not a matter of price but convenience. I do understand.

By Private Transport

I had a wonderful time with my rental car and the freedom that it brought me. I also spent about an hour trying to find Moulin de Mougins on the way from Grasse to Cannes (it's marked in the other direction, but not vice versa!). It was frustrating!

If being lost in the hills is not your thing, you may need some help. Enter my old buddy Piero Bruni, who now runs **E.T.S.**, which stands for Executive Transport Service. Piero and his wife provide all manner of transfers and transportation and complete tours of the Riviera (and Provence) from offices in Cannes. Call ☎ **04-92-98-06-29**; fax 04-92-98-98-58; e-mail: PBruni@compuserve.com. Piero speaks English fluently and spent years as a hotelier, so service is his business.

VIP Riviera Service handles transportation needs in Monte Carlo, Nice, and Cannes for groups or for individuals, and it even does airport pick-ups. The office is open daily, 24 hours a day. The local phone is ☎ **04-93-44-22-33**; fax 04-93-37-49-93.

By Train

Believe it or not, you can enjoy the south of France without a car. I did it for years. No problem. The heart of the Riviera, essentially from Cannes to Monaco, is totally connected by train, with any number of trains per hour. There's enough to do in the various towns that you can be set for many a day trip with only a few taxi rides, as needed.

St. Tropez is a little difficult to get to without a car, especially out of season, but you can take a train and bus combination, a train and taxi combination, or simply splurge for a taxi. I was able to get a Mercedes Benz taxi to drive me from St. Tropez to Cannes, so don't rule out taxis for solving transportation problems.

By Bus

Yes, they have buses in the south of France, and you too can ride them. They're great for some of the short hops in the Cannes area. Some working ability in French will be helpful. Most tourist offices print bus routes, so if you study these charts and point, you should do just fine.

THE RIVIERA SHOPPING SCENE

Although the Riviera is a tourist destination—even for the French—there are a lot of shopping surprises going on, even for the jaded who probably think that prices are jacked up in the Riviera because it is a resort.

Believe it or not, there are a number of price ranges, so not everything is out of sight. In fact, on the whole, *prices in the Riviera are less than those in Provence!*

There are plenty of designer boutiques, with the biggest concentration of the big money shops being in the big money towns—Monte Carlo, Nice, Cannes, and St. Tropez. There's also an overflow into Aix, which I mention here although the nitty-gritty on Aix is in the Provence chapter (chapter 12).

For the most part, if you are including a trip to Paris in this visit, you'll do better in Paris for perfumes and makeup/beauty products than in the Riviera, just because there are more discounters in Paris.

For everyday merchandise, all of the mass-oriented department stores have the same prices throughout France—the only exception being that the Champs-Elysées Prisunic is more expensive than others, but that won't affect you on the Riviera, will it?

Brocante seems to be less expensive in the Riviera than you would expect, while serious antiques are seriously expensive. Of course, they are expensive everywhere but are generally less in the provinces than in Paris.

As you do your town-to-town prowling you may want to note my simple rule of thumb—the cuter the town, the higher the prices. St. Tropez is more expensive than Cannes—that's all there is to it. Nice can be cheaper than Cannes. Real-people towns (and cities) have better prices and bigger selections.

Few of the bigger Riviera towns are in the "cute" category. Cute usually means a village, and village usually does not carry Chanel. The designer shopping cities are Aix, St. Tropez, Cannes, Monte Carlo, and Nice—Cannes being the best.

Nice's best shopping district is downright unappealing from a visual standpoint; Cannes has a casual Beverly Hills feel, but the shopping real estate is not stunning (aside from the view to sea and Esterel); and Monaco is picture perfect but sterile. Shopping in Corsica—that's a trick question, right?

MARKETS & FAIRS

. . . .

The south of France is one big market. The happiest news is that there are terrific flea markets on Monday—a day that can be totally dead for shoppers in many parts of France—every week, in and out of season.

As for flea markets, there are regular markets and then special events and salons, especially in Cannes and Monte Carlo.

For brocante, there's the **Marché Forville** in Cannes on Monday, with about 75 dealers, as well as **Cours Saleya** in Nice on Monday, where some 250 dealers congregate, and the Saturday market in St. Tropez, which isn't much to write home about in terms of brocante (and prices are high).

Brocante is sold on Thursday and Saturday at a teensy market in Antibes, and on Sunday in Villefranche, which has two separate little markets—a perfect Sunday browse. On Saturday in Cannes there's a different flea market at the Allées du Liberté, right across the street from the Palais du Festivals in the heart of town. Brocante is sold in Grasse on Wednesday. Sometimes there are special event brocante fairs, such as the **Grande Brocante de Printemps in Valbonne;** call ☎ 04-93-12-03-08 for dates.

CANNES

. . . .

Welcome to Cannes

Allo, oui; I send kisses on both cheeks and welcome you to Cannes. Air kisses darling. *Bisou, bisou!*

Cannes is my personal hometown when I am in the Riviera, although when I begin to look for a house to retire to, I think I'll go more for the Antibes area. Never mind, I have a very nice hotel room now and I can drive, so Cannes is home suite home.

Yes, there are parts of Cannes that are glitzy or even silly, but there's so much going on and so many types of things happening that it's the heartbeat of the Riviera to me. I particularly like Cannes out of season and hope you'll plan a winter trip here, carefully avoiding holidays and conventions.

Cannes is the perfect hub for enjoying not only the local scene but for getting out and about and up the hills and over to Monte Carlo and off to Provence. But, wonderfully, Cannes is also a real city and a walking town, so you don't need a car. If you stay in a centrally located hotel, you can dash in and out of the activity without ever having to worry about revving up the car.

Cannes is also the best shopping town on the Riviera. Just in the last year, **Zara,** the Spanish ready-to-wear firm, **L'Occitane,** the Provençal soap and suds maker, and **Sephora,** the LVMH Luxury Group perfume store, have all opened freestanding stores in Cannes. Shopping is hot, hot, hot in a town that has known how to simmer ever since it recovered from World War II.

Cannes isn't funky like St. Tropez, or small-town like Eze, or tourist trappy like Vallauris. The real Cannes has several personalities, because it's actually a very big city that spreads and sprawls, and there are real people who live here. But enough about them. What you come to Cannes for, aside from the very famous conventions and the film festival, are the sun, the sand, and the shopping. All are just a little bit bigger and brighter in Cannes.

The Lay of the Land

Cannes is located right smack dab in the middle of the Riviera, about a half-hour drive from Nice. While Nice is the big city of the Côte d'Azur for transportation and business, Cannes is the big city of the Riviera in terms of show biz and shopping.

To get around town, you only need to know these few things:

- The upper city is mostly for real people and fills in the tiers from the pay road to the sea; you will more than likely just drive through it. Or never see it.
- The old city is located around yet another hill, Le Suquet, which rises alongside the old harbor

Cannes

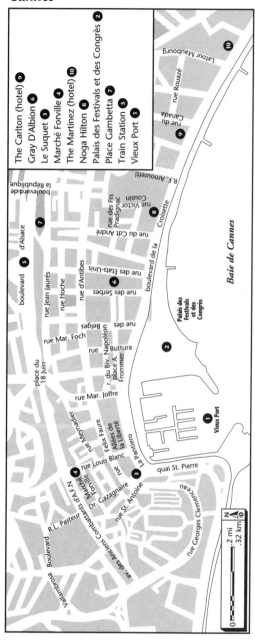

The Carlton (hotel) 9
Gray D'Albion 6
Le Suquet 3
Marché Forville 4
The Martinez (hotel) 10
Noga Hilton 8
Palais des Festivals et des Congrès 2
Place Gambetta 7
Train Station 5
Vieux Port 1

Baie de Cannes

Palais des Festivals et des Congrès

boulevard de la Croisette

R.F. Amouretti
rue Victor Cousin
rue des Frs Pradignac
rue du Cdt André
boulevard de la République
d'Alsace
boulevard
rue Jean Jaurès
rue Hoche
rue d'Antibes
rue des Etats-Unis
rue des Serbes
rue des Belges
rue Mar. Foch
rue Buttura
r. du Blv. Napoléon
place A. Frommer
rue Mar. Joffre
place du 18 Juin
rue Meynadier
Félix Faure
Allées de la Liberté
rue Louis Blanc
La Pantiero
rue
rue St-Antoine
quai St. Pierre
Dr. Gazagnaire
Marché Forville
R.L. Pasteur
av. des Anciens Combattants d'A.F.N
Boulevard
Vallombrosa
rue Georges Clemenceau

Latour Maubourg
rue Rouazé
rue du Canada

Vieux Port

N
0   .2 mi
0   .32 km

(Le Vieux Port). Wear walking shoes when you explore here.

- The new money is on La Croisette. By new, I mean post 1834, which is when Cannes suddenly became fashionable due to a cholera epidemic in Nice. Ever since then, the beach area and promenade in Cannes (boulevard de la Croisette) have been the in places to be seen in your tight bustle, tight hoop skirt, tight cloche, or tight Azzedine Alaia.

- The real-people shopping street is the rue d'Antibes, 1 block behind La Croisette and running parallel to it.

- The train station is in the heart of town, so if you don't drive, you can easily walk to and from the train station from just about any hotel.

Getting There

BY PLANE The easiest way to get to Cannes is to fly into the Nice–Côte d'Azur International Airport. From there you can now get a helicopter transfer to Cannes. Or you can take a bus. The bus costs 70 F (about $12) each way and departs from the front of the Nice airport every 20 to 30 minutes and takes you to downtown Cannes. You can actually buy a *carnet* of six tickets for 340 F ($57), if you are a regular. For information, call ☎ 04-93-39-11-39.

If you can't manage all your luggage (like me), then you will need to take a taxi from the airport. Note that taxi prices from Nice to Cannes are fixed; they don't go by the meter—ask and try to negotiate. There is also a surcharge for each piece of baggage. Ask the driver how much it will cost; be prepared to pay about 450 F ($75) from Nice to Cannes. I do not tip on rigged prices.

A taxi from Cannes to the Nice airport is less expensive, because the local politics are different (don't ask). You'll pay 350 F ($58) plus the surcharge for luggage. I usually add a small tip here because I appreciate honesty in taxi drivers.

Your hotel will gladly arrange a car and driver pickup at the airport for you. This service costs about $250, but that includes tip.

If you are doing any driving around the area, you really want to pick up your rental car right at the Nice airport. The airport is right on the highway; simply take the A8 and get off at the "Cannes/Mougins" exit. This is by far the best plan and you will feel like a genius for having saved the round-trip taxi fare. This cuts the actual cost of your car rental in half!

BY SHIP & YACHT   Numerous yachts, sailing vessels, and even the big luxury cruise ships call at the port of Cannes. The bay is too shallow for a large ship to come to the pier, so they send passengers to shore via tender, which lands right at the Maritime Center next to the Palais des Festivals on La Croisette.

But wait! The City of Cannes is redoing the harbor and the Maritime Center so that some cruise lines (with shallow draft) can come right up to the dock! This means the *QE2* will still be out at sea and need tenders but the Radisson *Song of Flower* will come right to shore, as will several other ships.

In many port towns, the pier is in a weird place—in Cannes, the pier is right where you want it to be, in the heart of everything and directly across the street from the city's Saturday flea market. Who could ask for anything more?

BY TRAIN   There are two so-called TGV trains from Paris per day; note that this is a bit of a misnomer since there isn't TGV track all the way to Cannes (yet; it's coming by the end of 1999). Still, this route will give you the best time: 6 hours and 5 minutes. Investigate Joker fares, which vary in price according to how far in advance you buy them.

Getting Around Town

Walk. Even if you have a car, don't drive in town if you can help it. Traffic is a nightmare and finding a parking space can take longer than the errand you want to run.

Getting Around the Riviera from Cannes

Like I said, rent the car. Otherwise, there are trains, buses, and special services that run in season only from some of the hipper cities on the coast—helicopter service between Cannes and St. Tropez and Cannes/Monte Carlo as well as ferry service to St. Tropez, though the ferry only runs when the sea is calm, so it's often unreliable.

Cruising by Car

You only need be in town for 10 minutes before you realize that the real way to get around Cannes is to have no place to go but to simply drive up and down La Croisette in your fancy car. If you didn't bring yours with you, call **Star Rent Prestige** (☎ 04-93-90-69-59). They will be happy to rent you a Rolls Royce Corniche for about $1,200 per day. Their showroom is right in the heart of the shopping district; do stop in, it's fun!

Sleeping in Cannes

The hotel situation in Cannes is tricky; here are a few general tips:

- Because Cannes has imported sand at its beaches and, therefore, has the best beaches in the area, the demand to stay in Cannes and use it as a hub city for the Riviera is high. Consequently, rooms in this town should be booked as far in advance as possible. Although you can get lucky at the last minute, this is not a last-minute kind of town.
- Cannes is not only a beach town but also a convention town—more shows than you can imagine play at the major convention facilities at the Palais des Festivals and the Palais de Croisette. If there's a convention in town, forget about a discount, and maybe even a room.

- Forget about getting a room in a palace hotel during the Cannes Film Festival.
- "Festival" is a season in Cannes and no longer refers to simply the famous (or is that infamous?) film festival in May. Festival is the highest rate on the books at palace hotels and is charged anytime a huge convention is in town and rooms are in short supply.
- August is the next most expensive month and it has deals, as most of the other times of the year do, except for festival.
- Hotels that are very similar to each other can have amazingly different prices. Trickier still, their promotional deals may sound similar, but the product each is offering at that price is not the same.
- The same hotel room at the same time of year may be marketed differently to different nationalities or in different parts of the world. Also note that some promotions require a minimum stay of a certain number of nights.
- Ocean-view rooms always cost more and are rarely included in promotional prices.
- Breakfast may be included with your room rate, but find out if it's a continental breakfast or a full breakfast—this makes a big difference, unless you happen to eat like a French bird. Breakfast for two people can easily cost $50, so look for hotels in which a full American breakfast or a breakfast buffet is included.
- While you're checking if breakfast is included, find out what else is included. Often a hotel will have several promotions going on at the same time. You'll discover that the hotel with more things included comes out to be a better value. If you are choosing a hotel for its beach club, please understand that you usually pay $25 per person per day for a chaise longue. However, most of the palace hotels have specific summer promotions that include a chaise longue with the room.

Ask! Few will volunteer to point out the inconsistencies of the various plans available.

- Speaking of inconsistencies, I just found an ad for a palace hotel that has a Forfait Azur package: During the spring and summer you pay for 6 nights and get the seventh night free. The same hotel offers this deal in the winter but you pay for 4 nights and get the fifth night free. But the rate for this deal is about $150 per person, which is higher for two people than other deals. You may have to make a chart of all the offerings and what goes with them just to find your best bet.

- Of course, your dog can come too. That's another $25 per night, more or less. Usually the car fee and the dog fee are equal. Dogs do cost more than children; up to the age of 12 or 16 (it depends on the hotel), kids are usually free if they stay in your room, although there is a charge for an extra bed, which can be very steep—it's 350 F ($58) at the Majestic. That's steep sleep.

- Local tax will be added to most bills unless you have an inclusive price. Local tax is 5 F (85¢) per night.

The Palace Hotels

Cannes, like all other cities in France, has no five-star hotels but has four four-star deluxe hotels that are classified in the French manner as "palace hotels."

THE CARLTON
58 La Croisette, Cannes

What becomes a legend most? Certainly the Carlton does; it is still the most famous hotel in town. The Carlton has been featured in numerous movies and even in a recent advertising campaign for a car. This hotel is so famous that anyone who sees royal blue and white striped awnings or beach umbrellas automatically thinks "Carlton."

None of this fanfare comes cheaply, and that bargain promotional rate advertised in print may be hard to nail in reality. The Carlton does get included in Inter-Continental promotions, although I made a blind call one May to make a reservation during August and was told there were no $292 rooms; there were just $1,300 rooms. So much for promotions in August.

But wait, even if you don't stay here, I insist you do lunch on the terrace of The Café, preferably during the film festival. There is no better definition of Cannes. For reservations in the United States, call ☎ **800/327-0200**. The local phone is ☎ 04-93-68-91-68; fax 04-93-06-40-25.

THE MAJESTIC
14 La Croisette, Cannes

Of the four palace hotels in Cannes, this is where I feel the most comfortable, but then I've never slept here, I just hang out in the lobby.

There's an out-of-season fixed price tea event in the Egyptian-style Le Bar de l'hôtel that is not only a bargain (50 F/$8.50 for tea and a pastry, and you can sit all afternoon and stare at everyone), but a must-do. The chef, Bruno Oger, has his first star. The convention crowds consider this a must-do and the new stores out front make the location ideal. What more could you want?

Rates vary with the season but begin around $250 and go to about $550. The local phone is ☎ **04-92-98-77-00**; fax 04-93-38-97-90.

THE MARTINEZ
73 La Croisette, Cannes

As a member of both Concorde Hotels and Leading Hotels of the World, the hotel does offer a large number of spiffy promotions, including rates frozen in U.S. dollars. It is at the far end of the shopping district, but when you get Annick Goutal amenities in the bathroom, it's worth the walk.

As much as I adore this hotel and love staying here, I must confess that this is an apples and oranges hotel: Because it is the largest in town (more than 400 rooms) and because it was built in the late 1920s, it has a number of small and bad rooms—more than most of the other palace hotels. So while you can get a great promotional rate in the hotel, you may not get a great room. Become a regular, spend plenty, and get pull with the front desk. Rates begin at about $200 out of season on special promotion and go up from there; the summer price I usually pay is about $300 a night, which includes the chaise longue on the beach.

The new Relais Martinez offers a terrific meal for 195 F ($33) per person; this is a good introduction to the hotel if you're just poking around looking at everything.

For reservations in the United States, call ☎ 800/888-4747. The local phone is 04-92-98-73-00; fax 04-93-39-67-82.

NOGA HILTON CANNES
50 La Croisette, Cannes

Location is this hotel's best claim to fame. The hotel is built into the Palais de Croisette, so if you go to conventions, you are truly in the right place. It also has its own small shopping mall. As for the hotel itself, it has a few choice secrets—such as a fabulous chef, a fixed-price gourmet formula, menu service at the beach cafe rather than just buffet service, various promotional deals, including Hilton rates and local promotions, and a house full of rooms that were created to be equal, so they are all the same size and there are no bad rooms.

There are 45 suites and some 200 rooms with either ocean view or city view. Rates are usually competitive with the Martinez, so what you are paying for is the location, the new plumbing, the better chance at a decent room, and the American glitz. Noga, despite its modern architecture and cold lobby, was named hotel of the year last year by the 1998 Champerard guidebook.

As a special courtesy to *Born to Shop* readers, the hotel's general manager is pleased to offer you a room upgrade, which will be granted based on availability. He cannot fax back a confirmed upgrade, but if he's got the space when you arrive, you've got a "suite" deal. From the United States, send a fax directly to Richard Duvauchelle, General Manager, Noga Hilton Cannes, fax 011-33-4-92-99-70-15.

You're looking at $250 to $289 in summer (with breakfast and beach chair included!). The Noga also offers rates frozen in U.S. dollars. For U.S. reservations, call ☎ 800/HILTONS. The local phone is 04-92-99-70-00; fax 04-92-99-70-11.

The Four Stars

HÔTEL GRAY D'ALBION
38 rue des Serbes, Cannes

You can't find a better shopping hotel when the hotel is located in the best mall in town, in the core of the best shops. This is a modern hotel, owned by the same people who hold the Majestic, but it is more modern and less expensive. The local phone is ☎ 04-92-99-79-79; fax 04-92-98-77-00

L'HORSET SAVOY
5 rue Françoise Einesy, Cannes

You call this The Savoy even though it's now owned by a chain called L'Horset; I call it one of the finds of the day. This old-style minipalais is a sneeze from the Croisette and has recently been refurbished in an Art Deco moderne style. Okay, so the rooms look more like a Holiday Inn than your French fantasy, but the room rate is lower than at the big hotels.

The hotel also has apartments. If you are the kind who doesn't care that much about the room and only wants to sleep in it, a "Type 17" room rents for $100 for two in the low season; this same room is $200 in season and almost $300 during festivals. For reservations in the United States, call ☎ 800/ 847-4249. The local phone is ☎ 04-92-99-72-00; fax 04-93-68-25-59.

HôTEL SPLENDID
4–6 rue Felix-Faure, Cannes

The location is truly splendid—and closer to McDonald's than any of the palace hotels. This hotel is not fancy, but it has a lot of charm and a super location in the heart of everything, basically across the street from the Palais des Festivals and 2 blocks from Le Suquet. It's almost on top of the Saturday flea market and deep in the heart of shopping land. Some rooms have kitchenettes and some have a sea view (more expensive). This place is a real gem for those who love funky charm. There are only about 60 rooms, so book early. Rates begin over $100 per room out of season. For reservations in the United States, call ☎ 800/462-7274. The local phone is ☎ 04-93-99-53-11; fax 04-93-99-55-02.

HôTEL BELLE PLAGE
2 rue Brougham, Cannes

I was at first upset to be booked into this hotel because it is on the other side of Cannes from the big hotels on La Croisette. Within 10 minutes I realized I was nuts, readjusted my attitude, and came away with the find of the century.

First of all, this part of Cannes is the best part of Cannes—truly another world apart from all that other stuff. It actually feels like the French Riviera, not Beverly Hills. Meanwhile, it's not far to the Palais des Festivals, so you aren't in no-man's-land. It's just a bit of a walk to the Carlton.

Meanwhile, I had a room with a view, a balcony, and a whole new life to live, and the rate is about $200 a night during the festival and less at other times! It's a family run hotel; I got to know everyone and to actually miss them once I had to leave. The breakfast is boring (old-fashioned continental style) and the hotel from the front looks far too much like Noga (modern and ugly). Once inside though, this is a prize, especially with a sea-view room.

The local phone is ☎ **04-93-06-25-50;** fax 04-93-99-61-06.

Dining Tricks

Cannes is now celebrating a totally new trend in dining; since you will be paying the bill for this marketing trick, you may as well enjoy it. The hotels are finding that people like to sleep late (because they party all night), then eat an enormous brunch/lunch and then go to the beach, have an ice cream or a snack late afternoon, and then go to dinner. This saves them time, money, and calories. As a result, all the hotels now have tons of food on the breakfast buffet—including selections of meats and cheeses—and you are expected to eat like there's no tomorrow. You will be charged far more than a continental breakfast, so eat up. If breakfast is included in your room rate, better still—follow this system and all you really pay for is dinner!

But wait, it's not *just* the Breakfast Club that's changed; many hotels (yes, ones with famous chefs) now have formula meals offering a three-course gourmet meal (including service and tax) for 195 F ($33) per person!

Big Tables/Big Deals

LA SCALA
Noga Hilton Hotel, 50 La Croisette, Cannes

What you have here is a combination of riches. The restaurant has a wraparound terrace that overlooks the Mediterranean, Provençal decor, and a flat rate formula meal that is the steal of the day—195 F ($33) for a three-course gourmet meal. New carte offered every 10 days.

For reservations, call ☎ **04-92-99-70-00.**

PALME D'OR
Hôtel Martinez, 73 La Croisette, Cannes

Possibly the most famous kitchen in Cannes is the gourmet restaurant Palme d'Or in the Hôtel Martinez, where the chef (Christian Willer) has earned two Michelin stars. With stars in their eyes, the stars of the Cannes Film Festival insist on dining here.

Here's the secret: The chef has a private table in the kitchen, which seats four, possibly five, so you can interact with the chef and watch the meals being cooked. This table is available to Born to Shop readers on a first-come, first-served basis. Reservations must be made as far in advance as is possible by faxing the hotel's general manager (fax **04-93-39-67-82**). Forget it during Film Festival.

The bargain is not so much in the price as in what you've bought for the money—something priceless. If you've never dined at a chef's table, you are in for a treat. This is a once-in-a-lifetime experience that is becoming trendy in famous kitchens around the world.

Lunch or dinner costs come off the regular Palme d'Or menu carte and includes everything—yes, memories too.

RELAIS MARTINEZ
Hôtel Martinez, 73 La Croisette, Cannes
Another formula restaurant with several choices at different prices and a flat fee lunch with one course or two. There's also a choice of two different Sunday brunch formulas.

Big Table Must-Do's

Naturally part of the experience of being in the area is to dine at some of the most famous tables in the area. There are a few nuggets in the Cannes area that require a car or a taxi to get to. These area chefs commingle with the Cannes chefs, but not the Nice-Eze chefs for some reason. Most of these chefs serve lunch and dinner; some even have rooms to rent.

If you are in Cannes for a day or two on a cruise ship, it's a nice treat to book a rental car ahead of time and to take off for a drive around the area and a gourmet meal—getting as far away from the cruise and the crowds as possible. All of these tables require advance booking, preferably by fax.

LA BASTIDE SAINT ANTOINE
45 av. Henri Dunant, Grasse

By the time you read this, chef Jacques Chibois may already have his third star. There's no question he will earn it shortly. This farmhouse (which has some rooms so you can spend the night) is nestled into the hills of Grasse and makes escaping Cannes a must-do. Allow about twenty or thirty minutes for the drive.

The setting is gorgeous, the food is to die for, and now he's got me addicted to a specific *vin cuit* that he serves as the house aperitif. The local phone is ☎ 04-93-09-16-48.

LE MOULIN DE MOUGINS
Quartier Notre Dame de Vie, Mougins

Although a lot of people like to say that this famed eatery isn't what it used to be, I find it a treat, visually and technically. Roger Vergé, who originally created the cuisine of the sun, has this adorable restaurant and inn (with a shop!) that is filled with visually creative touches—even in the kitchens there are walls of china and tile decorating the open spaces. On one of my last visits, Roger himself made the rounds (his English is perfect) and autographed menus for worshipping visitors. Denise, Roger's wife, runs the shop and is often around the house, giving lessons on the art pieces and charming us all.

Note, if you are driving, it is *very* easy to get here from Cannes and the road is well marked. Getting here from Mougins and/or Grasse is a nightmare!

If you are invited here during festival, yes, it's a lovely invitation, but try to come another time to get the real flavor of the food. The local phone is ☎ 04-93-75-78-24.

OASIS
Rue Jean Honoré Carle, La Napoule

Best-selling author Ken Follet first shared this secret with me, then I met the chef in the market through Richard Duvauchelle and now I count this as one of my best finds—the slightly out-of-town address assures that you are away from the American and glitzy parts of Cannes. If at all possible, eat on the courtyard in what is truly an oasis, a half block from the sea. While you can't go wrong with a table here, my best trick is that I book here for lunch when I arrive in town on a cruise. The tourists are busy doing their tourist things, while I have the real France and a fine table and some fellow foodies—*pas de tourists!* The local phone is ☎ 04-93-49-95-52.

VILLA DES LYS
Hotel Majestic, 14 La Croisette, Cannes

If you follow young, hot chefs, you already know about Bernard Oger, who earned his first star from Michelin almost right off the bat after opening in this truly grand space right in the heart of Cannes. There is a fixed-price menu at lunch and dinner, which makes trying out this talent an important step in being part of the culinary scene. For reservations, call ☎ 04-92-98-77-00.

Snack & Shop

If you're just out for a quick bite in Cannes, there are plenty of choices. Ice cream stores are all over town, even in the high rent districts.

The rue d'Antibes, Cannes's main real-people shopping and strolling street, is crammed with ice cream parlors (even **Häagen-Daz**), tea rooms, and fast-food joints. Near the Maritime Center, at the Allees de Liberté, there's a **McDonald's** (called McDo in French slang), with **Planet Hollywood** a few doors away.

All of the hotel beach clubs have restaurants on the beach, just down the stairs from La Croisette. If the weather is fine, dining alfresco can be part of the pleasure of Cannes—just check to see which restaurants have à la carte service, since some of them only serve a buffet at a flat price.

The Croisette is also lined with street-side cafes that feature average food at high prices but allow you to be part of the parade, especially if you sit outside. Note that this is more of an evening ritual than a daytime and shopping-break ritual, but the cafes are open for business and less crowded during off hours. **Caffe Roma,** across from the Palais des Festivals, is the hip in-spot for the young, Lycra-clad Eurotrash crowd but my fave is **Le Farfalla,** also on La Croisette across from the Palais, though for years it mystified me. From the street it looks very average but once inside and into the scene you not only enjoy a hot, young crowd, but these adorable waitresses with lighters in plastic sleeves on their uniform sleeves—yep, they flick their Bics for you. The scene, especially late at night, is truly outrageous. The food's okay, too, with enormous portions. It's just great fun and very much part of what Cannes is all about.

CAFÉ CARLTON
Carlton Hotel, 58 La Croisette, Cannes

Just because I don't stay at the Carlton anymore doesn't mean I am immune to its charms. If you want to have an affordable lunch or snack, let down your hair and set down your packages, be part of the in-crowd, and feel the special Cannes magic, then head for this coffee shop-cum-breakfast room in the front of the hotel. If weather permits, dine on the terrace. It's heaven.

Rohr
63 rue d'Antibes, Cannes

This is a tea room, thank you very much, and it is very special. It serves sweets and tea in a haven that is the essence of old-money resort chic. Open every day of the week. Monday through Saturday it opens at 8:30am (my friend Patricia Wells swears by their croissants) and closes at 7 or 8pm in summer. On Sunday, it's open from 9am to 1pm. You may have breakfast, lunch, a snack, a pastry, chocolates, ice cream, or buy takeout.

The Best Buys in Cannes

Are there any good buys in a resort town where the rich and famous hang? Yeah, as a matter of fact, there are. Here is an overview of the good, the bad, and the ugly.

DESIGNER CLOTHES If you are seriously shopping for serious clothes and you are not headed for Paris, Cannes gives you a better selection of big names than any other city in the Riviera, including Nice.

Best buys on designer clothes are those items (on sale!) that still qualify for a *détaxe* refund. Note, if you make a purchase in a designer shop but do not fulfill your needed 1,200 F ($200) requirement for détaxe, you can still get the paperwork and save up so that if another branch store of the designer you make another purchase and then qualify, *voila,* you're all set.

The savings are even more dramatic if you buy from a resale shop (*dépôt-vente*) or a store that cuts labels out (*dégriffé*). I have several really good ones that are among my regular haunts in town.

PERFUME, MAKEUP & BEAUTY GOODS
Cannes is filled with *parfumeries* and even a few discounters. If you spend 1,200 F ($200) and qualify for the détaxe, the savings can be up to 50% off U.S. prices. Aside from actual savings, let's talk

selection. Cannes has an amazing wealth of shopping opportunities in this category of goods from collectors' editions and cult brands (**Bouteille**), from supermarket style (**Sephora**), to brand-name boutiques (**L'Occitane**) and department stores like **Galeries Lafayette** and **Monoprix,** which sell all big brands as well as the low-priced mass market lines.

FOODSTUFF If there's a part of town called Food Town, you know this is a great town for buying gourmet foodstuff. Olive oil is a fabulous souvenir. Buy yours in the Marché Forville or a tiny store called **Cannolive.** However, you will have many other opportunities to buy olive oil so just warm up to the notion here or start tasting and learning. Meanwhile, I've got a little source (**Boutique des Landes**) right across from the market that sells homemade jam (*confiture*) complete with the gold medal it won printed on the label. The jam is so famous it is sold in fine stores in Paris.

SOULEIADO Americans have known this French firm as Pierre Deux, which at one time held exclusive rights to the Souleiado Provençal fabric merchandise. Pierre Deux now stocks Les Olivades, and Souleiado is hard to find in the United States. While there are numerous Souleiado shops all over France, the one in Cannes is one of my faves because the people are nice, which isn't always the case in Souleiado shops! Souleiado has totally revamped its line in the last year, so that while the traditional prints and fabrics we adore are still sold, there's also a line of ready-to-wear that is great. There are also gift soaps, small gift items, and all sorts of things that make the line as great a statement as ever and better than ever.

Cannes Prestige

A majority of the high-end shops in Cannes belong to an association called Cannes Prestige, which you can identify by the big C with feather logo. The association publishes its own guide of the member

Pierre's Lobster Farm: Crustazur

1 rue J.H. Carle, Mandelieu-La Napoule

Crustazur supplies lobster to the leading chefs in the area. There were 18 different varieties of lobsters on hand the day I visited. The lobsters are kept in different tubs with water of differing temperatures; it is a virtual zoo of activity and claws.

You can walk in off the street and buy at wholesale prices. Furthermore, each morning in the summer a small number of different types of lobsters are cooked and sit waiting to be taken on your picnic. They range in price from 35 F to 80 F ($5.80 to $13) per lobster; most are about 50 F ($8.50). I don't need to tell you that this may be the best bargain in all of France (☎ **04-93-49-38-38**). Merci, Pierre.

shops, and the member shops all agree to certain bylaws in order to offer the best service possible.

Among the amenities they offer is at least one member of the sales staff who speaks English. Look for the logo when you shop.

Shopping Hours

Regular business hours in Cannes are from 9am until 7pm. Most stores are closed on Monday mornings, but the glorious thing about Cannes is that Monday mornings are not dead; keep reading. Regular store hours are Tuesday through Saturday. Most stores are also closed on Sunday, although there is a small amount of Sunday morning action.

There are some variations in these shopping hours: some stores open at 9:15 or 9:30am and close at 7:30pm. There's also a group of stores that open at 10am and reopen after lunch at 3pm, not 2:30pm. Go figure.

There's also a loose feeling to Monday: During the summer, some stores are open on Monday mornings. During school vacations or holidays, almost everything is open on Monday. And, of course, there's a *brocante* market at Forville on Monday. So Mondays are far from boring.

A large number of the stores close for lunch, from 12:30 until 2:30pm. Stores that do not close for lunch often have the word *nonstop* posted, or the slogan *sans interruption*.

Summer season schedules can vary. Tourist-oriented stores tend to be open longer, whereas real-people stores tend to knock off earlier on Saturday afternoons to enjoy the summer.

Markets & Fairs

Cannes has plenty of market action just about every day of the week. While the **Marché Forville** is not quite as spectacular as the fruit and flower market in Nice, it's not at all bad, and you can spend many happy hours there. You can spend many happy months there.

The fruit and flower market is open every day except Monday. This is a morning event so people tend to pack up by 1 to 2pm. Sunday is a great day. On Monday the Marché Forville sells brocante.

There is a small daily market at **place Gambetta**, which is directly behind the Noga Hilton. It isn't much of a market, but it is open on Monday if you need something to do, and I personally find it hilarious. It sells dry goods (cheap shoes, cheap clothes, fake sunglasses) as well as fruit and veggies and has a very small-town, neighborhoody feel to it. I wouldn't go out of my way to get there, but it has a quiet charm and a funky flair.

On Saturday there is a flea market across from the Old Port, where La Croisette becomes La Pantiero. It's right next to McDonald's, which is probably the best way to get directions, or ask for Les Allées de la Liberté.

During the week, when Les Allées don't have antiques, they have a few vendors selling flowers. Some guidebooks go so far as to call this a flower

Sundays in Cannes

I was recently in Cannes on a cruise ship on a Sunday; passengers were really upset that most stores were closed. However, I noticed that Cannes is not nearly as dead as many French towns on Sunday. Marché Forville is wide open on Sunday and the Food Street, rue Meynadier, has about 50% of its shops open on Sunday until noonish. **Davis,** a great tourist shop, is open on Sunday, as is **Relais H,** a super newsstand that sells postcards, books, and supplies and is a good place to stare at people. By late afternoon, most of the stores on Le Suquet open and stay open until midnight. *Vive la France!*

market or a sight worth seeing. They also sell flowers in Forville, which is good enough for me, or you can wait for Nice.

Shopping Neighborhoods

The basic Cannes shopping neighborhoods all interconnect and can be walked, although if it's hot or you are wearing stiletto heels (isn't everyone in Cannes?) this will be more difficult.

LA CROISETTE   The main drag along the waterfront is called boulevard de la Croisette, or simply La Croisette. The beach itself is actually below the promenade, so you must go down stairs to get to the sand. All the major hotels and many of the major shops are lined up at attention facing the sea, stretching from the Palais des Festivals to the Martinez Hotel. The major hotels usually have a few shops in the lobby as well; Noga has a minimall attached to it.

There is no retail on the beach side, but there are restaurants and private beach clubs.

GRAY D'ALBION   Gray d'Albion is a large building, a mall, a shortcut through town to bring you from La Croisette to rue d'Antibes, and a local legend wrapped into one. Oh my, I forgot to say it's also a hotel.

There are in fact two buildings that make up the complex, so if you are shopping, note that you enter, exit, and enter and exit again, before you end up at rue d'Antibes. Once considered the best address in town if you couldn't get the Croisette, the malls house many big-name shops, including **Souleiado** and **La Perla**.

RUE D'ANTIBES Moving one street back from the sea, you've got the rue d'Antibes, which runs parallel to La Croisette. While it isn't the low-rent district by any means, it has more real-people shops, more branches of famous French multiples (such as **Kookai, Pimkie, Descamps**), and fewer big international icon names (**Lalique, Lancel**).

This street has a neighborhood feel to it, that has life to it at night (La Croisette has too much life), and that people enjoy strolling and just looking in windows. La Croisette is for looking at other people; rue d'Antibes is for shoppers.

MIDDLE ÉTATS-UNIS This is the name I have made up for the neighborhood of streets that connect the Croisette with the rue d'Antibes. The streets are in the center of town, in between the Palais des Festivals and the Hôtel Majestic. These streets are usually only 2 blocks long and each is crammed with stores. Many of them are upscale and some even bear designer names.

The central street of this neighborhood is rue des Etats-Unis, which is how I remember the name of the neighborhood and know where I am going. The rue des Serbes and the rue du Commandant Andre are also excellent side streets for browsing, prowling, and ruining your credit rating. Most of the stores in this cross-street grid are not big names, although you will find **Sonia Rykiel, Guy Laroche, Chacock,** and **Escada** here. Hmmm, is Escada moving to La Croisette? Well, come back next season to find out who moved where.

ROND POINT DU BOYS-D'ANGERS   Directly behind the Noga Hilton, about a block away, I direct your attention to a tiny, isolated group of shops that you would have never found unless you were lost or someone had given you directions to one of the stores. The chicest boutique in town, **Alexandra,** is here. I like it because my favorite *dépôt-vente,* **Contrapartie,** is also here. There's a men's shop to one side and a women's shop a few hundred meters away.

FOCH-HOCHE   This is another one of my own neighborhood names, based on the names of two great shopping streets. Rue Hoche runs parallel to the rue d'Antibes going away from the water; rue Marechal Foch is a small street that begins at the rue d'Antibes and runs to the train station.

The beauty of this neighborhood is that it's real. Foch is where you're going to find the famous French department store **Galeries Lafayette** and the famous French dime store **Monoprix.** On Hoche, you'll also find affordable cute stores (and tourist traps) and where you can buy truly French things used by real French people, not movie stars and glamour gals. If you look at a map of Cannes you'll note that Foch meets Hoche to form the letter *L* (on it's side), connecting through Galeries Lafayette.

FOOD TOWN   There is no part of Cannes that is actually called Food Town. I just call it that, and I bet you that if you asked my friend Patricia Wells, cold, where Food Town was she would name the exact same neighborhood I am about to describe.

Food Town is located behind the old port and consists of several parts: the Forville Market (coral stucco, you can't miss it); the rue Felix-Faure, where the market is located; the rue Meynadier, which juts off at an angle from the Felix-Faure; and Allées de la Liberte, where the flower market is held most days. All these many elements make for a neighborhood that is more than just a string of gourmet and real-people food stores and candy shops.

The rue Meynadier is filled with gourmet food shops. More importantly, if your idea of France is not all topless beaches and Chanel sunglasses, you will find what you are looking for in these back streets and byways. That it could also be chocolate is an added plus.

Please do not think that they only sell food in Food Town. The rue Meynadier is one of the main shopping streets in town, and it's filled with TTs (tourist traps) and other shops that service both tourists and real people. Prices are less than at Versace.

LE SUQUET   The oldest part of town and the part that most looks like a charming village, Le Suquet is also the place to eat, if we're talking fun or funky, not multiple Michelin stars. There are also some shops around here, but they tend to be either TTs or antique shops. Many shops sell the inexpensive Provençal fabrics, so they look cute.

Mostly this is an eating street, with dozens of cafes in a row. You simply march up the hill and decide which one you like. We've tried a variety of them and have no favorites. They do tend to be touristy. To get there, walk along rue d'Antibes in the downtown area until you pass the old port. Look for a tiny pedestrian street called rue Saint Antoine, which is mobbed and lined with cafes. It has recently been repaved with smooth cobblestones, but this is not the place for high heels. This is an evening parade, so forget it as a regular shopping district. The stores stay open late, sometimes until midnight in the summer.

Cannes Resources from A to Z

ANTIQUES & AUCTIONS

You can't in your right mind consider Cannes as a source for serious antiques, but if you like junk and flea markets and poking around, you'll be surprised not only at how much this town has to offer but at the fact that prices are beyond fair—they can be among the best in France. I do not even step foot inside any of the formal antique shops in Cannes; forgive me, but I'm not interested in formal antiques, and I go by the old rule of thumb that antique shops in resort cities are always overpriced.

Nonetheless, for those who like serious antiques and big-time dealers, there's a biannual show called **Salon des Antiquaires à Cannes,** held every winter and every summer for 2 weeks in the Palais des Festivals. For the specific dates each year, write the Association des Antiquaires de Cannes, Pascal Moufflet, 13 rue d'Oran, 06400 Cannes ☎ **04-93-38-13-64;** fax 04-93-68-99-79.

Note that the hours of formal antique shows all over France, not just here, are rather unusual by American standards. Shows may not open until 11am or noon and stay open until 9pm or so. Sometimes shows are only held in afternoons, beginning at 3 or 4pm and lasting until 10pm. Perhaps this is so Madame can bring her husband with his checkbook and patina.

If the kind of antiques you prefer are what the French call brocante, Cannes is a great place to shop. On Monday morning, beginning at 8am, the **Marché Forville** is filled with dealers, and it's fun and funky and quite affordable. Monday is also the big day for brocante in Nice—don't miss it if at all possible—so you can start in one town and finish up in the other. Doing the two markets together in one day will make your trip and fill your home.

On Saturday, the Allées de la Liberté (near McDonald's) is filled with dealers; this is also great fun although much more upscale in feel than the Monday show. The dealers are not the same, so don't feel like you've seen it and done it. Note also that this location is directly across from the ship terminal (Maritime Center), so if you are on a cruise ship and you come to port on a Saturday, *voilà—les puces.*

If you have a car, you can hit brocante markets in nearby villages on just about every day of the week. On Thursdays it's brocante day at the *marché paysant* in nearby Mandelieu. This is a very low end affair on blankets in a parking lot, but if you have transportation, you might enjoy it because prices are quite low and this is the real thing sans tourists.

Antibes has a tiny but yummy little flea market in the street right off the old port held on Saturday and Tuesday. There are also dealers on the roads that reach outside of Cannes and into the nearby villages—head off toward Grasse and Mougins or toward Antibes and just find 'em.

As for real antique shops in Cannes, well, along the boulevard de la République, a real-people street in downtown Cannes, there are a few dealers not too far from each other. These are more serious dealers, not funky junk stores. Start with **Lucienne Lai,** 99 bd. de la République.

Those interested in antiques should also know that Nice has a big antique community and that Monaco has some fancy shops and a very big time show (see chapter 10). There are also auctions in the winter season. For information on specific auctions or antique events, check the local newspaper.

Big Names

If you are sophisticated enough to know who Chanel and Versace are, I figure you just need an address, not descriptions of the merchandise or the architecture of the store.

Note that the trend in this town for years has been that there are a handful of fancy-schmancy boutiques that are named after their owners, and these shops carry several designer lines. Sometimes the store has a theme—only Italian designers, for example. I have listed these shops under "Boutiques." More and more designers are opening freestanding shops in Cannes, so this type of store will eventually die out or move further away from tourist real estate and into the realm of local shopping.

The following is a list of freestanding big-name designer stores.

ALMA
67 La Croisette, Cannes

ARMANI EMPORIO
52 La Croisette, Cannes

BULGARI
14 La Croisette, Cannes

CARTIER
57 La Croisette, Cannes

CÈLINE
24 La Croisette, Cannes

CERRUTI **1881**
15 rue des Serbes, Cannes (men)

65 rue d'Antibes, Cannes (women)

CHANEL
5 La Croisette, Cannes

CHARLES JOURDAN
47 rue d'Antibes, Cannes

CHRISTIAN DIOR
38 La Croisette, Cannes

CHRISTIAN LACROIX
14 La Croisette, Cannes

CHRISTOFLE
9 rue d'Antibes, Cannes

DUNHILL
14 La Croisette, Cannes

ESCADA
15 rue des Serbes, Cannes

FRED
21 La Croisette, Cannes

GIANFRANCO FERRE
67 La Croisette, Cannes

GIANNI VERSACE
9 rue Saint-Honoré, Cannes

GUCCI
17 La Croisette, Cannes

GUY LAROCHE
17 rue des Belges, Cannes

HERMÈS
17 La Croisette, Cannes

JEAN LOUIS SCHERRER
17 La Croisette, Cannes

JOSEPH
116 rue d'Antibes, Cannes

KENZO
65 rue d'Antibes, Cannes

LALIQUE
87 rue d'Antibes, Cannes

LANCEL
34 rue d'Antibes, Cannes

LA PERLA
Gray d'Albion, 17 La Croisette, Cannes

LAUREL
123-125 rue d'Antibes, Cannes

LÉONARD
45 La Croisette, Cannes

LOLITA LEMPICKA
9 La Croisette, Cannes

LOUIS VUITTON
44 La Croisette, Cannes

MAX MARA
79 rue d'Antibes, Cannes

PIERRE CARDIN
9 La Croisette, Cannes

SONIA RYKIEL
15 rue des États-Unis, Cannes

THIERRY MUGLER
45 La Croisette, Cannes

UNGARO
55 La Croisette, Cannes

VAN CLEEF & ARPELS
61 La Croisette, Cannes

YVES SAINT LAURENT/RIVE GAUCHE
44 La Croisette, Cannes

ZARA
32 rue d'Antibes, Cannes

BOUTIQUES

ALEXANDRA
Rond Point, Du boys-d'Angers, Cannes

The leading light in the biggest French and Italian names, the most famous of the specialty boutiques, and the last word in chic. I don't need to tell you that we are into expensive garments and high style. But of course, darling. Now you are a member of the club. We must have lunch.

REUSSNER
4 rue Ctdt. André, Cannes

Another of those small, special shops for those in the know. This one is bought for the cutting edge: Alexander McQueen, Ann Demeulemeester, Dries Van Noten, and so on. Top drawer.

VIA VENETO
91 rue d'Antibes, Cannes

The good news is that this is a string of three fabulous shops that have all the big, hip Italian designers and some of the French ones too. If you love fashion, you will adore these boutiques, where the staff is used to a very with-it but service-oriented customer. The bad news is that the Versace jeans that I thought I couldn't live without cost $175. Much fun just to touch everything and dream about the look. Certainly Cannes is the place to wear it.

CHILDREN'S CLOTHING

For affordable kid's clothing, I shop at **Monoprix!** For rich grandmas or those who never look at price tags, a stroll through both parts of the mall at Gray d'Albion will knock your socks off—there are numerous fancy-schmancy boutiques here for kiddie style, including shoe shops and designer clothing shops.

BILL TORNADE
Gray d'Ablion, 17 La Croisette, Cannes

This designer has a very specific style with wild flourishes and bold artistic strokes and he does kids clothes as well as adults. I very much wanted to buy for my 6-year-old niece in this shop, the kiddie venue, but the prices almost struck me deaf and dumb. Very hip and hot.

CATIMINI
Gray d'Albion, Cannes

Absolutely adorable. Reasonably priced for designer kids' wear.

DOMINIQUE
7 Rond Point du Boys-d'Angers, Cannes

Absolutely adorable. Old-fashioned smocking for infants and young girls and traditional baby items. One block behind Noga.

FLORIANE
60 rue d'Antibes, Cannes

Absolutely adorable. Fun and colorful and traditional with enough of an update to not be out of style. Some TinTin styles for boys. Very upscale French middle class. Back end of Gray d'Albion mall.

DEPARTMENT STORES

GALERIES LAFAYETTE
6 rue du Marechal Foch, Cannes

If you're thinking about the Galeries Lafayette in Paris or even the store in Nice, try to calm down now. This particular branch store is nice but not as big as the Nice store nor particularly complete.

Please note that it is standard GL procedure to give those with foreign passports a flat 10% discount on perfume and beauty products. Ask before you shop.

MONOPRIX
9 rue du Marechal Foch, Cannes

Monoprix isn't really a department store; it's what an American would call a dime store. It's one of my favorite places to shop.

There is a grocery store upstairs; this is a fine browse and a good place to buy mustard and various foodstuff for gifts. It's also the best place for postcards.

DISCOUNT, DÉGRIFFÉ & DÉPÔT-VENTE

CONTREPARTIE
Rond Point du Boys (corner of rue de Lerins), Cannes

We are talking Chanel suits for $700, which is, by the way, almost exactly the same price you will pay for used Chanel in New York. In fact, I saw the same suit I saw here in New York for exactly the same price. However, the one here was in my size. And I didn't buy it! How do I sleep at night?

This store is small, packed, and also has shoes and handbags. The best stuff is in the windows and up front. There is a separate men's store.

This store is directly behind the Noga, so you may want to get up from lunch now and run over there. Oops, my mistake. They close for lunch.

INTEMPORAL
3 rue d'Oran, Cannes

Ignore the hard-to-read name and don't let the address throw you. This store is right off the rue d'Antibes, right near the Noga, and it is a must-visit, especially for those who wear a French size 38 or 40 (although they offer a whole range of sizes). For a size conversion chart, please turn to page 380.

I adore this shop. Every big name in France is represented here; I'll never forget the Léonard dress for $150! They also carry shoes, handbags, and some furs.

J. VOGEL
13 rue Jean Riouffe, Cannes

This is really an insider place. You will be floored the first time you enter and think I'm nuts to send you here. Chances are the clothes you see on the racks will bore you silly. But wait! Voilà! The good stuff, all the designer names, is brought from the back. Why? Because the labels have been cut out so the name-brand clothes can be discounted.

If you are shopping for serious designer clothes, introduce yourself and play the game. It helps to speak French.

FABRICS

There are three top fabric firms with gorgeous goods that are in competition with each other, although they do have stylistic differences: Souleiado, Les Olivades, and, maybe, Valdrome. The rest pale in the pale moonlight. Daylight is even worse.

Cannes, and all of the south from Nice to Avignon, is filled with stores selling copies of these fabrics. For the most part, the copies look cheap. (They are cheap.) I've been known to buy such goods, and I try to direct you to the lesser-priced sources in addition to the big names, but, academically speaking, you cannot compare the quality. You get what you pay for.

CANNOLIVE (VALDROME)
16 & 20 rue Venizelos, Cannes

LES OLIVADES
8 rue Chabaud, Cannes

SOULEIADO
Gray d'Albion, Cannes

FESTIVAL SOUVENIRS

If you happen to be in town during the film festival, don't think you have to be invited to walk the red carpet in order to play. Although there are three official screenings a day, the 7:30pm screening is the biggie and everyone comes all dolled up, beginning around 6:30pm. Freelance photographers stand nearby the red carpet to take photos, which will be on sale the next day. You need not have tickets or passes to the festival in order to get your photo taken.

There is sort of a system to it. Some photographers pop out in front of you, snap a few shots and hand you a card. Others don't say a word. You can also ask shooters to take your photo and ask for their card. The next day, you go to the address printed on the card (after noon) or go to the boards under the tents alongside the Palais and you look for your photo. The proofs are on the boards—you mark the number, pay, and wait for the print.

Prices vary from 80 F to 200 F ($13 to $33); the time it takes for the print can be 10 minutes to 4 hours. In my case, the photos from one of the sources had to be mailed to me—I didn't think they'd ship to the United States so I left a local contact, my hotel concierge. The hotel forwarded the photos to me.

There's a chain of stores called **Davis,** with one shop right on La Croisette across from the Palais and one shop at the back end of the mall Gray d'Albion: This store sells high-class souvenirs as well as other items.

Souvenirs are also sold in the streets (I got a great tote bag in the street for 100 F/$17) as well as in official booths under tents at the Palais. The souvenirs with the proper date of the festival come out just 2 weeks before the festival and then stay on the shelves for the year, so it could be the year 1999, but up until May 1 they are still selling 1998 festival stuff.

Aside from the director's chairs, my favorite souvenir is the T-shirt, which comes packaged in a tin reel can, another 100 F ($17). These kinds of things are sold up and down the rue Meynadier.

FLOWERS

MELONIE
80 rue d'Antibes, Cannes

Provençal-style dried arrangements of lavender, roses, grasses, and so on. They ship.

FOODSTUFF

There's no lack of fine food and foodstuff in Cannes. If you aren't into checking out specific addresses, then merely browse the rue Meynadier, which is crammed with specialists and has a branch of the Champion grocery store. This isn't the best grocery store I've been to, even in the area, but it's there and you're there, so why not?

Monoprix has a small supermarket upstairs; for gift items this may be all you need. I buy coffee and mustard here; I've bought my little wheely red nylon market cart here. (I don't recommend the cheapie house brand; it's too short for a tall person. Splurge for a more expensive one with a longer extension handle.) You can get picnic items here or just browse around enough to feel that you are French.

Remember that there is one fabulous fruit and veggie market (Marché Forville) and one small market (place Gambetta). Also note one of the tricks my friend Pierre, the executive chef at the Noga, taught me: The stands in the Marché Forville are ranked. The chefs buy wholesale from dealers who surround the market but are not under the market roof. If they want something special, they go to the area where the top vendors are located, which is in one specific far corner—prices are higher here than at the other stands, but the quality is better. Almost all markets in all towns have a secret like this to them.

I don't really think you need a map of the marché, since it's square, but take a look around as you arrive, so you can understand the layout. The market stands on the place called place du Marché (so simple, these French). Surrounding the market and facing it are more suppliers; these are mostly wholesalers. The fruit broker that Pierre uses (Vincent) is here. There's a dry goods store across the way that sells everything, including a wide variety of market baskets, which may come in handy. (I keep mine at the Noga waiting for me for each trip.) Any store with an address "place du Marché" is in the circle that surrounds the market square.

If you are standing under the arch that says Porte Forville at the market, your back is to Vincent, the wholesaler, and the covered market is to your left. In the near corner of the top right of the market is the niche where the best quality goods are sold.

Most food shops open relatively early in the morning but close at 12:30pm; some close for lunch, some close for the day. Those that reopen do so at 2 or 2:30pm. Many are open Sunday in the morning. Some close in November. Hours during the summer season and school holidays—when tourists are in town—may be more liberal than usual.

CAVE DE FORVILLE
3 Marché Forville, Cannes

This local wine shop also sells some hard liquor and much champagne. You'll have a ball here. Some gourmet foodstuff for picnics, too.

CHEZ BRUNO
50 Rue d'Antibes, Cannes

Perhaps this store considers itself the rival of Maiffret (they are virtually across the street from each other), but I find it very different. There's something funky and friendly about Maiffret, whereas this store, with its very proper packages of just the right candies for gifts and entertaining, is very formal, stiff, and makes me think of weddings. It's a local status symbol, though.

La Boutique des Landes
13 place du Marché Forville, Cannes

This is a small, sometimes dark and unassuming shop in the area around the Marché Forville. It sells canned and packaged French foods, such as duck and mushrooms, but the specialty of the house is the gold-medal *confiture* (jam). It comes in a variety of flavors. The shop is open on Sunday.

La Ferme Savoyarde
22 rue Meynadier, Cannes

The most famous cheese shop in Cannes is also one of the most famous in France and has been recognized with honors from the French government. They fly cheese to various luxury hotels around the world, supply the local big-name chefs, and have been cited by many food writers as the place to worship the cow or the goat or the sheep. Three generations of the Ceneri family run the shop. You can spend weeks here. My favorite is the cheese rolled in raisins.

Maiffret
31 rue d'Antibes, Cannes

This is a branch of the famous Parisian candy maker. Their specialty in the south of France is candied and dried fruits (*fruits confits*), but they also sell many chocolates, various hard candies, bonbons, and things for kiddies. Very high-status gift item. They also sell cakes and a variety of regional goodies— enough to make a true foodie go nuts. Forget the diet. Note that the store is very deep so keep walking back; there's more and more selection.

Schies Chocolatier
125 rue d'Antibes, Cannes

This chocolatier is toward what I call the uptown end of the rue d'Antibes. I went here during Carneval one year to find they were making wafer-thin chocolate masks! Divinely French.

HAIR

Worried about having your hair done for the festival? Didn't bring your own hairdresser along? Not to worry, I'll lend you mine.

Carita
21 rue du Cdt. Andre, Cannes

I go to Carita in Paris; they are new to Cannes and I am devoted to Didier. Still, this is the place where you'll never go wrong. To book, call ☎ 04.92.99.22.00.

Jacques Dessange
Galerie Noga Hilton, 50 La Croisette, Cannes

I've been going to Didier at Jacques Dessange for years now; I first started to go to him because Catherine Deneuve suggested him. During the festival you can get appointments in the morning, but it gets tough later in the day. Didier is a master technician; I trust him with anything. His English is so-so; if you need to communicate a lot, try speaking French. A cut and a blowdry costs about $50. For an appointment call ☎ 04-93-99-00-30.

Jean Louis David
21 rue des États Unis, Cannes

The same formula as everywhere in France and the United States—no appointment needed. It's not too expensive and you won't get the world's best blow dry, but it just might be good enough.

HOME DESIGN

My girlfriend Tracy returned from Cannes with the demand that I immediately write up a store that sells wrought-iron furniture—the most divine she has ever seen. I went to check it out, right there on the rue d'Antibes (**Ligne Metal,** 111 rue d'Antibes), and she's right, it is truly fabulous. But I don't think most of us are going to ship home a garden table and set of chairs. Therefore, I am limiting this to just a few thoughts.

BENITO ET FILS
109 rue d'Antibes, Cannes

This large store is one of the leading dealers in town for chic to chic, for seeing and buying French arts d'table. Please check out the finest firms in crystal, tabletop, and dishes, dishes, dishes. Make that porcelain, *chère*. They represent Christofle, Daum, Baccarat, Limoges. This is the place to register for your wedding gifts.

MIS EN DEMEURE
Gray d'Albion, 17 La Croisette, Cannes

Walk through the first part of Gray d'Albion and outside, before you walk into the second part of Gray d'Albion (this will make perfect sense when you are standing there), look to your left. There it is!

This store is sort of like a very tony Pottery Barn but a little more French and more creative and definitely snazzier than Habitat. But not weird and not Philippe Starck. There's also linen and some furniture.

SIFAS
73 rue d'Antibes, Cannes

This is Sifas, not Sofas, so don't worry. It's a home decorating shop, and they do sell furniture, but they also sell wonderful candles and my beloved Lampes

Berger, which are catalytic burners to eliminate odors. Fabulous for smokers or cat owners.

This store has five or six branches around the south; there's a bigger showroom on the edge of Cannes that you will pass on the way to the autoroute.

The in-town store will do the trick if you are looking for French style and gift items, or a Lampes Berger. Very chic. Be sure to get downstairs where there's more style crammed into every nook.

VOG
61 rue d'Antibes, Cannes

Although from the street this shop just looks like a showroom for fancy vases, they carry a good selection of the crystal jewelry now being made by the big names—Baccarat, Daum, etc. I'm in love with the Baccarat necklaces.

JEWELRY

There happen to be real jewelry stores in Cannes, too—I just don't happen to shop in them. Ever. Their names and addresses are listed in "Big Names" (see above). If you are interested in Hermès jewelry, check out the duty-free shop Hermès runs in the Nice airport. Chanel jewelry and accessories are not sold in the airport in Nice; they are available in the boutique on La Croisette.

CLÉOPATRE
20 rue Meynadier, Cannes

This is a chain, and they sell cheap junk and in no way do they belong in the same category as the other listings. However, this is a great place where almost everything I like costs about $3. You can buy earrings, hair doodles, and gift items.

NIL
41 rue d'Antibes, Cannes

Lots of glass, spangle bangle, hotsy totsy, glorious chic. Don't miss it. Prices start around 200 F ($33). This is inventive designer rah-rah fun in creative works for resort, beach, and even back home.

VANILLE
13 rue Cdt-Andre, Cannes

Not to be confused with Nil, because they look quite similar and have similar names.

LINGERIE

EVE
6 rue Fréderic Amouretti

This is really a cultural lesson in what French lingerie should be. First of all, like all good French lingerie shops, they sell bathing suits as well as underwear. Second of all, they carry extremely expensive goods so that Americans may faint dead away when they see the prices. They also carry pantyhose and bodysuits. Just watching the women who shop here is a real treat, even if you buy nothing.

MA MIE
89 rue d'Antibes, Cannes

I call this shop Mamie (as in Eisenhower)—they carry all the big names in French lingerie, but what attracted me into the shop is the stupidest little red feather G-string you have ever seen, which I spied in the window. It's really not that kind of shop, but I loved the idea of a G-string as the perfect souvenir of Cannes.

SAMY
27 rue d'Antibes, Cannes

This is a small chain that carries top French lingerie brands, but not the outrageously expensive ones.

LOCAL HEROES

CANNOLIVE
16 & 20 rue Vénizélos

I cannot in good conscience list this store as a tourist trap, although the undiscerning eye might question me on this. Cannolive is a celebration of local goods, items from the Riviera through Provence including one store devoted mostly to foodstuff and one store, a few doors away, for fabrics, santons, trays, and gift items. I can spend hours here. Note in the food store that olive oil can be tasted and poured from the spigot.

Now, let's talk about the address. This is the correct address. The street is only called this particular proper name for 1 block and in fact, you are on this street (which is virtually unmarked) as you walk from Monoprix toward rue Meynadier. The stores are only 50 meters from Monoprix; hidden in clear sight.

CORDONNIER BOTTIER
51 rue Meynadier, Cannes

If you're looking for a pair of honest espadrilles, not the ones they sell at Hèrmes, this is the source. The shop looks so much like the local shoemaker that you wouldn't think to enter, but check out that wall full of shoes.

NICOLAY SICCARD
Place Gambetta, Cannes

You were perhaps in the mood to play French maid tonight? Step this way. If you are looking for a uniform for your housekeeper or a *veste du cuisine* (the cute jacket the chef wears), this is your local source. It's right behind the Noga, so don't panic about the address.

MENSWEAR

ANDRÉ GHEKIERE
69 La Croisette, Cannes

More preppy, but with a touch of the beach and a
serious touch of the yacht crowd. Bathing costumes
with matching robes, and so on.

CLAUDE BONUCCI
Noga Hilton, 50 La Croisette, Cannes

Primarily a menswear designer, Bonucci is one of
the last couturiers in the Riviera and certainly the
most famous to locals with the big bucks. He makes
some women's clothing and sells handmade ready-
made clothes off the rack as well as bespoke (made
to measure).

   Aside from the fact that every known musician,
cinema star, and festival-goer wears his clothes,
his genius is for original elegance translated into
the very distinctive rock and roll of the Côte d'Azur.
We're talking resort elegance, which is a hard
thing to do without looking like you died and went
to Palm Beach. This is the only man in France who
can cut a man's suit in pale turquoise and make it
work.

   Although the clothes are expensive ($1,000-plus
for a silk blazer), they have a classical finesse that
actually makes them worth the money. I've got to
tell you, I was a skeptic at first, but after a fashion
show and a serious browse through his stores, I am
hooked. Now I just need to win at the tables.

   Next time you tour with your rock band, break
the bank at Monte Carlo, or need to look absolutely
with the team à la the local luxe, this is your only
stop.

TRABAUD
48 rue d'Antibes, Cannes

Selling a modified version of Bonucci, but not handmade and not glitzy. This is where you come for

those chicer than thou linen blazers in just the right color of the season. The clothes have a preppy touch without being conservative. Ralph Lauren goes French resort.

Multiples & Chain Stores

Chacock
7 rue du Cdt-Andre, Cannes

Wild patterns and bright colors; good for resort wear.

Descamps
111 rue d'Antibes, Cannes

Bed and bath; pretty expensive.

Et Vous
84 rue d'Antibes, Cannes

The Ann Taylor of France.

Kookai
18 rue d'Antibes, Cannes

Teen angel, can you hear me?

L'Occitane
14 rue du Maréchal Joffre

Masses of soaps.

Marithe & Francois Girbaud
Gray d'Albion, Cannes

$150 for a pair of jeans?

Pimkie
42 rue d'Antibes, Cannes

Low-cost teen angel, can you hear me?

Rodier
13 rue Hoche, Cannes

Great French knits.

SEPHORA
53 bis rue d'Antibes

More makeup and scent than an airport.

MUSIC (TAPES & CDs)

Musical recordings, be they records, tapes, or CDs, are usually frightfully expensive in France and aren't a tourist's best buy. However, if selection is the issue not price, you will be in heaven. There are scads of recordings that never come to the United States; there is also a bit of a business in bootleg tapes that were illegally recorded at events and then made into "real" CDs.

There are branches of FNAC in many cities, but not yet in Cannes. You may want to wait for another town for a chance to shop FNAC (Nice, Monte Carlo, and so on). But if you want to shop in the heart of Cannes, try **Rapsodie,** which faces the parking lot of the train station. (That's the real address as printed on their shopping bag: *face au parking de la gare.)*

Rapsodie is also the place to go if you are looking to buy concert tickets to any of the many big events in the area. I mention this because we were driving around the south and saw scads of posters for the Joe Cocker concert in Juan les Pins but didn't know how to get tickets. In Cannes, call **04-93-38-31-18** to find out if they have the tickets you desire.

LA MAISON DU DISQUE
12 bd. de la République

Where my friend Dominique buys me Johnny Hallyday CDs and tapes; it's right behind the Noga.

PARAPHARMACIES

A relatively new concept in French retail, a *parapharmacie* sells prescriptions and drugs and health needs along with the many beauty products and cures made by the big French pharmaceutical firms. They also usually discount by 20%. Go to several as they do differ. The best one in France, by the way, is a chain called **Euro Sante Beauté**, which does not have a branch in Cannes (yet).

ANGLO-FRANCAISE PHARMACIE
95 rue d'Antibes, Cannes

A good place to warm up to the notion, not far from the Noga. They don't carry a huge selection, but the store is spacious so you can see everything and begin to learn brand names.

PARA PLUS PHARMACIE
113 rue d'Antibes, Cannes

This is a small parapharmacie located in the heart of town. They offer discounts on every purchase—never mind about détaxe or whatever.

PARALAND
22 rue Meynadier, Cannes

This is a small shop but has become sort of my regular because it's part of my ritual stroll from Marché Forville into town. I just wish they would open on Sunday. I stock up on my basics here: Lierac's Teint Lift Transparent and Galenic Orphycée Creme de Renovation Cellulaire.

PERFUME, MAKEUP & SOAP

I can't imagine why you came to France if not to load up on these essentials of life. I find new ones to buy just about every day and I shop the entire area, not just Cannes.

- If you will be in Paris during your visit to France and have time to shop there, the prices on perfume and makeup at major discounters in Paris are better than in the south of France.
- If you don't use discounters in the first place, don't worry about Paris.

- If you are indeed buying in the south, buy everything at one time, so that you can get détaxe if you spend 1,200 F ($200).
- If you are planning to wait to shop for makeup and perfume in the duty-free shop at the airport of your last city in the European Union, you are making a mistake—especially if you are planning on spending 1,200 F ($200) or more.
- Don't wait for the duty free at the Nice airport either. I recently bought a bottle of perfume in a regular perfume shop on the rue d'Antibes in Cannes that was 30 F ($6) cheaper than at the duty-free shop in the Nice airport.
- Don't forget to shop the dime store (a place like Monoprix) for cheap makeup and fragrance. The drug store and/or parapharmacie can also be great for beauty treatment products.
- The rue d'Antibes is filled with at least a half dozen perfume shops. Most have the same prices because prices are set by the manufacturer, as well as what the local market will bear. There are some discounts during promotions.

SEPHORA
53 bis rue d'Antibes, Cannes

The biggest story to hit the Cannes shopping scene is the arrival of Sephora, the American-style beauty supermarket owned by the Louis Vuitton Moet Hennessey luxury group. Sephora is a rather large chain, with stores in other cities including Nice, Aix, and Avignon—all of these branches are bigger and better than the one in Cannes. But if you've never been to a Sephora or you aren't going to another city, well, well, well have you got a treat in store for you.

Where to begin? Hmmm, some details:

- The clerks wear cute uniforms with hats and white gloves.
- Everything is organized by color group; this is more apparent in other branches, but you'll figure it out.

- Along the side walls there's a wide range of scents with testers and paper scent strips if you don't want to spritz yourself to death.
- The dime store brands of French makeup (Bourjois, for example) are sold in the rear.
- There's a house line of great stuff, including tiny travel sizes and great gifts for teenagers. There's a do-it-yourself box that you fill with product; a wonderful gift in the 240 F ($40) range.
- There's the Makeup Forever line of professional makeup from Paris, as well as makeup tools and hair doodads and makeup cases and all that stuff.
- There are a few pharmacy brands, but not many in this branch.
- Finally (am I sounding a little breathless?), they do an automatic, electronic détaxe for you—very convenient.

Okay, if this is heaven, why are other stores still in business? Read on.

BOUTEILLE
59 rue d'Antibes, Cannes

A member of Cannes Prestige, Bouteille has earned the reputation among locals as the best shop in town. They not only carry more brands than any other shop, but they get exclusive items and they provide the kind of service and knowledge that you can't find in American supermarket-style stores.

Bouteille has the expected full range of all of the designer names in fragrance and skin care, as well as some of the hard-to-find ones (like the special-edition releases and the collectors bottles and groups). They carry Annick Goutal, so you don't have to steal it from your hotel room at The Martinez. (Goutal is not carried at Sephora.)

They also offer fragrance for the home and scented candles from big designers such as Canovas and Rigaud as well as a new range, which includes scented madeleines for your drawers. (Honest.)

Meanwhile, Bouteille is old-fashioned in the service approach. Sephora is young and modern and American but the salesgirls don't know a lot about skin or product. They're cute and they've been trained well, but they aren't experts who have a career in skin care. At Bouteille, they really know something and can give you treatment and product advice. This is especially important if you are over 35.

Bouteille is open on Monday, and stays open during lunchtime. Of course they do détaxe too. And they give out tons of little samples when you buy stuff.

STARLETT/BERNARD MARIONAUD
18 rue d'Antibes, Cannes

I met a man from Beverly Hills once who was overburdened with shopping bags (my kind of guy) bearing the logo of this shop. The store offers discounts on promotional items. Although prices are lower here, they are often sold out of your favorites.

Now then, there is a full Bernard Marionaud in Nice and I have written gobs about it and if you can, shop here instead.

L'OCCITANE
14 rue du Maréchal Joffre

L'Occitane is one of the most famous Provençal brands in the world, with global distribution and stores everywhere, including London, Paris, and the United States. They've been expanding like mad the last few years, and they now have their own freestanding shop in Cannes. The line is enormous; the prices begin around 14 F ($2.30) and you can go stark raving nuts with the touching and the sniffing of everything.

I have tested tons of their products and find some are really special and others are average products in great packages. Regardless, they make attractive gifts. My friend Betsy just tested their lipstick and pronounced it the best she has ever used, and she's been a lipstick freak since we were 15 years old.

I like the scented candles but find that the incense doesn't do much. The shea butter cream for heavy-duty winter damage is excellent. Most of the soaps are sensational; the shampoos and bath foams are average.

The store is a big plus in Cannes and shouldn't be missed. It's on the corner of the small part of rue Meynadier and the rue du Marechal Joffre, between Monoprix and the regular pedestrian street rue Meynadier, a small one block offshoot of rue Meynadier.

Personal Needs

French pharmacies are designated by a green neon cross and carry most items you could need, including condoms. In fact, right on the rue d'Antibes, there's an outdoor condom machine in front of the **Lienhard Pharmacie** (no. 36).

Feminine supplies can be bought at pharmacies, supermarkets, drugstores, and places like Monoprix. For some reason, the big hotels do not seem to have those little sundries shops that sell these emergency items. They sell caviar in the lobby of the Noga but not condoms.

There's a branch of American Express at 8 rue de Belges, right off La Croisette. There are bank machines all over town and exchange booths in most hotels.

If you need inexpensive items, everything from pantyhose to sand buckets, from suntan oil or beauty aids to picnic supplies, head for that one-stop shopping haven: **Monoprix,** 9 rue Marechal Foch. There is a grocery store upstairs.

The **Cannes English Bookshop** is in the heart of town (don't let the address scare you). It's run by a lovely British man, so most of the English-language works are actually British, but you'll have no trouble finding beach or travel pleasures. Check it out: 11 rue Bivouac-Napoléon, near the Palais des Festivals.

If you need a liquor store and your hotel minibar just won't cut it, **Sunshine** is an excellent wine and spirits shop right in the heart of town where you can buy anything from favored vintages to Scotch single malts (5 rue Marechal Joffre).

Postcards

I buy my postcards at **Monoprix,** where they cost 1.60 F (26¢) each; they are also 1.60 F in the TTs (tourist traps) along the rue Meynadier. There are better postcards in terms of price and style of cards (selection of unusual styles is what I really mean) in Nice.

Shoes & Leather Goods

Of course you know about the big names such as Hermès and Gucci, Vuitton, and all that; even Chanel has handbags and shoes. These are more specialty related.

CHARLES JOURDAN
47 rue d'Antibes, Cannes

Jourdan is getting harder and harder to find in the United States, so if you love the look, now's your chance. Maybe your last chance.

JACQUES LOUP
21 rue d'Antibes, Cannes

The best shoe store in town, with a round-up of every line including Prada, which is not sold at bargain prices despite the fact that Italy is just an hour away. Excellent selection for men and women makes this good one-stop shopping for any need from sandal to silk.

LANCEL
34 rue d'Antibes, Cannes

This is one of the fanciest boutiques on the rue d'Antibes offering a terrific line of leather goods, from handbags to luggage. They have fabulous colors, and items are cost considerably less in France than in the United States. They also make luggage. I like the fact that they often have unusual colors—I got an olive green bag for last fall and a honey-colored hemp bag for this summer.

L'ETRIER
51 rue d'Antibes, Cannes

A rather average handbag shop with a few absolutely fabulous copies of big-name bags. This is the kind of store you might walk by without paying notice. Don't. A very good Kelly bag goes for about $200.

ROBERT CLERGERIE
17 rue St. Honoré, Cannes

This is dedicated to whomever interrupted my dinner one night to ask me for the address of the nearest Clergerie store because she needed a shoe fix. Voilà! This is on a small side street in the heart of town.

Souvenirs, TTs & Novelty Gifts

There are scads of tourist traps (TTs) all over town. There are a few unusual stores that sell gimmicky silly gifts that I guess you can only call souvenirs, although they may not have CANNES emblazoned on them. **Bathroom Graffitti** (52 rue d'Antibes) is a chain of gift shops, whereas **Davis** (1 La Croisette and Gray d'Albion) is an original kind of place offering film festival souvenirs, unusual items that you've never seen anywhere else, and all sorts of gadgets. Davis is open on Sunday.

I'm into kitsch and love the junky stores on the rue Meynadier that sell everything from lavender

sachets to Provençal print toilet paper holders to
snow domes made of plastic frogs.

CHEZ MON ONCLE
87 rue d'Antibes, Cannes

This is my favorite TT because it's not quite trappy;
it can give you a headache if you pay too much
attention to the chirping of the electronic cigalles or
if you breathe too many soap fumes, but around all
the junk there are some excellent finds. Stay, spend
some time, touch everything, give it your best eye-
ball—there is treasure here.

LA JARDIN DE LAURA
79 rue Felix Faure, Cannes

This one isn't as good as the two listed above, but
it's in another part of town and is quite close to the
Palais, if you're in town for the festival and need a
TT fix fast.

LA MAISON DU LUCILLE
41 rue Hoche, Cannes

This is a chain of stores all over the south of France,
but franchise owners are only required to buy 50%
of their stock from the mother store, so the branch
stores do vary somewhat. Each sells so much local
soap that you could have a sneeze attack, as well as
various other almost-cute touristy gifts and
Provençal doodads.

LAETITIA
13 rue Meynadier, Cannes

Attention shoppers: This is a Suzy find. This is one
of many TTs specializing in T-shirts, sweats, and tote
bags. I normally shun these things, but I confess that
they used to make a white plastic tote bag with
CANNES FRENCH RIVIERA in Chanel-style letters on it
for $12 that I found sublime. Unfortunately they no
longer have the white version, but this is still a good

shop for totes and tees. Hours are unusual by local standards: open at 9am; closed Monday mornings.

Cannes Shopper's Stroll & Tour

1. Begin your tour no later than 9:30am, earlier if you can cope. Start at the Forville Market, which is the fruit and vegetable market that serves not only Cannes locals but the various chefs of the city's best restaurants as well. You have to be at the market around 6am to catch a real live chef; by 9:30am, you'll still see the glorious produce. And olive oil. And flowers.

   This market is open every day of the week, including Sunday, so there are no excuses here.

2. From Porte Forville cut over to the rue Meynadier, which is really just around the corner. Turn left on rue Meynadier and, behold, you are in Food Town. It is a pedestrian street, so no need to worry about traffic.

3. Prowl to your heart's content. This used to be the main shopping drag in town and has the quality of a real-people, real-shopping street. Enjoy the regular shops that are in both the real people and the TT category; nothing here is too chic or too expensive. Also check out the gourmet food stores, and don't miss the famous cheese shop **La Ferme Savoyarde** (no. 22) which is next door to **Paraland,** my regular *parapharmacie* for drug store beauty brands.

4. Walk to the end of rue Meynadier (it's 1 big block long) and get ready to hang a right on rue Marechal de Joffre. But wait! Don't turn yet, cross the street and pop into L'Occitaine (14 rue du Maréchal Joffre), then proceed toward the sea on Mr. Joffre's streeet. Next stop: tabletop design store Genevieve Lethu.

5. Now walk straight ahead, which will take you right to La Croisette at the **Palais des Festivals.** Turn left on La Croisette. First hit the TTs and a really unusual boutique called **Davis,** right

there on La Croisette (no. 1), for film festival souvenirs and more, and then work your way toward the heart of town. The big-name French designer fashions (**Chanel,** for example) are soon to be yours. As you pass the big-name designer shops, shop or stare—whichever is more your style. Be sure to work up an appetite.

By 12:30pm or so, the shops will close and you'll find yourself in the middle of La Croisette. It wouldn't be a perfect day in Cannes without lunch on the beach or overlooking the beach, so now you choose one of the luxury palace hotels.

I pick the Noga partly for the location, partly because they have menu service on the beach (the Martinez has a set-price buffet), but mostly because my friend Pierre is the chef and he would kill me if I went somewhere else.

6. By 2pm, you are back on your feet. Head out the back end of the Noga toward Rond Point Duboys and get to **Contrepartie,** the best spot in town, for used designer clothing. When you're finished there, walk the half block to the rue d'Antibes and hang a left, walking back toward the Forville Market.

7. Follow the rue d'Antibes, shopping as you go, back the way you came. This is west, in case you have your compass on you. You can shop all the way back across town, or you can shop for the few blocks it takes to get to the Gray d'Albion mall (**Souleiado, La Perla**) and then out, back on the street. On rue d'Antibes you can make a double header out of a visit first to Bouteille, the fanciest perfume and make-up store in town and then to Sephora, the American-style makeup store.

8. When you get to the **Pharmacy Leinhard,** look at a map here so you can hit the rue du Marshall

Foch, not to be confused with the rue du Marechal Joffre.

9. Although you are getting tired, keep shopping along rue Foch for some real-people French style. Also be sure to take a quick look at **Galeries Lafayette** (you can't miss it when you almost dead-end into the doors). When finished with your tour of GL, go out the front door (not the way you came in) and then cross the street right into **Monoprix.**

   If at any time along this part of the tour you think you need more than a bag of coffee beans, there's a cafe inside the mall Gray d'Albion where you can get a coffee. You can also stop at one of my favorite places in town, **Rohr,** a tea room with fabulous French pastries. Then you will be refreshed enough to study the map, get on with the show, explore rue Foch, and hit those major French landmark department and dime stores.

10. From Monoprix, cut out the back door toward the train station, but don't go into the train station. Turn left and walk a half block to a two-part store called **Cannolive.** One part has foodstuff, the other sells Provençal fabrics and goodies. Note that there is a public toilet across the street if you are so inclined. Or reclined. Two francs, SVP.

11. If you can still walk, cut back toward rue d'Antibes to explore the small grid of streets between rue d'Antibes and La Croisette in this middle part of town—the rue des Serbes, the rue des Belges, and the rue des Etats Unis— they have many small but fancy boutiques lined up in neat rows. Prowl these side streets as long as strength holds.

12. Limp back to La Croisette. Collapse at **Farfalla,** the cafe on La Croisette, for coffee or a stiff drink. Bottoms up! Or, at least, feet up!

BEYOND CANNES

· ·

The beauty of using Cannes as a hub is that you can get to all the villages in the area. Each makes a perfect day trip and most can be reached by public transportation. Although St. Tropez and Provence could be done as day trips from Cannes, there's a lot of driving involved there. I don't suggest it. For me, I usually group it geographically. Then I get Mike or Pascale-Agnes to drive me. I have done both Nice and Monte Carlo as day trips on the train from Cannes, and that's a breeze. Here are my suggestions for how to organize your day trips:

- Mougins and Grasse
- Nice
- Antibes and the hill towns (Vallauris, Biot, St. Paul de Vence, Eze)
- Monaco (Eze can be combined with Monaco if your schedule gets too tight)

MOUGINS

· ·

Mougins is almost a suburb of Cannes; most tourists visit because it is home to world-renowned star chef Roger Vergé. It's also the winter home of cabaret performer Bobby Short: He doesn't perform in the south of France, so you must catch him at the Cafe Carlyle in New York or on the sly in the local Champion supermarket. Roger Moore used to live here, too. That's the kind of place Mougins is: intimate and in. There are also several golf courses.

For those who do not like the shimmer and shine of Cannes, you can choose a hidden location in Mougins and still be far away but close. Not too many destinations offer those polar choices.

There's a bit of a trick to getting to the right part of Mougins. Much ordinary countryside is within the city limits of Mougins; what you want as a tourist is Mougins Village. Follow signs to an adorable little town perched atop a hill.

It's so classic (read touristy) that you park your car in a town lot and walk to town—no cars allowed. I've heard cynics claim the town is too cute. I'm not certain if there's such a thing as too cute; maybe it's just a matter of too many tourists.

I think the place is adorable and very much worth a pit stop. Or more. And I like to shop here, if only to buy gifts from Roger Vergé's shop.

If you are not staying nearby, you will be in town probably only long enough to eat and to shop. The stores are mostly TTs, offering an enormous selection of postcards done in arty styles. My favorite store in town is at the bottom of the hill, right near the parking lot. It's the gourmet food shop where Roger Vergé sells his packaged foodstuff (La Boutique Roger Vergé, place du Village).

Although Vergé is one of the most famous chefs in the world, his prices for things such as confiture (jam) and tapenade are no higher than the prices in the markets and groceries around town. You'll pay about 20 F ($3.30) per item. Bergdorf-Goodman in New York sells some of the Roger Vergé products for more.

GRASSE

. . . .

Now that I've fallen in love with chef Jacques Chibois, I welcome you to Grasse with new enthusiasm. I used to have a love-hate thing with Grasse. I mean, I can't imagine that you would come this close and miss the opportunity to visit a town that represents the perfume business. But I am sad to send you to the mostly touristy places that make up the town, and I am appalled at how much the city has changed in recent years in order to accommodate the tour buses.

But, here's the good part: When I know I can also send you to eat (and even sleep) chez Chibois, my heart sings. I also think I need a drink, as Jacques has gotten me hooked on a local brew that is heaven in a glass, *vin cuit*.

If you have been to Grasse and have memories of it, if you are using an old guidebook, or if you are merely curious, forget anything you ever remembered or heard about the old system wherein the many perfume houses in town sold copycat fragrances. Nowadays there are no copycat fragrances, there are no charts saying "If you like Chanel No. 5 you will like . . ." and no little vials of anything that smell suspiciously like the real thing. So the Grasse I welcome you to is far different than it used to be or than you imagine it to be.

The Lay of the Land

Grasse is located a mere 15 kilometers (a little more than 9 miles) from Cannes, perched in the hills slightly to the north. It is the industrial and emotional heart of the perfume industry.

There is sort of a downtown Grasse; even a cute street in Old Grasse. However, most of center Grasse is neither cute nor charming, it's just vertical. It sprawls up and down and around and feels like the kind of place where you can get lost without having fun being lost.

You don't come to Grasse for the cute; you come for Chibois. Then, maybe the perfumes.

If you have fantasies about fields of poppies or the smell of flowers in the air or of friendly worker bees in cute native dress with baskets on their heads, you can think again. Imagine instead TTs, tour buses, and zillions of schoolchildren wearing name tags.

Getting There

If you haven't got a car, you can take public transportation from Cannes. I took the bus once—great fun. I felt like a genius for a week.

Shopping for Scent

Grasse is not one enormous duty-free shop, nor is it nearly as much fun as any branch of the French makeup chain Sephora. You don't come to Grasse to get discounts on designer perfume or to find a bigger or better selection of designer anything. In fact, Grasse is not a designer fragrance town as far as tourists are concerned.

None of the big names allow you into their factories or to sniff their poppies. Even though Chanel keeps its own fields to grow its own flowers in order to ensure their purity and that of their essence, Chanel does not appear to be represented to the public in any form.

What Grasse has is a few renovated mansions that have been turned into museums and shops selling their own brands. What Grasse has is a lot of tour buses. Power to the petals.

But Wait

A brocante market is held on Wednesday. It makes it all worthwhile.

Grasse Trick

Follow the signs for **Monoprix**—in so doing, you get a tour of the town and know which fork to take every time you have a choice of roads. Then you can park in the Monoprix parking lot and explore the heart of the old town on foot.

Grasse on Tour

There are an enormous number of package tours that go to Grasse, including shore excursions offered by cruise lines that come to port along the Riviera. Like most package tours, these are marriages between one perfume house and the firm offering the tour.

You will not be able to cope with more than one factory tour—how perfume is made is fascinating only once. (Sort of like the "How Wine Is Made" speech.) Note that tours at all of the big factories are guided in a variety of languages and are free.

The Big Three

Grasse has three big names in the tourist perfume factory business. Two of these three names have factory shops in other parts of the Riviera.

I have ranked the Big Three according to my opinion of their charms.

MOLINARD
60 bd. Victor Hugo, Grasse

There's no question that Molinard is the classiest of the three. If you are only going to go to one of the three houses, this is the one to pick.

The villa in which the showroom is housed is gorgeous; the costumes in their museum arcades are gorgeous; some of their scents are even gorgeous.

The house has a full range of lines, most of which are sold at Bergdorf-Goodman in New York and a few other fancy-dancy shops. Most Americans are not familiar with the perfume house itself or any of its brands. Not to worry.

Perhaps its most famous scent is Habanita, which comes in a very distinctive (and highly collectible) Lalique bottle. This is the kind of scent you either love or hate.

My favorite part of the collection is a complete line called Les Senteurs, which is a range of eaux de toilette made from natural flowers, spices, or herbs, such as vanilla, lime, orange, and cinnamon. There is a baby scent, Les Cherubins, to compete in this new area; a great gift for the baby who has everything.

They conduct a perfume-making workshop, usually booked by small groups and arranged ahead of time, whereby you can create your very own scent.

To arrange your perfume workshop, fax **04-93-36-03-91**. The price is based on the number of people in your group.

FRAGONARD
20 bd. Fragonard, Grasse

Les 4 Chemins, route de Cannes and Eze village

Fragonard sort of owns Grasse; it has two shops/factories in Grasse, one downtown and one on the road from Cannes. There are two other retail factories: one in Eze village and one in Paris near American Express on rue Scribe.

Fragonard's main headquarters are in a magnificently restored villa in the heart of the center of town; its museum and tour are excellent. I just don't happen to like their products very much. Sorry.

Should you pick up any of the free literature distributed in hotels or tourist venues, you'll note a discount coupon for 5% off your purchases.

GALIMARD
73 route de Cannes, Grasse

Galimard has a little old lady type of showroom in downtown Grasse and a big factory-style outlet on the road outside of town. There is also a shop in Eze.

My mother always told me that if you haven't got anything nice to say about someone, don't say anything. So do you want to talk about Jacques Chibois some more?

ANTIBES

I welcome you to Antibes if you come out of season. I welcome you to Antibes in summer if you come on a yacht. Okay, you can come by train any time. Otherwise, watch out, I don't think you want to even be welcomed here—you won't find a parking place and the traffic may make you nuts.

Don't give up.

I wouldn't dream of coming to Antibes on a Saturday; God knows how early you must arrive to find a parking space. My day is Thursday, the other of the two regular, weekly flea market days. Any day is a good day if you aren't driving; Thursday or Saturday are preferred if you like markets.

There are actually two markets in Antibes on Thursday; do them both because the contrasts between them gives an academic lesson in French marketing. If you can't find one of them (hey, we had trouble), ask. One market is right along the waterfront; the other is in the center of town. They're not far apart, but they do not merge and no neon signs indicate that there are two different types of venues for your shopping pleasure.

The new market, where new merchandise is sold, is right on the waterfront and rambles throughout a parking lot or two. Here you can find a few pieces of brocante but mostly new household and clothing items. A few tables sell factory overruns. One dealer had fake Hermès-style handbags. There is more of the new market in the heart of Antibes; only the small portion at the lower end of the main street is a truly good flea market. Dealers lay out their wares on tables, the street, and the curb. Prices are excellent!

The only thing that disappointed me about this flea market was the fact that there were so few dealers. I will add that in all my research in all the flea markets I scoped out in France, this market had the lowest asking prices on similar and traditional French merchandise.

BIOT
. . . .

Welcome to Biot, *bienvenue*. Forget about the glass factory you've read all about and get into the spirit of the south of France, the spirit of the hill towns. I'd been going to Biot for years to take in the glass factory, which is in the outskirts of town, and only recently went into the actual city of Biot. Trust me, friends, this one is a winner. What a difference a few miles makes.

The heart of downtown is only about 2 blocks long. Although the main street is lined with TTs, they are exactly the kind of places you expect to see and actually want to see. There are several cafes and we ate at the local crepe restaurant, which was perfect for us.

Several TTs sell locally made monochromatic pottery. There's also an abundance of Provençal fabrics, sold by the bolt or made up into table items, clothing, and accessories—everything from eyeglasses cases to toilet paper holders.

The main shopping street is called rue St. Sébastien; my favorite TT is **Gabel** (no. 28). My notes about the shop that I wrote on their business card are simple: "All my dreams come true." There's also a branch of the chain **La Maison de Lucille,** no. 36, where you can get touristy gifts. I found a small sisal rug with a needlepoint inset there, the likes of which I've never found elsewhere in France. It was $6.

The glass factory, **La Verrerie de Biot** (Chemin des Combes, right outside Biot center), has been made famous to Americans because the bubble-encrusted glass works are often featured on tables set with Pierre Deux or Souleiado linen. There's no question that the glassware is nice, but they are also very expensive. To complicate matters, the store does not ship items bought from the bargain corner, where you can find some true bargains. Be prepared to schlepp!

The glass factory is a major attraction for tourists from all over—not just Americans in search of Pierre Deux—and is off in its own little complex before you get to town. On the complex there is also a relatively plain crafts shop that sells ordinary enough stuff (and has clean bathrooms upstairs).

The glass showroom is rather big, by local standards, and has tons of nice merchandise, but it's expensive. Prices are no less in the factory than in town.

The showroom does ship to anyplace in the world, but only items that are at sold at regular prices. A bargain is any item in the shop that costs $50 or less.

VALLAURIS

. . . .

Years ago I would have extended a warm welcome to Vallauris, a city I have enjoyed. I would have welcomed you to the city where Picasso got into the lay of the clay, where studios selling locally made dishes dished out their wares, where the name Studio Madoura meant something.

Today: Phooey. Yankee go home. The town is loaded with tourists, the TTs are overwhelming, and the soul of the city has been destroyed by crass commercialism. Yuck.

Despite the tourists in St. Paul, it has managed to stay serene and peaceful. Vallauris is a riot of cheap ceramics, bad taste, and tour buses. Picasso is turning over in his clay.

If you insist on visiting Vallauris, I can tell you that there are plenty of places to shop. Few of them are charming, but here and there you'll find a few special resources.

The main drag is avenue Georges Clemenceau; check out the part with the higher numbers (like 65 bis) rather than the lower numbers, which tend to be more touristy.

My favorite shop from years ago is still open and wonderful. You'll have to look hard to find it, even though it's in plain sight, because of all of the junky stores that have been built up along the way. My find is Foucard-Jourdan, 65 bis av. G. Clemenceau; I also like Potterie Provencale (no. 54).

Because of the overwhelming amount of TTs, all with merchandise spilling out of their stores and piled high on the curbs, you'll be tempted to do some of your souvenir shopping here. Compared to elsewhere in France, prices on souvenir items are actually quite good in Vallauris.

Prices on packaged lavender are the best in the area (four sachets for 17 F/$2.80; five for 19 F/$3.20!). These same sachets cost 50 F ($8.50) at similar tourist traps in Paris. Marseille-style block soap costs 9 F ($1.50) for 400 grams (14 ounces), which is a very good price. I usually pay 12 F ($2) for the same gift, although I buy my block soap from a very fancy place in Cannes.

As much as I hate to admit this, I'd rather pay more for these very same items and buy them from someplace that I love. Vallauris couldn't be more tacky if it were in the Caribbean.

SAINT PAUL DE VENCE

. . . .

Welcome, welcome, and again welcome to Saint Paul de Vence, a tourist town that knows how to get it right. This town is so perfect that I refused to shoot the cover of this book here, because it's almost a cliché in perfection. Ah, Saint Paul de Vence, so easy to love. Ah, yes, Saint Paul de Vence, so easy to hate because it's so easy to love.

On the whole, the shopping scene within the walls of this medieval town is what you would expect—lots of TTs selling everything from postcards to plastic swords and armor for the kids. There are some art galleries with high prices and a handful of very nice boutiques dotted here and there, so that even a person with a real sense of style can get a sense of well being when out strolling and window shopping the rue Grande.

What seems to make the difference here is the level of taste. While a few stores sell cheap tricks, the good fabric houses are in place, and the overall quality of the goods and the storefronts seduces the visitor into thinking this is not an ordinary tourist town.

One trick: My girlfriend Jill lives near St. Paul, and she suggests that you come in November or early December, because, although some stores are closed, the winter is mild and the galleries and restaurants that are open are empty of tourists.

Les Olivades (1 rue Grande) and **Souleiado** (17 rue Grande), the two biggest names in quality Provençal fabrics, each have boutiques on the cobbled main shopping street. **L'Air du Sud** (56 rue Grande) is an extraordinary store—a local dollop of design, crafts, color, and the look of the south of France in tabletop and gift items.

Around the corner, check out **L'herbier de Provence,** another chain that is enjoyable in almost any town. It sells Provençal-style gifts and its Marseille soap sells for 15 F ($2.50) for 400 grams (14 ounces).

But wait, I think I forgot to tell you one of the most important things in the world. St. Paul is open and I mean wide open on Sunday!

OPIO

. . . .

I welcome you to Opio in a totally different manner than to anyplace else on your tour of these French hills. I welcome you as an accidental tourist, a person who made a wrong turn and who found God. Or, at least, an olive oil mill.

When you have no expectations and you find something wonderful, it's just that much more wonderful. I had read about Opio. I knew it was an olive-producing region. When we made a wrong turn somewhere in the hills (easily done) and then saw the signs for Opio, we took it as a sign. It was also 1:45pm. Another sign.

The village itself has no particular shopping, but on the road, down the hill, we saw a sign that simply said "Le Moulin." At the door of Le Moulin, it said, in handwritten scrawl, *"magasin"* (store). The doors opened at exactly 2pm, and in no time I was jumping around like an American, hugging and kiss-ing every olive in sight. (Those little dishes on stands are for the pits, thank you.)

MOULIN DE LA BRAQUE
2 route de Châteauneuf, Opio

A movie set couldn't look better than Le Moulin Huile Michel, also known as the Moulin de la Braque (it's owned by Roger Michel, hence the two names). The mill makes olive oil and sells a number of vari-eties of olives, olive oil, and olive oil products such as soap. They also sell some fabric, some touristy items, and a few gifts.

But we came for the olives.

While the oil is sold in any number of tins, it can also be tasted, tested, and bought straight from the vat. If you bring your own container it costs less. If you were so silly as to leave your container at home, you can pick from a number of different types, sizes, and packages. Tins are easier to pack than glass bottles.

Tasting the different olive oil flavors was very interesting. Pascale-Agnes said that my choice was typically American and touristy. When I bought a tin of oil for a French friend, Pascale-Agnes insisted that I pick the French-style oil—the kind she liked, not the kind I liked. When I handed over the oil to the Duvauchelles, and explained the story, Richard thanked Pascale-Agnes for making me see the light and buy the right one.

Without further supervision, I bought airtight bags of olives in a variety of marinades and a giant package of olive oil soap. I paid with a credit card. It was fabulous. The hours are 9am to noon and 2 to 7pm. The local phone is ☎ 04-93-77-23-03.

VALBONNE
· ·

We never got to Valbonne, so I can't quite give you the proper welcome. But I have written down the name of a famous honey shop that I wanted to track down: **Ruchers Mazzini,** 12 rue Emile Pourcel. Supposedly this is the secret celeb source for honey and royal jelly beauty products. *Note:* Friday is market day in Valbonne.

NICE

· ·

You probably won't have much trouble having a nice week if you use Nice the same way I use Cannes—as a hub city. Even if you just come to Nice on a day trip or a shore excursion, I think you're going to like it. The best part of Nice can be seen in a day.

I welcome you to a part of the French Riviera that has a hidden side and plenty of shopping secrets. Nice is not picture-perfect cute, like some of the surrounding hill towns, but Nice has some places with soul and is worth discovering.

It's a huge city, sprawling all over the hills, and is home to industry galore. It's the true business, transportation, and communications capital of the south of France. When I welcome you to Nice, I don't welcome you to all that, to metropolitan Nice. Instead, I welcome you to Old Nice, to downtown Nice, to a bit of Nice. To a Nice day or two.

While I happily welcome you to the modern international airport, the Nice I welcome you to is a combination of old-fashioned values with just a few new twists. While there is a big modern mall on the edge of town (remarkably close to the airport), I don't really use that mall, and I refuse to welcome you to the Nice of malls.

I welcome you to the Nice of flowers, of Carneval, of hotels along the sea, of olive oil, *fruits confit,* and antique shops. Lots of antique shops.

Although rue Paradis is the main pedestrian shopping street, I don't find it paradise at all. I think it's sort of limited, in fact. Cannes has better big-name shopping than Nice, so don't shrug and wonder where paradise has gone.

True paradise is around the corner, in Old Nice. Welcome and step this way.

Getting There & Getting Around

You can fly directly to Nice–Côte d'Azur Airport from New York via Delta. Air France and Air InterEurope have flights from Paris on an almost hourly basis. (The flying time is a little over $1^1/_2$ hours.) Many, many other carriers serve this airport, which I consider a great hub for this part of the world—I even use it for getting to Morocco!

I will not go into a spiel about politics in Nice, because this book could end up with Jimmy Hoffa, but I will warn you that taxi fares are outrageously expensive and controlled by some higher deity. There is little competition and not much room for bargaining. A taxi from the Nice airport to a hotel on the Promenade des Anglais—about a 7-minute drive—will easily cost $25.

I think the trick to getting around Nice is to stay in a hotel that is well situated so you can walk everywhere. Even if you have a car, you may find that parking is hard to get. I found that parking tickets were easy to get.

If you don't have your car with you, you will need to take a taxi to the antique neighborhood. Otherwise, everything is accessible by foot.

To get to Nice by train from neighboring towns, you want the St.Raphael–Cannes-Nice-Monaco-Ventimiglia line from the Region Provence-Alps, TER. The free timetable at the station comes in English and French. The timetable chart is fairly conventional, so you shouldn't have any trouble reading it.

Do not forget to *composter* (validate) your ticket (see chapter 2 for details). You can also use the Nice train station for catching small trains to small nearby cities, such as Biot.

Nice

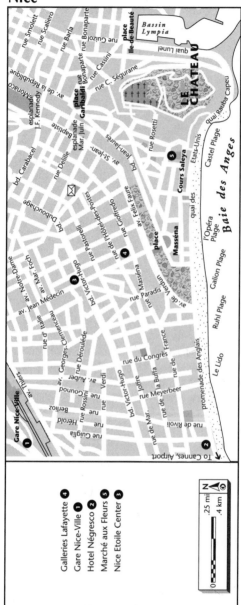

Galleries Lafayette **4**
Gare Nice-Ville **1**
Hotel Négresco **2**
Marché aux Fleurs **5**
Nice Etoile Center **3**

0   .25 mi
0   .4 km

N

Sleeping in Nice

HÔTEL NÉGRESCO
37 Promenade des Anglais, Nice

Although Cannes has an international reputation for its belle epoque, sugar plum hotels, Nice has one or two left too. The most famous of them is the Hôtel Négresco, which is downright sumptuous inside and out.

Located right on the Promenade des Agnlais and overlooking the sea, the Negresco is also within walking distance of everything and is considered the place to be. Every star in the world has stayed here, and Richard Burton even accidentally left Liz's 69-carat diamond on the bar one night. The Beatles wrote a hit song here.

Rooms begin around $250 per night, but they have gold-sparkle bidets. Honest. They also have promotional rates and all sorts of things. It's just one of the world's best treats to stay here because the decor is so over the top and the mixture of old world grandeur with modern art is so stunning—and silly. Good bar; big fat hotel cat.

Even if you can't afford this hotel, please come visit. The staff here is incredibly nice. I've asked the concierge for help many times, even when I wasn't staying at the hotel. Two of the hotel's restaurants are must-dos—pick from casual or formal. Or have a drink in the English-style bar. Pet the cat. Go to the ladies' room; you've never seen a bathroom like this, I promise.

There are some stores in the lobby; use them as your excuse to poke around. Don't forget that the new chef is young, gorgeous, and fantastic!

If you thought hotels like this do not have any bargains or secrets, think again. The best bet at this hotel: Guest parking is free!

For reservations in the United States, call **Leading Hotels of the World** at ☎ 800/223-6800. The local phone is 04-93-88-39-51; fax 04-93-88-35-68.

Hôtel Plaza Concorde
12 av. de Verdun, Nice

This hotel is located in the core of the shopping district in downtown Nice and just across a garden from Old Nice. It's within a sneeze of the rue Paradis, where all the designer shops are located. It is not on the seaside, but is just a block from the sea. That makes it 1 block closer to Galeries Lafayette. For those who want to combine price with chrome, glass, mirrors, and an old-fashioned facade, this hotel can be yours for about $150 per night.

For reservations in the United States, call ☎ 800/ 888-4747. The local phone is 04-93-16-75-75; fax 04-93-82-50-70.

Hôtel Westminster Concorde
27 Promenade des Anglais, Nice

It was my friend Richard who chose the Westminster for me. He described it as "the poor man's petit Négresco." Located only 1 block from the Négresco, the hotel is light years away otherwise. Make that 100 years away. You see, while the rooms of the Westminster have been redone in the last 100 years and an elevator has been put in, not too much else has been done to the hotel. The result: marvelous shabby chic snuggled behind pink stucco.

If you can take it funky, if you are very relaxed, and if you love the idea of a hotel that costs between $130 and $150 per night, this one has a great location and a lot of charm. The breakfast buffet—an enormous affair—is served in a grand ballroom. This hotel should be a landmark and is one of the best finds of my life (thanks R.D.).

I've had big rooms and I've had a room so tiny that two people wouldn't have survived, but the hotel is still grand. Front rooms have the view but they are noisy; there are enormous bathrooms and good amenities.

For reservations in the United States, call ☎ 800/ 888-4747. The local phone is 04-93-88-29-44; fax 04-93-82-45-35.

Markets & Fairs

FRUIT & FLOWER MARKET Daily except Monday, Cours Saleya, from 7am.

BROCANTE MARKET (FLEA MARKET) Monday, Cours Saleya, from 7am. More than 200 dealers. Year-round.

ANTIQUE MARKET Quai de la Doune, daily except Sunday, 11am to 7pm, about 18 stalls. Year-round.

USED & OLD BOOKS MARKET First and third Saturday of each month, place du Palais du Justice, 8am to 5pm. The first Sunday is old books; the third Sunday is postcards and ephemera. Some 24 stalls. Year-round.

CARNAVAL Carnaval is organized by Roy du Cinema; admission to the gated-off areas is 50 F ($8.50) (otherwise you can't see anything). Tribunes (solid seats with backs almost like movie theater seats) are 100 F ($17), and loges (box seats) are 200 F ($33). I never even saw any loges. Our tribunes were great; I got them by faxing one of my regular hotels in Nice (Hôtel Westminster) and asking them to save me two tickets.

Assorted Carnaval gear—noise makers, plastic hats, confetti, masks, paper parasols—is sold from tables along the main drag of Nice (avenue Médecin). However, the most important ingredient for Carnaval is foam string, which is sold in atomizer cans and which you spray until you have lost every care in the world. String battles with total strangers ensue at the drop of a plastic hat. String sells for 6 F ($1) a can or three cans for 20 F ($3.30). Don't waste money—buy in bulk.

Shopping Neighborhoods

NICE AIRPORT For a small airport, the Nice airport has very good shopping. Half of the stores are located near the gates after you have gone through immigration, but wait, if you're on an intra-Euro flight they have more stores and duty-free shops so that even if you don't go through immigration, you can still shop. The stores include a tiny **Hermès** boutique (where I have found things with fair prices), a newsagent (newsdealer), a duty-free shop, a shop that sells Provençal fabric–style souvenirs, and a gourmet food store that sells fresh cheese, olive oil, and so on.

Right near the airport is a big American-style mall called **Cap 3000** that has a branch of every big chain in France.

COURS SALEYA   You can have the rest of Nice, I'll keep the airport and the Cours Saleya, the main square in the heart of the Old Town where a flower and vegetable market is held every day (yes, Sunday too) except Monday, which is brocante day.

I cannot tell you that this is the cutest town square in France or that the Old Town in Nice is adorable and worthy of a postcard. The fact that the area is real and not perfect explains some of the charm. The visual here is color, from striped awnings to gorgeous fruits and flowers. Several cafes that line the way make for the perfect opportunity to stop, have a coffee, stare, and wonder at the fact that this is a way of life for some people.

In the market stands you'll find a variety of prices for seemingly the same things. Don't buy until you've surveyed the lot. Then choose from the fruits of the season, homemade jams and tapenades, various types of olives, and assorted candies.

This is one of the best fruit and flower markets in the south of France; go out of your way to get here. Old Town is adjacent to the market, so be sure to allow time for both.

VIEUX NICE   The Old Town, comprised of a small warren of streets surrounding the Cours Saleya. You do the two together. Again, I won't tell you this is the most picturesque old town in France or even on the Riviera. It's actually kind of gritty.

With any luck, you're staying at a hotel on the Promenade des Anglais or right in the center of town, so you can walk to this area. There's something fabulous about strolling along the ocean side of the promenade and then cutting into the Old Town and coming upon these old-fashioned little stores and TTs as if you were in a dream.

If you are driving and arrive for the day, there is municipal parking right at the Cours Saleya. A computerized sign above the lot tells you how many parking spaces are available. If the lot is full, the sign will say *complet*. If you park there, do take time to wander over 1 block to see the ocean and the promenade.

QUAI DE LA DOUANE   This is the antique neighborhood. On a map it looks like it is an easy walk from the Cours Saleya. However, because of the size of Le Château, on a mountain between the two parts of town, you'll be happier if you take a taxi.

Ask for Le Marché Aux Puce du Quai de la Douane and you will be dropped where you need to be. The marché has about 18 stalls and isn't impressive, but there's a candy factory next door (**Confiserie du Vieux Nice,** 14 Quai Papacino) and many more warehouses of antiques around the corner. So don't panic.

The candy factory is small, but it gives tours and sells samples. They make chocolates and fruits confits; upstairs there's a rather large shop with free tastings and great products to take home for gifts including many unusual items such as jasmine jam.

Don't panic that addresses seem strange; there are 3 blocks that run alongside the tiny boat harbor, and each block has a different name.

But don't bury your nose in a map, sniff the air and look around. This is a part of town virtually unknown to tourists.

Walk alongside the quay for antique shops and cafes (ignore the karaoke bars), then turn left onto rue Antoine Gauthier for a 2-block stretch filled with warehouses of used furniture and antiques. Most of the houses here will ship; few dealers speak English. The specialty in these warehouses is large pieces of furniture. Prices, even with shipping added, are at least half of what you would pay for similar pieces in the United States.

Prices are listed in the warehouses, but the more you buy, the more flexible the dealer will become. The warehouses all keep more or less the same hours: Monday through Saturday, 9am to 12:30pm and 2:30 to 7pm. They are closed on Sunday.

Because this is not a touristy neighborhood, you should be able to find street parking. You use the meter to buy a ticket. The meter costs 3 F (50¢) per minute.

A final neighborhood note: The flea market stalls next to the candy factory opened in May 1995. Marché Aux Puce de Nice Brocante is open from 11am to 5pm on a regular basis, with longer evening hours during the summer. If you have used an older guidebook or printed materials that have not been updated, you may be directed to another address for Antiquaires du Port at the place Guyenmer. That flea market is gone.

PARADIS   The main fancy shopping street of Nice is called the rue Paradis. I don't know how to break this to you gently, but if you think this is paradise, you have come to the wrong book.

Don't get me wrong, there's nothing wrong with the rue Paradis or with the stores that are on this 2-block stretch of upper-class French mall. It's just that by giving the street a name like that, one has hopes. And the street is boring. I'll buy my Chanel in Cannes, thank you. There's just nothing elegant about the rue Paradis, nor anything funky or fun. It's neither this nor that. It's simply there, with stores to serve locals who have money and need expensive things.

REAL-PEOPLE MASSENA   The rue Paradis is a short little street in the greater pedestrian shopping cluster of downtown that branches off away from the main shopping thoroughfare. The place Massena, with **Galeries Lafayette,** is the anchor of this shopping area. However, the bulk of the nieghborhood is off to one side, past the rue Paradis and snuggled behind a portion of the Promenade des Anglais. Note that one of the perimeters of this shopping district is the rue Verdun, which becomes avenue Felix-Faure, another main drag. Check your map to see how the streets converge and intersect.

Some of the stores here are branches of real-people shops selling cheap shoes and sportswear. Most of them are tourist traps (TTs) and cafes or pizza places. I just love it back here because it's very real. But you will never confuse it with Cannes.

But wait. On the surface all of this looks tacky and cheap. That's because most of the good stuff is hidden. On the very side streets that sell the T-shirts, and along the boring rue Paradis and rue Massena, there are a few addresses, that will knock your socks off once you get inside.

As is the tradition in many places in France and Italy, local boutiques sell many of the bigger names. You need to check out places like **Pink** (rue de France), **Jelly** (place Magenta), or even **Claude Bonucci** (rue Massenet), which sells Claude Bonucci made-to-measure clothes from a very small and discreet shop. Bonucci, which also has shops in Cannes, makes old-fashioned, finely tailored togs for rock stars, movie stars, and Riviera elite.

REAL-PEOPLE MÉDECIN A spoonful of shopping makes the Médecin go down, even if the shopping has very little glamour and represents the basic multiples and real-people resources. Avenue Jean Médecin is where you'll find the French record store chain **FNAC** (CDs, tapes, books), the dime store, and all the real-people multiples, as well as branches of the affordable famed ones: **Zara, Sephora, La Redoute, Prisunic**. These stores are larger than the ones in Cannes.

My husband was out on the town one day and found **Régence** (8 av. Jean Médecin) where he bought some fabulous faux Souleiado fabric for $8 a meter (just over 3 feet). The perfume discounter **Bernard Marionnaud** is located at no. 46, a block after the

Nice Etoile Center. This is a little confusing, because there is another perfume shop at no. 48, but if you go into the Riviera Center, you'll find Marionnaud has a big shop on the ground floor, and what a shop it is.

Marionnaud is a renegade retailer. He was one of the first discounters in France and began in the suburbs of Paris. He now has stores all over France. Prices are better than at duty frees, and locals have gone nuts for the opportunity to save money, since locals cannot get détaxe.

If you arrive in Nice via train, the train station is right off this main thoroughfare. You can easily walk along it shopping your way to the rue Paradis, the place Massena, the Cours Saleya, and everywhere else.

Finds/Old Nice

ALZIARI
14 rue Saint Francçois de Paule, Old Nice

If I had to pick one store to send you to in all of France, one place that to me best captures the soul of what shopping in the south of France should be, I would send you to this hole-in-the-wall little mill. You can buy olives, olive oil, and olive oil soap.

The olive oil, famed for the design and colors of its royal blue can, is sold outside Nice in various gourmet food stores for two to three times what you pay for it in Nice. If you can't get to the mill in the Old Town, note that the gourmet food shop in the Nice airport sells two sizes of the olive oil. It's not cheap, even in Nice, but it is a very special souvenir.

AUER
7 rue Saint Francçois de Paule, Old Nice

This ice cream parlor and sweets shop looks like a movie set. It will enchant you as you study the storefront and then again when you step foot inside. You may have tea or get an ice cream cone or do what generations of tourists before you have done: Send off some local sweets to your friends back home. Check out the mailing labels.

CINNAMON
10–12 rue Jules Gilly, Old Nice

This large store sells furniture and decorative items. It's located in the area right past the Cours Saleya. The entire street has several shops with antiques and furniture. This is sort of the professional cute look.

LA COUQUETA
8 rue François Saint Paule, Old Nice

This street is crammed with TTs, many of them selling Provençal fabrics. The best of the bunch is this shop, which sells Valdromme brand, one of the better makes. Prices are higher than in the surrounding stores, but the quality is better.

LA MAISON DE L'OLIVE
18 rue Pairoliere, Old Nice

This will take some time to find until you are familiar with the maze of pedestrian streets in Old Nice, but it's worth it because the store is very authentic. It actually has two parts: a TT portion for gifts (this part is touristy) and the food part, which is not touristy at all. Great source for 28F ($4.70) (very expensive!) lavender soap. Open Sunday in the morning but not on Monday.

LE MOULIN DES CARACOLES
5 rue Saint Francçois de Paule, Old Nice

Of the several TTs in a row in this part of the Old Town, this one is my favorite because I like the shop, the merchandise, the display, the wrap, and even their business cards. This is where I buy packaged olives (airtight; they can legally be brought into the United States) as well as some gift items.

Nice Resources

BIG NAMES

ARMANI EMPORIO
1 rue Paradis, Nice

CACHAREL
rue du Paradis, Nice

CHANEL
6 rue Paradis, Nice

CHRISTIAN DIOR
6 rue Paradis, Nice

ESCADA
8 rue de France, Nice

FACONNABLE
Rue du Paradis, Nice

HERMÈS
8 av. de Verdun, Nice

LOUIS VUITTON
Rue du Paradis, Nice

KENZO
5 rue Alphonse Karr, Nice

LANCEL
Nice Etoile, av. Jean Médecin, Nice

LACOSTE
6 rue du Gustav V

YVES SAINT LAURENT
4 rue du Gustav v

ZARA
10 av. Jean Médecin, Nice

CHAINS & MULTIPLES

CAMAIEU FEMME
21–22 rue Massena, Nice

Cheapie teen thrills for all ages.

CLEOPATRE
Nice Etoile, av. Jean Médecin, Nice

Cheap teen jewels.

DU PARAEIL AU MEME MAISON
44 rue Pastorelli, Nice

Adorable kids clothes.

LA REDOUTE
54 av. Jean Médecin, Nice

Store for the catalogue firm.

PIMKIE
Nice Etoile, av. Jean Médecin, Nice

Hot teen cheapie looks.

SECRETS DESSOUS
4 rue Massena, Nice

Lingerie in all price brackets.

SEPHORA
8 av. Jean Médecin, Nice

Makeup Forever.

DEPARTMENT STORES

Galeries Lafayette (GL) has a rather large store at place Masséna; get a discount card at your hotel to entitle you to a 10% discount on all purchases. You must present the discount card before payment. This is not the détaxe refund, which at GL is an additional 13%.

Marks & Spencer has a really big place a few doors away, about a block up avenue Jean Médecin toward the train station, right after the mall Nice Etoile.

C&A, the Dutch department store for low-cost clothes and things, has a branch at Nice Etoile.

REAL PEOPLE NEEDS

AMERICAN EXPRESS
11 Promenade des Anglais, Nice

Open only in season from May through September but open daily from 9am to 9pm.

FNAC
Centre Nice Etoile, 30 av. Jean Médecin, Nice
Right near the train station and on the main shopping street in the big mall in the center of downtown. A super store for books, CDs, computer needs, and so on. Open 10am to 7pm Monday to Saturday, closed Sunday.

PARASHOP
5 rue Masséna, Nice

New modern chain of parapharmacies with most brands in a clean, well-lighted open space that's easy to use. Fidelty card available.

INTERMARCHÉ
5 bd. Gambetta, Nice

This is a grocery store, a block from the Negresco, away from town (toward Cannes) but convenient if you are on foot. There's a much nicer supermarket (**Stoc**) near the Radisson SAS Hotel, but its not walking distance. Intermarché is fine for loading up on basics.

CORSICA

Right near the candy factory and the antiques shops in Nice is the ferry for Corsica. There are also other ferry ports in various French coastal towns, as going to Corsica is considered a treat by many locals.

It's my firm belief that there are Fire Island people and Hamptons people and Connecticut people, which may only make sense to you if you live in

New York and have had to pick a summer retreat. But I think you get the general idea. I relate this to Corsica because I know many, many Corsica people. They adore Corsica. Me? I don't get it.

This is possibly because you don't go to Corsica to shop, but hey, that's just my opinion. Because I've now been there several times and because your cruise ship just might come to port in Corsica, I'll give you a bit of the lowdown.

Why Corsica Was Invented

Simple:

- last chance for a French pharmacy.
- last chance for French mail system.
- last chance for French perfumes with detaxe.
- last chance to use French phone card.

Otherwise you have to consider that this is where Napoleon came from. It was good enough for him to leave for the City of Lights; it's good enough for you to leave if you have shopping in mind, although Corsica does have great beaches.

Foodies Delight

Foodies like local wines, cheeses, honey, and sausage.

Chapter Ten

· · · · · · ·

SHOPPING MONACO

MONTE CARLO

· ·

Monte Carlo is about glamour. In fact, Monte Carlo defines glamour.

Unlike Cannes, it has nothing real about it. The streets are clean and perfect. Not that Cannes isn't clean and perfect, but Cannes seems human, French, lived-in, *alive.* Monaco is pink and tight and laced up. You get a ticket for crossing in the middle of the street.

Sometimes I think that Alain Ducasse is the star of the town because, sure, he's a great chef, but he's also the most alive person in the city. Sometimes I think the reason Monte Carlo has such wonderful performers who visit and such great circus events is that they need to import the energy.

Once you get past the idea of what it's like to actually live there, you can decide to sit back and giggle and really have a ball. A Red Cross Ball or any other ball. Monte Carlo has tons of them, especially during the summer season. So kick off your pumps, loosen your black tie, let down your diamonds and let's eat and laugh and shop a little. No, let's eat a lot.

Don't forget, Monaco has a new world-class spa in the Hermitage Hotel (Thermes Marins de Monte Carlo), American-style bars and burgers (try Stars 'n Bars if you want to see Prince Albert up close and personal), and the yacht scene for all you sea gods and goddesses. There's also the car scene. If you've got a really good balcony and it's time for the Grand Prix, *ooh la la*, glamour is guaranteed. Along with a whole new set of friends.

Lots of cruise ships turn around in Monte Carlo, lots of passengers on cruise ships in other ports jump into rental cars just to see what it's all about. So what's it all about, Alfie?

It's about money, *bien sur.*

Monaco is what it is because there's no personal tax. The rich get richer and the old come to party before they die. Come to think of it, everyone comes to party. Everyone but me—I'm here to shop.

The Lay of the Land

Monte Carlo is perched on top of a cliff; the town is in levels that are connected by stairs. There are also more parts of Monaco than Monte Carlo; each area has its own name and its own shopping. The various neighborhoods make up the principality. Tourists will most likely stick to Monte Carlo but shouldn't—there is more to town than town.

There is no border to cross from France to Monaco, so it is hard to know when you are where. Note that before you enter Italy, you go back into France and then enter Italy. You'll know it when you're at the border to Italy; you won't when you're at the border of Monaco.

Getting There

You may arrive in Monte Carlo by train from Nice, Cannes, or elsewhere, or come through the Nice airport and arrive by taxi, bus, or helicopter. Two helicopter firms are **Héli-Air** (☎ 04-92-05-00-50) and **Heli-Inter** (☎ 04-93-21-46-46). The helicopter arrives in the Fontvielle district of Monaco, right near McDonald's; the flight from the Nice airport is all of 6 minutes. Round-trip airfare is 722 F ($120) on Heli-Inter.

Crossing the Border: Ventimille with Pascale-Agnes

Getting there was a nightmare. We took the motorway, but we spent a lot of time at the border. There is no border control, but there were so many cars that it takes a long time to pass by. Once you arrive in Ventimiglia, it's hard to find a space to park. If you come from France, it's better to take the train.

This border between France and Italy is not under the Schengen Convention laws, so you still must cross the border formally as you return to France. As for fake merchandise, they are cracking down. Americans may be in a better position than the French, but authorities are trying to break up the business in fakes in France.

In the market, however, there are plenty of fakes and they are out in the open. I noticed that it's easier than ever to find them, especially Vuitton. Bags are well displayed, and you can choose in better conditions than behind a door or under a cloak. The same goes for Chanel and Gucci. Aside from these items, there is nothing interesting in this market. We found prices on many things the same in Cannes and the Thursday market in Antibes far better for prices and fun.

If you don't want to come back with empty hands but are too scared to buy fakes, try the Provençal-style seat covers: $7 for a set of four or $13 for the thicker ones.

Should you be staying in Italy or onboard a cruise ship, and are not worried about the French border, here are some basic prices for fakes: Chanel classic style purse, between $80 and $100; Vuitton, Epi style, between $70 and $80; Vuitton documents holder, $100.

Many arrive, or depart, by yacht.

If you come by train, note that the train station is in the real-people part of downtown Monte Carlo. You will want to taxi from there to the heart of town. I take my taxi to the Hôtel de Paris, which is in the center of the action.

A new train station is being built; there will also be a subway system, so that you can park your car at the edge of town and commute by subway to various pedestrian zones. Car traffic will be restricted to local plates. Did I mention that life in Monte Carlo is restricted?

The train ride from Nice takes about a half hour; it takes an hour from Cannes. A first-class ticket from Cannes to Monte Carlo costs about 65 F ($12). There is no reason in the world to travel first class; second class is fine. Both classes of service are air-conditioned in summer.

Trains to Monte Carlo may be marked Ventimiglia instead of Monaco: Ask!

If you are a Sea Goddess, a Silver Sea passenger, or you are meeting up with your yacht, the port is below most of Monaco, and you have a lot of stairs to climb or a taxi to take. If you are taken directly to the boat from the Nice airport and want to poke around town, flag a taxi and head for Hotel de Paris.

Indeed, my Monte Carlo begins and ends at the Hôtel de Paris.

Phoning There

Since you may want to call Monaco for hotel information, you should know that they changed the phone systems in France and Monaco a few years back. Monaco got its own area code (377), which you use as you would any other international country code. If you are calling from France, dial 00 for an international line, then 377 and then the Monaco phone number.

Bargains in Monaco

Okay, so there aren't a lot of them. However, for $45 a year you can join Le Club Diamant Rouge de Monaco and get a quarterly newsletter and a very cute little credit card–like object that entitles you to free drinks at participating hotels and restaurants, upgrades, and additional values and perks. To get yours, call the **Monaco Government Tourist Office** at ☎ 800/753-9696.

Sleeping in Monte Carlo

The **Société des Bains de Mer (SBM),** which essentially runs Monaco in terms of hotels and casinos and everything that's chic, has a series of hotels in the heart of town, carefully chosen in different styles and different price ranges. There are four types of hotels and three different seasons, and prices vary accordingly. In the United States, call ☎ 800/221-4708. If you think any SBM product has to be deluxe beyond words and expensive beyond belief, you are only half right. It's all very fancy, but out-of-season prices can begin at $210 per night; packages usually require a minimum 2-night stay.

SBM is not the only game in town: There's a terrific Loew's as well as Le Meridien Beach Plaza, both of which are incredibly reasonable; rooms in the $245 to $250 per night range!

Hôtel de Paris
Place du Casino, Monte Carlo

The Hôtel de Paris is SBM's most expensive property; it goes for $390 per night in a promotional deal and more in season or if you are Harry Connick Jr. The hotel was built in 1864. It is grand like there ain't no tomorrow, and it is Alain Ducasse's home. For U.S. reservations, call **Leading Hotels of the World** at ☎ 800/221-4708. The local phone is 377-92-18-30-00; fax 377-93-25-59-17.

Loew's Monte Carlo
12 av. des Spélugues, Monte Carlo

This is the American-style cousin to all of the up-the-hill rococo. This hotel is down a mountain of stairs and closer to the water and is not an SBM property. Because it is below the town, it costs less—rates begin around $200 out of season. Rates vary with the season and the package. For U.S. reservations, call ☎ 800/23-LOEWS. The local phone is 377-93-50-65-00; fax 377-93-30-01-57.

Dining in Monte Carlo

Café de Paris
Place du Casino, Monte Carlo

Not to be confused with the Hôtel de Paris, this cafe has an outdoor and an indoor part. The outdoor part is the chic part. This is where you sit all day to see and be seen. You can eat a meal or simply have coffee. They even sell postcards, so you can sit, sip, soak up the atmosphere, and smile while you scribble. Reservations are not required, and a proper tip will probably get you where you want to sit, but you can try calling ahead if you want (☎ **377-92-16-25-54**).

Louis XV
Hôtel de Paris, Place du Casino, Monte Carlo

Perhaps Monte Carlo was always a good place to eat; I only know that these days, the name Alain Ducasse and the name Monte Carlo are synonymous with glamour. One does not come to Monaco without at least considering a meal at the world-famous, Michelin three-star dining room Louis XV.

I had read so much and heard so much and nervously tittered so much about Alain Ducasse and the legendary Louis XV that I don't think this can be assessed as a meal: It's a myth, a legend, an experience, a part of what Monte Carlo is. I really didn't even like Monte Carlo that much until I met Alain Ducasse. I now worship here not because he's famous or because the food was so good (both simple facts), but because this man is one of the few people in the world who can combine drop-dead elegance with salt-of-the-earth down home. That is the secret to his cooking, his presentation, and his heart.

I'm not even going to talk about the food since of course it was spectacular. Instead, I'll pass on a few consumer tips that I learned along the way. Okay, I learned them from Alain Ducasse himself.

- Lunch reservations are far easier to come by than dinner reservations.
- Dinner reservations should be made in advance, possibly months in advance for summer reservations. The dining room only has 50 tables. I met one couple that always makes a reservation for four, figuring that they can always go down to two but that they'll never get space for another couple should they meet someone interesting.
- Make your advance reservations by fax. If you are up to it, write a personal note to M. Ducasse telling him why you've chosen to dine there, what you're looking forward to, what you like. You can even mention that this suggestion comes from me. The point here—reach out and touch. His English is so-so; a note in French would be brilliant. He doesn't come to the table or do anything in public, but reach out to him and it will make a difference.
- Look at the menu because it's fun to look, but don't order from the menu. Do note that the ladies' menu has no prices. Remember that letter I asked you to write ahead of time? Now comes the payoff. M. Ducasse has a phenomenal memory and a very good secretary.
- Tell the maître d' that you have written ahead and that you leave the menu up to the master. Make sure you have learned the difference between a menu and a carte (see chapter 5). Use

the word *menu*. This is going to save you a lot of money.

- Specify if there are any foods you don't like or can't eat.
- Let the chef and the sommelier choose the wines for the meal.
- Do not ask if you can have the menu as a souvenir. You will be brought two menus as you leave; one is the formal menu you just looked at and one is a miniature version, done by laser printer while you were eating, that lists your personal menu for that particular meal. God is in the details.
- The complete menu is about 850 F ($142) per person; with wine, expect to pay about $500 for the event. That doesn't count what you wear to the event. What starts out as a simple little $500 lunch could cost thousands if you get carried away with your attire.
- That little stool next to one of the chairs? It's for Madame's handbag.
- Leave a 100 F note ($17) under Monsieur's plate. Service is included, but this is just a little something extra to make the evening perfect from everyone's point of view.

PRINCES TEA ROOM
26 av. de la Costa, Monte Carlo

This is my own little find that is the perfect place for the tourist who wants to nibble at the veneer of the glamour but won't waste the money on the big-time silliness. This combination tea room, pastry shop, and candy store has just a few tables where you can grab a bite to eat and feel like Eloise at the Plaza Hotel. It's 1 block from the Place du Casino in the heart of town.

REPLAY CAFÉ
57 rue Grimaldi, Monte Carlo

Replay is a huge part of the scene because it is owned by Princess Stephanie, who is often seen here, so everyone who wants to say they saw a real live princess likes to grab a coffee here and try to get lucky. Light meals or snacks; American style.

Spa Day in Monte Carlo

So it came to pass that Prince Rainer got tired of going out of town to the spa (he favored la Baule and the works of Dr. Yves Treguer). So, Le Prince decided to build one of his own and bring over the good doctor. *Voilà!*

Les Thermes de Monte Carlo, nestled between the Hôtel de Paris and the Hôtel Hermitage—two SBM properties—is the last word in thalassotherapie; there are even private cabanas for the royals and would-bes. And do check out the tile work in the steam bath.

I was hoping that they would sell their own line of products, but they didn't have any when I visited. Stay tuned.

Treatments can be booked individually with a day program or with a total spa package. There is an entire tariff booklet, because prices vary depending on how often you book. The more treatments you have, the less they cost. There are also weekend and multiday spa cure packages. My favorite is the Sejour Anti-Stress. I'm not sure what it is, but I know I need it.

In terms of à la carte prices, it's not too outrageous in the water of the Grimaldis. An algae bath (seaweed) costs 190 F ($32). An application of seaweed costs 200 F ($33). These are more or less the standard rates for all spas and cruise ships. Massages begin at 170 F ($28).

Fax your reservations to **377-92-16-49-49.**

Shopping Monte Carlo

While Monte Carlo has some beautiful shops, you do not go to Monte Carlo to shop. Please, I beg you, don't think of this as a shopping destination. You may well do some shopping, but go for the whole of the experience and let shopping be only a portion of your time here. Maybe you should shop for a bigger size, because after a few meals with M. Ducasse, you may need it.

I mean, let's face it: There's neither a Monoprix nor a Prisunic in downtown Monte Carlo. Maybe that's the way they want it to be. For me, without a little variation in the shopping scheme, it can get boring fast. Just how many Chanel suits can you wear at one time, anyway?

But wait. I'm hyperventilating. There is a branch of **Carrefour,** the hypermarché, in Fontvieille. We have to allow that to count for something. It's part of a mall with 38 other shops and a branch of McDonald's, so Monaco is not without its own vulgarities. Carrefour happens to be great fun.

The mall in downtown Monte Carlo does have **FNAC** and quite a few other shops worth browsing, even if some of them are American big names.

It's not all Harel, Harel and the having to know who in the Harel that Harel is (a very, very exclusive shoe maker).

As for me, I'm so in love with Alain Ducasse that I'm ready to move to Monaco. Put me in a chaise longue at Les Thermes Marins de Monte Carlo, let me stare out to sea or thalaso my therapie, and I am yours. I cannot complain about all those 25 F ($5) gants de toilette that I scarfed up at Porthault, right there in beautiful downtown Monte Carlo. There is even a real flea market at the edge of town. Come to think about it, I just can't grouse at all.

The heart of the shopping—and yes, most of the shopping in Monte Carlo is drop-dead fancy—is downtown, around the casino and the Hôtel de Paris. You can walk just about everywhere you need to go, unless you need to be trailed by your car and driver so you don't have to carry any packages with you.

- The fanciest stores (the designer freestanding shops like Chanel) are on the avenue Beaux Arts and the two allées that run alongside it, right near the Hôtel de Paris.

- On the underside of the Hôtel de Paris, closer to the water but on the curving avenue de Monte Carlo, is another strip of more designer shops, such as Lalique.

- There's a real live American-style mall in the Hôtel Métropole, called Le Métropole. It's across the street from the Hôtel de Paris on avenue des Spélugues and avenue de la Madone. It has more than 100 boutiques, many of them recognizable names and French multiples. This is where you can find **Genevieve Lethu** (who does great tabletop), some bed and sheet designers (not Porthault but Yves Delorme will do, *merci bien*), and some almost normal French stores.

- Park Palace is one of the smaller malls. It's on the avenue de la Costa and houses a few big-name European designer shops and some local big names of moderate interest. Of course, we are talking $1,000 handbags at **Delvraux,** but it is Monaco. And some only cost $820.

- The avenue de la Costa is the main shopping thoroughfare. Easing away from the casino, it even gets a little real. You'll find a pharmacy, a hairdresser, and my little Porthault shop, home of the big bargain, where I was able to buy *gants de toilette*—French style washcloths—for a mere 25 F ($4.20) each. The avenue de la Costa becomes the boulevard des Moulins in the heart of town, right where the tourist office is located.

- There are a few shops in Loew's Hotel, which is located beneath downtown. Take the stairs along the cliff.

- There are gift shops in most of the museums. However, I feel compelled to tell you that I clipped an article from *Condé Nast Traveler* that contained a major complaint about a watch bought at the gift shop of the Musée Océanographique and the difficulty in exchanging it or getting credit.

Shopping Hours

Most stores in Monte Carlo are open from 9am to noon, and from 2 to 7pm, Monday through Saturday. Almost everything is closed tight on Sunday.

Finds

Louis Sciolla
Boulevard des Moulins, Monte Carlo

This is a very snazzy, sort of BCBG man (preppy) meets the yachting crowd look that is ever so internationally chic for George Hamilton wannabes.

Manufacture de Monaco
Le Metropole, Monte Carlo

Cute tabletop and design shop in the mall. The store seems average and just nice until you realize that everything they sell is a copy of something from Monte Carlo, be it a museum or a royal home. There are two designs in exclusive china and dinnerware. Sort of a chic museum store. Wake me when they sell a copy of Alain Ducasse.

Massimo Rebecchi
Alleé Lumieres, Monte Carlo

Chic, chic. We are talking chic and fun and funky designer clothing that is a tad over the top, but why not? I mean, this is Monte Carlo, isn't it?

Monaco Resources

Antiques

Monte Carlo is the home of many antiques. Chuckle, chuckle. Seriously, folks, the Biennale International des Antiquaires, Joaillers & Galeries d'Art, held every other year in odd years for about 3 weeks at the end of July and through the first 2 weeks of August, is a major, major show. It is held at the Sporting Club, Place du Casino, and it is the kind of shopping venue that Marie Antoinette would enjoy. In fact, she'd probably feel right at home.

The important antiques sold at this event are most often of museum quality and offer one of the few opportunities for people to see and touch this kind of workmanship. Consider it a museum where you can touch and ask questions. We are talking about sweet nothings that cost $60,000. But then, there are clocks for $600,000. It's all a matter of perspective. Remember, value-added tax (VAT) is now added to antiques as well, so if you spend over 1,200 F ($200) (which shouldn't be too hard), be sure to apply for the détaxe refund.

Although I find expensive antiques boring and intimidating, some 30,000 people don't seem to mind. This is a major event, planned to be part of the summer season. Don't forget to wear your best tan. Dealers will give tickets to their favored clients; otherwise you can buy at the door, about $10 per person.

Note that the hours are unusual and vary with the days of the week. For the most part, this is an afternoon affair, from 4 to 9pm. For more information, write c/o 2A bd. des Moulins, MC 98000, Monaco.

If you don't care for hoity or toity, you may be pleased to know they have a Foire la Brocante every Saturday at the Fontvieille port. It is a casual little thing and not at all intimidating. I never would have found it on my own, but there it was, spilling onto a few steps, surrounded by yachts headed away from Monte Carlo on their way to Nice. Hours are 9:30am to 6pm, year-round.

There are a few antique shops here and there in the heart of Monte Carlo. Every time I look at them I simply think, "You've got to be kidding."

What to Wear to the Louis XV

There are rather simple rules, so don't panic. For dinner, especially Saturday night in season, women cannot get too dressed up. Men do not wear black tie, but a dark suit is appropriate. Jewelry is good, especially for women. Real jewelry is better.

Lunch is a completely different story. I had planned to wear a red and white striped silk halter dress, since it was August. My darling Barbara Cady, who is the chicest woman in America and is married to a Frenchman, had a fit when I told her what I had chosen. Only Americans wear red, she announced. No, she was quite firm, the day dress would not do.

I was to wear the perfect summer suit, preferably Chanel, in a pale color with short sleeves and a very short skirt. Then, I was to wear very high heels, no stockings, and "important jewelry."

We finally compromised on a beige linen Calvin Klein suit, a beige Kelly bag (faux), a beige silk flower (pas de important jewelry), pale stockings, and Chanel-style black toe beige pumps. And tortoise Ray-Bans.

I felt very comfortable in the hotel, with Alain, and at lunch. But the whole psycho-drama over to what to wear became a joke when I looked around the room. At one table was a group of five Japanese women, each wearing a kimono sashed with a Western-style belt, no obi! At another table, two tourists sat in T-shirts and madras Bermuda shorts. At another table, two businessmen were eating in short-sleeve dress shirts with contrasting neckties.

What do you wear for lunch? Anything you want.

The auction season is another hot ticket. It begins in the fall, as elsewhere; there's a second round in April and May. Both Sotheby's and Christie's have local offices.

The Big Names

BULGARI
Avenue des Beaux Arts, Monte Carlo

CARTIER
Avenue des Beaux Arts, Monte Carlo

CÉLINE
Avenue des Beaux Arts, Monte Carlo

CHANEL
Place du Casino (Allée Serge de Diaghilev), Monte Carlo

CHARLES JOURDAN
Boulevard des Moulins, Monte Carlo

CHRISTIAN DIOR
Avenue des Beaux Arts, Monte Carlo

DELVAUX
Park Palace, 29 av. de la Costa, Monte Carlo

ESCADA
Park Palace, 29 av. de la Costa, Monte Carlo

GENEVIEVE LETHU
Le Metropole, Monte Carlo

GIVENCHY
Avenue des Beaux Arts, Monte Carlo

HANAE MORI
Allée Serge Diaghilev, Monte Carlo

HAREL
Galerie du Sporting, Monte Carlo

HERMÈS
Avenue de Monte Carlo, Monte Carlo

JACQUES FATH
Avenue des Beaux Arts, Monte Carlo

LALIQUE
Avenue de Monte Carlo, Monte Carlo

LANVIN
Allée Serge de Diaghilev, Monte Carlo

LOUIS VUITTON
Avenue des Beaux Arts, Monte Carlo

PORTHAULT
26 av. de la Costa, Monte Carlo

PUIFORCAT
2 av. des Spélugues, Monte Carlo

YVES SAINT LAURENT
Avenue des Beaux Arts, Monte Carlo

VALENTINO
Avenue Monte Carlo, Monte Carlo

VAN CLEEF & ARPELS
Place du Casino, Monte Carlo

FOODSTUFF

CHOCOLATERIE DE MONACO
Café de Paris, Place du Casino, Monte Carlo

COMTESSE DU BARRY
Le Metropole, Monte Carlo

HEDIARD
Le Metropole, Monte Carlo

MAISON DU CAVIAR
1 av. Saint Charles, Monte Carlo

Chapter Eleven

. . . .

SHOPPING SAINT-TROPEZ

Hang on to your bathing suit top and welcome to Saint-Tropez, which got its reputation as the tony beach of the rich and famous in the early 1950s. St. Trop is the opposite direction down the beach from Monaco.

Monaco is where you wear everything you own, probably with diamonds and high heels at the same time. Saint-Tropez is where you wear very little at all. Except maybe a diamond in your belly button.

St. Trop now attracts so many tourists that the number-one sport here has to be staring at all those people and what they think passes as fashion. Okay, let me concede the point; maybe the number-one sport is looking at the topless women and wondering why the ladies who should least go without a top are always the ones who are topless. But I digress. Welcome to St. Trop, as we say, a nice little pun since *trop* means "too much" in French.

This is the village where being a little bit more outrageous than the next guy is part of your fashion statement, and where trends are set and reset with the changes in the tide. Think of it as Laurel Canyon with a beach.

There is an edge of country charm to St. Trop that doesn't exist in a lot of other famous hangouts. It is not an authentic cute, but it's not bad at all. Saint-Tropez isn't particularly Provençal—although there are Provençal-style shopping opportunities—but as soon as you step away from the beach and are into the hills, as nearby as Gassin and Cogolin, well then, suddenly you are in Provence.

If you're looking for more than a superficial thrill, head for the hills. If you want to get away from the parade, all you need do is head off on your own. First, get away from the port and those expensive cafes: Work your way through the winding warren of medieval streets in the Old Town, and then wander into the cute parts of the city flats. Venture even farther to the edges of town, where locals shop at the *hypermarché* and tourists rarely dare to go.

Real Francophiles will want to go to the hypermarché, *mais oui,* but they will crave much more. That's because Saint-Tropez is in Var, and Var really does reach into Provence. The area surrounding Saint-Tropez represents some of the best of the real France. Salernes, did someone say tile factories? Lorgues? You want a real market? You want to eat? And for heaven's sake, can we head for Gassin now?

Don't forget that once you've gotten yourself to Salernes, you're halfway to Moustier-Ste-Marie, which is the home of the tiny inn owned by superchef Alain Ducasse, where you eat, sleep, and make menu. By the time you get there, you are also in a very particular corner of Provence, a tad off the beaten track for American tourists (see chapter 12).

But I don't want to push too hard on the Provence button; there are plenty of people who will do Saint-Tropez as a day trip from Cannes—the contrast between the two is worth experiencing, especially during the film festival. Saint-Tropez is a place unto itself, a different state of mind. There are Cannes people and there are Saint-Tropez people, sort of like Martha's vineyard and Nantucket, *n'cest pas?*

If Saint-Tropez is your hub city, all of these thoughts become day trips or a weekend away. Indeed, if you've never heard of these little towns, welcome to the real Saint-Tropez. Welcome to a town that has everything because beyond the beach there's more.

GETTING THERE

. . . .

It ain't easy to get to Saint-Tropez—and therein lies its fame. For a place to be a genuine haven for the rich and famous, it has to be inaccessible to mere mortals and only easy to get to by those with the ways and means to be the right kind of people.

Therefore, the best way to get to Saint-Tropez is by yacht. If not your own yacht, someone else's yacht. Or the Sea Goddess' or any of the small but luxurious cruise ships that can come to port here.

You can drive, which is perfect if it's not summer. Saint-Tropez is only about 1½ hour's drive from the Nice–Côte d'Azur International Airport (NCE). But in summer, the drive can take 4 hours. *Mais oui!* (The traffic is *mere merde!*)

You can take a helicopter from the airport or between towns; there is service between Cannes and Saint-Tropez. If you don't mind regional airports, you can fly right into Toulon, which has service by AOM, Air Liberte, and so on. Should you be traveling from Paris, there are about five flights a day directly to Toulon from Orly Sud, and almost a dozen flights a day to Nice from Orly Sud, and more from CDG.

There is also summer ferry service between Cannes and Saint-Tropez, but it's not a reliable form of transportation because it only runs if the sea is calm. Also, the times of the service are meant for day trippers, not commuters, so you may not find this very useful. There is similar shuttle service by boat between St. Raphael and Nice, for those using the Nice–Côte d'Azur airport.

For more direct airport service, there is a bus from the Nice–Côte d'Azur airport to San Raphael, called Aviabus, which you catch right in front of the airport, easy as *gâteau*.

This forces us to discuss the train. Hang onto your chapeau, because there is no train track along the Riviera that connects to Saint-Tropez. This is the meaning of exclusive. The train ends in Saint Raphael, which isn't enormously far away, but it's not within walking distance. In summer, when the traffic makes the road as slow moving as cold honey, you'll lose your mind trying to connect on the bus. Furthermore, the bus station is next door to the train station, and if you have a small tote bag you can easily connect. If you have luggage, however, it could be problematic—made worse by the fact that frequently the connect time between bus and train is a mere 5 minutes.

Oh yes, another thing about the train: Schedules change with the seasons.

Your hotel may not give you the right train schedule! Since this happened to me, it can happen to you. I needed to get from Saint-Tropez to Cannes and the Nice airport. I had my usual load of luggage and actually made a deal with a taxi driver, sort of impromptu style. My hotel in Saint-Tropez quoted me an outrageous price for a taxi to Cannes (1,100 F, almost $200). Instead, I decided I needed the taxi to St. Raphael (400 F/$67) so I'd be at the train station since I thought I'd have a nervous breakdown with a 7-minute connection. Once I was in the taxi, the driver volunteered to take me to Cannes for another 100 F ($17); I was in a luxurious Mercedes Benz and happy as a clam. In a word: Investigate. My guy: **Taxi Robert,** home phone ☎ **04-94-96-31-10;** mobile phone ☎ 06-09-62-67-29.

Also ask your hotel if they have a driver and a hotel van that can be hired to get you to the airport or wherever you need to go.

GETTING AROUND
. . . .

In town, walk. For the real soul of the area, you do need a car, and several days. Hotels on the edge of town have shuttle service to town. Some people like to rent scooters for getting around, but not me.

SLEEPING IN SAINT-TROPEZ

. . . .

HÔTEL BYBLOS
Avenue Paul Signac, Saint-Tropez

Right in the heart of town, this hotel takes up a city block in a sprawl of up and down and layers and levels—with a swimming pool at the core. There are several shops here. There's also a nightclub that is the chicest place to boogie in town. There's no admission charge, but drinks are very, very *chèr.* Hotel rates begin at an affordable $250. For U.S. reservations, call **Leading Hotels of the World** at ☎ 800/223-6800. The local phone is ☎ 04-94-97-00-04; fax 04-94-97-40-52.

HÔTEL CHÂTEAU DE LA MESSADIERE
Route de Tahiti, Saint-Tropez

This is my latest discovery, a triumph of luxury, intimacy, and privacy. Although it is not in town, there is shuttle service to town if you don't have a car. The hotel is above town and therefore gives you rest and respite in an incredibly glamorous surrounding. It is the last hotel visited by Princess Diana before she died. Even if you can't stay here, I suggest a visit to have a look see and a lunch; or spend a day in one of the cooking classes.

The hotel does have some unusual shopping opportunities. It has a very chic little gift shop on the premises, and they sell the artwork off the walls of the restaurant—work by Victoire de la Messadiere, which I bought in poster form since I could not afford the originals. There's also shopping down at the beach, a local *trendlet.*

Room rates are available at different deals depending on the time of year and whether or not you buy a package; in season, the hotel is half the price of Byblos, or about $200-something per night.

There are dollar rates as well; call Concorde at
☎ 800-888-4747 in the United States. One of the
hotel's most interesting deals is the "Holiday at Saint-
Tropez" package, which includes an airline ticket
from any number of French cities (including Paris),
car hire, hotel, lunch, and assorted other goodies.
U.S. bookings can be made directly with Concorde
Hotels or through Leading Hotels of the World. The
local phone is ☎ 04-94-56-76-00; fax: 04-94-56-
76-01.

HÔTEL DE LA PONCHE
3 rue des Remparts, Saint-Tropez

If you're looking for the charming little four-star—
not the deluxe luxury required by a princess—you
may want to consider this in-town beauty right in
the heart of the old town and meters away from
many of the best stores. There are only 18 rooms;
prices range from $150 to $300, certainly less than
the fancier hotels. Romy Schneider is a regular and
the bathroom amenities come from Roger & Gallet:
What more could you want? The local phone is
☎ 04-94-97-02-53; fax: 04-94-97-78-61.

RESIDENCE DE LA PINEDE
Plage de la Bouillabaisse, Saint-Tropez

If you're as devoted to the Relais & Châteaux members as I am, you'll want to note this local find—
only 37 rooms and five suites. This hotel is directly
on the beach (which the others are not) but slightly
out of town. The local phone is ☎ 04-94-55-91-00;
fax 04-94-97-73-64.

SNACK & SHOP/SAINT-TROPEZ
. . . .

Okay, so it's hard to have a bad meal anyplace in
France, and you aren't exactly looking to me for
restaurant suggestions. But wait! Saint-Tropez happens to be a great little area for buying gourmet foodstuff, snacks, and edible gifts.

One of the most famous shops in town happens to be a bakery, Patissier Senequier, quai Jean-Jaures, behind a cafe of the same name. This is the most famous cafe in town for hanging out, seeing, and being seen.

One of the reasons people like to drive around the nearby suburbs and hill towns is to stop at farms, shops, wineries, and markets to buy locally made honey, wine, and other yummies.

Around the corner from Patissier Senequier is Carmen et Dominique, Epicurie du March (7 place aux Herbes); here you can buy fresh local cheeses and other goodies for the perfect snack or picnic.

Also note that the surrounding hills are dotted with wineries where you can pop in for a free tasting. I've always had my doubts about just how many of these places you can take (and still be sober enough to drive), and whether or not the quality of the local wine was worth my time and trouble. I was driving around said hills with American cooking expert Patricia Wells once, and our guide asked if she wanted to stop at any of these wineries. *"Non,"* she smiled sweetly. I take that as the definitive answer.

THE SHOPPING SCENE

Let's face it: You don't come to Saint-Tropez just to shop. And it's not a place people go to be seen in their clothes—the converse is true. But, hey, while you're here, you might as well browse. You'll do your big-name, big-time shopping in Cannes, or even Aix. Saint-Tropez is for funky little shops, for boutiques filled with specialty resort wares, and for home-style méditerranée.

Don't get me wrong, there is a very good, big parfumerie in town (**Parfumerie Berton**, 19 quai Suffren) and there are a handful of designer shops, but that's not really the shopping action in

Saint-Tropez. Sure, there's everything from Hermés to Sonia Rykiel, with Soulieado as well. But the fun is not in the nationally known brands.

Shopping the Beach

Saint-Tropez is very much about the beach—especially two famous beaches, Pampelonne and Tahiti, with their clubs and places to hang out. It's common practice to have your own beach for your crowd, and to only go to that beach. Of course you also have your own café or club there where you eat. After you order your lunch, you pop up and shop at the beach shacks, which sell outrageous bathing suits and wraps and beachy things.

Big Brands

AGATHA
Rue Allard

ALAIN MANOUKIAN
Rue Georges Clemenceau Benetton

Rue Allard

BLANC BLEU
Place de la Garonne

CARTIER
Passage du Port

CERUTTI 1881
Rue de la Ponche

DIEGO DELLA VALLE
Passage du Port

GIANNI VERSACE
Passage du Port

GUCCI (AT LILLY)
Place des Lices

HERMÈS
Rue de la Ponche

LACOSTE
Rue Allard

MANRICO
Place des Lices

PRADA (AT LILLY)
Place des Lices

SONIA RYKIEL
Place des Lices

SOULIEADO
Rue Allard

SAINT-TROPEZ STYLE

In Saint-Tropez, the flavor-of-the-month boutiques in the old town offer the best browse. They change almost every season as hopefuls set up shop on a bikini string and a franc with hopes of becoming rich and famous. Or merely rich. Some of these shops are no bigger than your closet. They are located on the little streets that curve around in the village's ancient center, next to the port.

Because of its location on the sea side of Provence, Saint-Tropez is one of the better areas to buy Provençal-style merchandise and items for the home. There is a small Souleiado in town, at the edge of the main shopping area, near the post office.

There are other brands of cotton print fabrics besides Souleiado available—some famous (Les Olivades), some unknown. The look and feel are similar, but a sharp eye will soon discern each maker and his or her special traits. Fabric is also sold in the market. I buy mine there for 40 F ($6.50) per meter.

While you can indeed buy Provençal-type merchandise in Cannes, Saint-Tropez is a better location for a better selection of items that comprise "the look." The look, in terms of home design, includes cotton Provençal copycat prints, and also includes tiles, pottery (glazed and unglazed), wicker, wrought iron, and plenty of wooden items, preferably rough hewn.

What Saint-Tropez lacks in big-name designer clothing shops, it more than makes up for with home style and tabletop design showcases. And market day? Wait till you go to the market in the place des Lices.

Shopping Style

Saint-Tropez is devoted to looking cute. The stores are organized along that theme. It's faux cute, but if you've never been here before and you don't know any better, you will love it.

Even I can be seduced by this kind of cute.

Many stores are located in small malls and passages. While there are many big-name shops, they are not in a row on one high street.

There are a large number of different shopping neighborhoods in a small area, which leads you to constant surprise that there's more to Saint-Tropez than you imagined. And I'm still talking about the city center.

There is also a big business in locally owned stores that carry French fashion icons that you may not be that familiar with. Most of the stores carry French brands, but there are also some Italian and even English lines. Patrick Cox's Wannabe line of shoes is very hot in Saint-Tropez, as is Diego Della Valle's JPTods collection. Must be those pink driving shoes that are sooooo Brigitte Bardot.

Shopping Hours

Stores usually open around 10am and close at 12:30pm for lunch. They reopen at 2:30pm or later, maybe 3pm, depending on the type of store and the season. They stay open until 7pm out of season and 9pm in season. Real-people stores tend to open at 9am.

Most stores close for the midday break, although a few tourist traps (TTs) stay open nonstop. The pharmacy is open during lunch.

The season is July and August, and some of the stores close when the season is over. Of those that close after the season, about half will not return the next year.

Saturday and Sunday are both big days for retail; this is one of the few towns in the Riviera where the stores are wide open on Sunday. *Bon dimanche.*

Market days are Saturday and Tuesday, making Saturday the biggest, and most congested, retail day in town. On summer Sundays, there is also market at Petit Village. Petit Village is open daily but has a farmer's market only on Sunday in season.

Markets & Fairs

Every day is market day someplace in the area. Some markets just happen to be better than others. How good a market you get depends on luck and wheels. If you want a real French market, you had better get out of town—although the Saint-Tropez market is a marvelous affair, almost theatrical in character. Saint-Tropez market is what Central Casting would put up on the back lot if called to bring on the *marché.*

This is sort of a hippy, dippy market; it does not feel like France to me, but it's busy and energetic and filled with a wide selection of wares and even has *brocante* in the rear, although no bargains, believe me. It's a good start, and it's not one of those things merely set up to fleece tourists. It's a genuine market: Buy everything from local products, fabrics, and spices to foodstuff and baskets.

If you aren't a shopper, grab a coffee at the Café Des Arts on the place and watch the parade.

There are two market days in Saint-Tropez: Tuesday and Saturday. Market is better in the summer, but it's also more crowded with tourists.

Many of the vendors seen in Saint-Tropez rotate from town to town, and, of course, locals know them and their merchandise and go on at great length. Without the local crowd, the market would be totally bad Disney. As it is, it's small time, but if you keep low expectations, you'll find it charming.

Unfortunately, some of the locals who show on Saturday don't come back on Tuesday. *Dommage.* My fabric vendor sells in Lorgues on Tuesday and in Saint-Tropez on Saturday. This is the guy I've been buying faux Pierre Deux from for many years. On Wednesday, you want Cogolin; Thursday, it's Les Arcs; Friday, Cuers; and Sunday, Le Muy.

Brocante is sold in the Place des Lices market in Saint-Tropez, as well as in all the markets. For information on specific events or brocante fairs, you can contact **l'Union des Brocanteurs du Var,** ☎ **04-94-59-56-13.** There is usually a printed schedule available for each season.

For example, on every fourth Sunday from May through August, there is a brocante in Frejus-Ville. Also on Sunday, depending on the weekly cycle, there can be brocante markets in Brignoles and Les Arcs sur Argens. Once a month on a Thursday, there's a market in Hyeres.

On Sunday in summer only, there is a farmer's market in the parking lot of Petit Village, La Foux, Gassin; the local phone ☎ **04-94-56-32-04.**

Special Events

There's also a September fete for regional costume that is very sweet; there are summer saints days that are big deals—namely St. Pierre and St. Anne. There are Christmas events during the entire month of December and, best of all, is the annual affair done by *Côte Sud* magazine to show off the entire lifestyle of the south of France.

SHOPPING NEIGHBORHOODS

· ·

The Port

Yes, the port is where the boats are and isn't actually the best of shopping neighborhoods. It's more a shipping neighborhood. But, as in most port towns, the main street facing the water is the high street.

In Saint-Tropez, the name of this street is quai Sufferen. It not only hosts the big perfume shop I told you about (Parfumerie Berton), but it also has a ton of artists' stands and stalls on the water side. There are also quite a few TTs selling T-shirts, sweats, sunglasses, and hats.

Old Town

If your back is to the quai Sufferen and you are facing the port, the right-hand side of the port U is called Quai Jean Juares. It is strung with famous cafes. Behind those cafes and to your right is the Old Town, identified by two landmark towers, Tour du Portalet and Tour Vielle.

Be sure to check out the tiny little arcade that is the fish market. Even though it smells, it's covered with tiles and fishy country charm.

The little street leading away from the Old Town is rue de la Ponche, which is where Hermés and all those fancy shops are found.

Gambetta: Main Street

The main shopping street in town in terms of regular retail is rue Gambetta, which leads away from the Old Town and out yonder toward Hotel Byblos. Check out **Galeries Tropeziennes,** no. 32, which has charming tabletop designs, household goods, gifts, and is on my list as one of the best stores in France.

Lots of natural fabrics and country looks that aren't full of hype.

Rue Gambetta is sort of a cross between a real-people street and a tourist street. There are a number of multiples here, and I also found a small grocery store, a toy store, and an ice cream shop in the area closest to theport. Gambetta moves out of town, and it becomes avenue Foch. Right around where the name changes you'll find a branch of Jardin En Plus, a French multiple for home design, and the Hôtel Byblos, which also has stores. Very good stores worth looking at. But wait, as Gambetta moves into the old port part of town, it changes its name to rue des Commercants.

You can also cut through some of the medieval maze by using Passage Gambetta, a mall, as your tunnel. Shop till you come out the other side.

La Citadelle

Two of the good shopping streets in town are at odd angles and aren't where you'd expect shopping streets to be, so watch for them. If the Old Town and the water are to your back, then the rue de la Citadelle is to your left and curves a bit, then straightens out.

Allard: Port & Center

If you stayed on Gambetta thinking it was the only main shopping street in town, you goofed. Rue Allard, which veers off from behind the quai Sufferen and to one side as it leads away from town, has its own share of high-rent retail. In fact, this is really the town's high street.

There's lots to see and buy here, much of it local with only a few big-name French multiples. This is where you'll find my pharmacy **Mouton,** which is where you can buy toys or beach supplies for the kids (sand pails, floats).

You'll also find ice cream cones and chocolate shops (such as **La Pause Douceur,** no. 11) and even a very good art supply store. The rue Allard becomes the rue Leclerc as you head out of town toward Saint Raphael.

Louis Blanc: Edge of Town

Farther from the madding crowd and therefore more used by locals, this street is packed with home furnishing and design studios. Don't miss **Fred Prysquel,** no. 34–36, for the rustic country look of your dreams; **Pierre Basset** for tiles (he supplies Alain Ducasse!); and **La Maison Marine,** no. 2, for tabletop designs.

Clemenceau: Cute & Center

This street is truly the heart of the cute retail in the center of town. It's sort of halfway between Gambetta and Allard—Gambetta runs parallel and Allard curves around to become almost parallel. Photo ops galore.

Les Olivades has a store here, no. 17. Rodini (no. 16) is one of the most famous makers of sandals in the local style and is considered an icon. The other big name for tropezienne sandals is K. Jacques. Failure to wear sandals from one of these two places immediately places you in jeopardy of being discovered as an American, and a tourist at that.

Rue Sibille: Side & Center

This is a little bit of a side street that's right off the place des Lices and runs all the way to the waterfront. It is one of the more chic addresses for locals in the know. Versace is located nearby. Claire L'Insolite (no. 1) is one of those boutiques that sells a mélange of big-name Italian designers, including Max Mara and Genny.

Finds

Blvd. Des Rues
Rue de la Ponche, Saint-Tropez

One of the most unusual shops I've found in France, this tiny boutique sells items made from street signs or can make up your name into a French-style street sign. Prices begin at 190 F ($32); a must-do.

JJK
24 rue George Clemenceau, Saint-Tropez

Delightful store for fun gift items. I think the owners are English (hence the name from their initials); cute mélange of gift items.

Kiwi
20 rue Gambetta, Saint-Tropez

A small boutique that sells resort wear and clothes that are simply perfect for the Riviera without being glitzy, gold lamé, covered in rhinestones, or tacky. Soft colors, some batik-washed styles, pleasant palm trees, and lush, plush soft drape and sarongs.

L'Occitane/Les Olivades
11 rue Clemenceau, Saint-Tropez

L'Occitane is a Provençal brand of soap, bath, and beauty products that is sensational. The products are sold all over France and in fancy stores in the United States. This particular boutique also carries Les Olivades, the Provençal line now sold at Pierre Deux shops in the United States.

Le Byblos
Hotel Byblos, Saint-Tropez

This is one of the best hotel logo shops I've ever encountered. It has classy merchandise that you would want to have that does not seem cheapened by the hotel logo. The little terry-cloth travel pouches are fabulous.

MAISON OTOU
9 rue des Commercants, Saint-Tropez

Actually I didn't find this one, my friends Ken and Foxy did. They bought beautiful tabletop in Provençal styles, but not cheap touristy stuff.

MOSAIQUE
4 rue Henri Seillon, Saint-Tropez

While you're wandering around looking at the silly tourists and their ice cream cones and tacky clothes, you can stumble into this shop and find sheer elegance, class, and perfect harmony in southern French mosaic charm.

PETIT VILLAGE
La Foux, Gassin

Located on the road right into town, this modern complex is a one-stop shopping mecca that shouldn't be missed. Basically this is a cooperative where wine from regional grossers is bottled and sold; there's also an outdoor farmer's market held on Sunday in summer, and there's a boutique selling regional products including foodstuff, soaps, and fabrics/gifts.

PHARMACIE MOUTON
9 rue Allard, Saint-Tropez

Yes, of course it's a regular pharmacy but they also have their own house line of products, which is unusual. I buy the house brand of bubble bath in assorted aromatherapy and natural scents. They cost 60 F each. I buy lavender, vanilla, and a woodsy pine scent. It's one of the best lavenders I've ever bathed in. Because the plastic bottle is imprinted with the name and address of the pharmacy, I consider this a fabulously seductive gift-cum-status symbol for 10 bucks.

THIERRY DERBEZ
Route D98, Gassin

Nearby in Gassin (but you need a car) is this farm-stand-cum-garden-cum-nursery-cum-real-people-gourmet, where you can load up with goodies for serious foodies.

VO
Avenue du 8 Mai 1945, Saint-Tropez

Just down the street from Souleiado, this showroom sells garden furniture and rustic charm that will enchant you, even if you can't bring home the garden and lawn set. There are also smaller accessories, gifts, and decorative items.

BEYOND SAINT-TROPEZ

Some of these neighborhoods are suburbs and others are halfway across the hills on the way to Aix. You'll note that a few of the addresses above are actually located in Gassin. Be sure to consult your map.

Gassin

Gassin is so close to Saint-Tropez that it's almost a suburb. Some people go just to look at the view. I go for the house of jams. Honest. Maison des Confitures, Route de Bourrian, carries more than 250 different varieties, from the regular to the unusual in terms of flavors and combinations. There are low sugar selections as well.

I don't want to ruin this for you by offering too much hype, but I can't think of a more perfect French experience in all of France than for you to spend a half hour in the stone cottage shop of the Confiture House. The names of the jams are in French, so you may need a dic-tionary. There are some unique combinations that will leave you drooling. I couldn't resist buy-ing "Chocolate & Cinnamon." They do little gift baskets for you and wrap in cellophane. Heaven.

Ramatuelle

Ramatuelle is that little medieval walled city fortress town not far from Saint-Tropez (just past Johnny Hallyday's house) where everything appears to be perfect. There's not really any serious shopping, but there are the usual tourist places selling pottery and printed fabrics. My fave is Poterie Provencal at the top of the town.

Grimaud

It's not that the village of Grimaud is the best shopping neighborhood outside of Saint-Tropez, I just happen to like it because it has a lot of soul. Everything about this village is what you want it to be—hills that overlook hills into the sea, crumbling this-and-that ruins, little farmhouses with flowering window boxes, curvy hill streets, and *charme, charme, charme.*

If you're looking for someplace for lunch, I suggest Hostellerie du Coteau Fleuri, a fantasy stone villa high on a hill just past town (Place de Pénitents). It's hidden behind flowering bushes and offers a wonderful lunch on the terrace. You probably won't need a reservation, but you can call or fax in case you're the type who likes to plan ahead. The local phone is ☎ **04-94-43-20-17;** fax 04-94-43-33-42.

While you're there, be sure to stop in at the pottery and tile factory, **Potterie des Trois Terres.** (Do learn this word in French: *carrelage*—it means tile.) They have baked earthenware goods as well as glazed and painted wares; they specialize in both tabletop and garden ware. One of the styles they do is a white glaze with a single color trim—the blue and white is the most sensational, but other colors are also available. Nothing is cheap here.

There's an outdoor part, an indoor part, and a workshop where you may be able to watch tiles being painted. There's a back wall with merchandise that has been marked down, but again, breakables pose a problem unless you are willing to ship or hand carry.

Port Grimaud

Not to be confused with Grimaud in any way; Port Grimaud is down and Grimaud is up, and that's how you must remember them. Grimaud is a hillside village; Port Grimaud is on the waterfront alongside Saint-Tropez and is a fake tourist town. It was created à la Disney as a French version of Venice. You tour by boat and pop out to shop. There are some stores, but it's not to-die-for magic because it's almost too perfect for words. Often included in shore excursions offered by cruise lines. Not on my hit parade.

Cogolin

Cogolin has a long main street (rue Carnot), a great Wednesday market, and an assortment of manufacturing oddities dotted around on nearby roads that make it fun to spend the day here. There's the famous pipe maker and a carpet tufting factory, which may sound like a yawn but is actually pretty neat—they make carpet for many design firms, including Souleiado (Les Tapis et Tissus de Cogolin et Maurice Lauer, boulevard Louis Blanc; ☎ 04-94-54-66-17).

The market in Cogolin is one of those dream-come-true country markets. It's not very big, but it's extremely authentic—tables set up to sell homemade foods, mounds of cubes of locally milled soap, bolts of Provençal-style cotton prints, old postcards sold from a shoe box, some brocante, honey in heavy glass jars.

Speaking of brocante, there is a tiny antique and junk shop that I like, Foire à la Brocante, on the route St. Maur just outside of town. It's not big, and there's not a lot to write home about, but it's fun and adds to the perfection of the day. In fact, there are a number of brocante shops on this road—you can just pick and choose all day long.

La Garde Freinet

Ever come upon a new village while you're out just tooling around in your rental car and suddenly feel, "This is it"? That's how I felt the first time I saw La Garde Freinet. It spoke to me as my perfect French village, the kind where you hope to retire someday.

The fact that it's filled with antique stores doesn't hurt. I always like to stop at La Maison de la Freinet for locally made foodstuff and souvenirs.

Lorgues

Actually we're going to Lorgues for two things: market day (Tuesday) and Bruno, where we will eat lunch. Bruno has one of the most celebrated tables in the south of France. If it's not market day, don't worry. Head for the road between Lorgues and Taradeau to visit Maison Vassal-Teisseie, where *Madame et Monsieur* spin their honey into nougat. Just drive 9 kilometers ($5^{1}/_{2}$ miles) southeast.

Salernes

The entire town is filled with tile factories. Among the most famous is the showroom of Pierre Basset, who has shops dotted wherever rich people hang out in the Riviera and can be found in Salernes in the Quartier des Arnaud. On the route de Draguigan, there's Maurice Amphoux, another local name. Nearby is La Forge de Saint-Romain, an ironmonger. Local craftsmen and studios are closed on Sunday but otherwise open usually from 8am until noon and then from 2pm until 6 or 6:30pm.

Chapter Twelve

· · · · · · · · ·

SHOPPING PROVENCE

WELCOME TO PROVENCE

· ·

So here we are in our rental cars zooming along the *autoroute*. Welcome to Provence, which begins above Cannes and drapes itself across mountains and fields of vines and lavender. Welcome to tiny villages of postcard perfection and to ring roads of confusion and congestion. Welcome to colors like ochre, washed turquoise, burnt umber, and geranium red. Welcome to a host of cities I know you'll want to explore, the purposeful exclusion of some famous cities (crummy shopping in Nîmes and Arles), and the basic knowledge that each time you return, you'll dig deeper into the real roots of Provence.

I recently found a house for sale in Crillon le Brave; I'm thinking about buying it, opening a store (Ma Chere Suzy), and settling in. I hope you'll join me. This is the life we all fantasize about.

Indeed, millions of people are dreaming that they will retire to an old stone house where they can fight with the plumber, share in the olive harvest, and make fun of the natives while downing pastis. If it's your dream too, dream on. Come fly with me.

The legends are all living here, whether they are actually alive, like superchef Alain Ducasse, or a little bit dead, like Cézanne, Van Gogh, those legions of Romans and their ruins, and Charles Démery, who

Provence

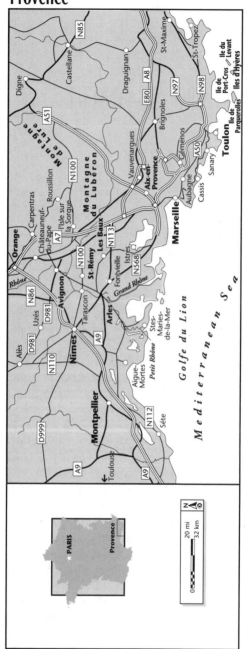

was head of the fabric design firm Souleiado, now carried on by his children.

Welcome to the land of legends, where the rustic arts are the best buys, where your souvenirs may cost more than in other parts of France but will take on added value because they come from a region that whispers the soul of France.

Getting There

By Plane

While Marseille in no way can be considered a true part of Provence, it has a fabulous international airport, so that you can fly in from many destinations in Europe, as well as from Paris. The Marseille airport lies directly between Marseille and Aix, which is why it is officially named the Marseille-Provence International Airport. Note that you don't go into Marseille to get to Aix, you just drive the other direction.

Should you prefer the Nice–Côte d'Azur International Airport (NCE), it's not a bad choice at all and has the benefit of the nonstop Delta flight from New York. Nice is about a 2-hour drive on the autoroute from Aix-en-Provence. The road is clearly marked as you get on the A8 right near the Nice airport. Better yet, there is a wonderful emotional connection between the Riviera and Provence, so that combining them in one trip makes perfect sense.

By Train

Important train announcement: France is in the process of completing the TGV Mediterranee, which includes new train stations at major stops such as Avignon. Do know what you are doing before you do it.

Many people mistakenly think that there's been TGV service to the Riviera for years. Wrong.

Regardless of which train you are on, your main hub cities will be either Marseille or Nice, but you can start in Avignon, especially if you are coming from Paris on the north-south axis. There is existing TGV service from Paris to Avignon; about 3 hours by fast train.

There are some rather amazing bargains to be had on train tickets, especially from Paris to Marseille. There are differing rates for those who reserve and pay for their tickets in advance—the Joker 30 ticket means you pay 30 days in advance; the Joker 8 means you pay 8 days in advance. Day trains (meaning no couchette) from Paris to Marseille cost about 180 F ($30) for a Joker 30 ticket and 300 F ($50) for a Joker 8 ticket.

You may want to take the overnight train from Paris to Marseille and then rent a car to get to Provence or anywhere else in southern France.

The overnight train is the slow train, but you save on the cost of a hotel room and you wake up in Marseille at about 7am.

Also note that Marseille does have TGV service from Paris, so you can get there in about 5 hours. There will soon be TGV service directly to Aix.

Getting Around

You really can't do Provence without driving. Well, you can, but you won't get to fight with your spouse or your family or your loved ones.

By Bus

Provence is very well connected by regional buses because this is how the local workforce commutes. If you find the right hub city, you can do a good bit with buses, although you won't have a lot of flexibility in terms of scheduling.

By Car

First, you will need two types of maps: a big one that gives an overview of the area and then another one with smaller details and back roads. If you have not done so before arrival in the area, get out the bigger map and circle your target cities and have a daily plan. Yes, that's a pun in French, but a good one: A *plan* is a map, and you need a map plan.

Many of the most attractive cities, towns, and villages in Provence are close to each other, but it's hard to know how to get to them all or how to plan how much time you're going to need. Without planning, you may not be able to connect the dots in a sensible way. Furthermore, there's a good bit of spread to Provence, which you may not grasp until you factor in how far apart places are and how difficult the road there can be. I've never endured a longer (or slower) 39 kilometers (25 miles) than the last little bit that brought me to Bastide Moustier right near Moustier-Ste-Marie. Don't bite off so much territory that the vacation becomes a chore.

You may also find that a village you read about or dreamed about does not touch you the way you thought it would, or that getting into town and parking are such a nightmare that you are no longer enchanted with that town. After a day or two, you may want to remap your assault.

Much of how you enjoy your trip is dependent on which routes you pick and what time of year you drive them. It is impossible to do Provence in a weekend or even 4 or 5 days.

Just like the Riviera, there will be parts that will excite you and parts that will leave you cold. There will be cities that you have never heard of that end up forcing themselves on you because of one inn, one restaurant, one store (or two) that you have to visit.

Ever plan on going to Lorgues? Maybe not. But any foodie knows that no visit to Provence is complete without dining Chez Bruno. Suddenly you reconfigure your trip to include Lorgues. Then you look at the map and realize that Lorgues isn't so far from St. Tropez. And so it goes. Back on the road again.

Here are some other tips on driving Provence:

- Driving in Provence may not be the romantic interlude you dreamed it would be. My husband and I went on a 2-week driving trip a few years ago. I soon found that getting in and out of the famous towns was grounds for divorce, and that's after 20 happily married years with the same driver. We were only living our dreams on back roads and in small towns that we had never heard of. We quickly gave up Arles and Nimes and limited our explorations in Avignon and took on towns that were easy for us. Easy became more fun. Unheard of and not-so-famous became our finest memories. God help the couple that drives in July or August—the traffic is unbearable.

- Driving is a better two-person sport than one person. I have done it myself and sometimes you have to pull over to study the map if there's no one to call out the directions every time you come to a *rond point* (rotary). Or sometimes you just have to drive around the rotary two or three times until you can do it while reading the map.

- In making your map plan, also take into consideration the days of the week, since you will want to hit certain cities on market day. Get to the market early. Markets that sell food almost always close by 1pm. There is also more traffic on market day, since there are more people in town.

- Remember to gas up at *hypermarchés* and to avoid the gas stations on the autoroute or in the center of town.

- You can pay tolls with a credit card.

- There's usually a bathroom at each pay station on the autoroute and they are clean. They may not be marked but usually if you look for the *P*, which means parking, you'll find a pay phone and a toilet.

- Driving around eats money like mad. If you aren't used to driving in France, maybe this is a good time to tell you that pay roads are outrageously expensive and gas is frightfully high. Expect to pay $300 to $500 in gas and tolls for a week's driving in the Riviera and Provence.

- Please remember that the larger the city, the more roads, the more suburbs, and the more complications in getting to the center of town. Very often there are so many one-way streets, even if you can remember how you got into town, you can't use the same route to get out of town.

- In approaching a major city, follow signs to *centre ville*. If you are spending the night in the town, have directions to your hotel and the hotel's address and phone number handy, not buried in your suitcase. If needed, call for specific directions in English before you arrive.

- A telecarte will help you call your hotel from a pay phone while you're on the road.

- Once you've chosen a village for exploration, make sure you understand how to pay for the parking. See chapter 5 for more on parking.

- One of our best tricks became locating the part of town we wanted (*centre ville*) and then, before looking for a parking space, driving around to check it out and to see exactly what the spread was. This also gives you an idea of directions, of street parking, and of parking lots. After once around the town, you'll know where the shops are, where you want to go, and maybe even how long you want to spend in town.

  If you don't get a parking space anywhere near where you want to shop, your drive around town has stimulated your brain so that you know what to expect. You can then decide how far from town you are willing to park, and what degree of trouble you are willing to undergo to take in the charms of any particular town.

- Each day you leave your hotel for a new hotel and a new city, get detailed directions, preferably marked on a map. Do not waste time with road numbers, as they are rarely marked and are never marked when you have to make a quick decision. You need city directionals. My concierge at Noga in Cannes gave me the best directions— a map that was marked plus a list of the directional choices and which one to pick. The worst directions I was given from another concierge at another hotel were "Follow the signs to Avignon; it's always marked for Avignon." In fact, it's not, and in one major decision I had to choose for Lyon, Marseille, or Other Directions. That is not pretty. The only good directions are based on city place names.

By Train

If you don't like the idea of driving, you may prefer to create your own version of Provence and/or the Riviera through a train trip of your own devising. Major towns are served by rail. Once the new TGV is completed around the turn of the century, things will be even more fun. You will also be able to more easily tackle Provence from either end: Paris down or Nice up.

You will miss the almost religious ritual of driving in the countryside, but you get a look at a different kind of Provence, and it may be a marvelous first taste. There's no question that Avignon is a great 3-day town, a magnificent choice for a weekend.

If you plan a train trip punctuated by 3-day stays, and move across the south of France by train, you will indeed see a lot—and never know the emotions involved with traffic, tour buses, French cars that don't start without a computer code, or signs that point to all directions. Bigger cities like Avignon that have so many museums, stores, and flea markets give you a nice feeling for the region without forcing you onto the road.

I'd consider a Paris-Lyon-Avignon-Cannes trip to be a successful search for the soul of France. And each city is on the main train line. When the new train is operational, you can also include Aix. Coming from the other direction, one of the most unique options is to celebrate the 151 kilometers (94 miles) of travel from Nice to Digne on the special Train des Pignes.

Taking the train will never give you the feelings of Provence that you get when you drive, but it may help you learn your way around when you're starting out.

Warning: Do go light on the shopping as many train stations in Provence do not have luggage carts.

Sleeping in Provence

Even with a car, I find myself torn between two different methods of booking hotels: choosing those that are located in city centers, so that I can at least walk around in that town, and choosing those that are romantic and adorable and fairy-talelike and are in the middle of nowhere, but possess great charm and a fair kitchen.

Your own choice in this matter will lead you to specific hotel choices and overnight destinations.

You must also decide if you like staying in a different hotel every night and want to keep moving on, even if you are only moving 50 miles, or if you like to use a certain city as a hub and return to it each night. And no, Marseille is not an appropriate hub.

There are no Hilton hotels in Provence, no American-style places that know your needs and offer a weekend promotional rate with an American-style all-you-can-eat breakfast buffet included in the package. There's funky and there's funky grand deluxe.

The easiest way to get around Provence is to pick one rather centrally located hub hotel and stay for a few days (weeks, months, years). Then you go out on day trips from there, even if this means a little extra driving during the days and some doubling back. At least you don't have to pack up your belongings (and purchases) each night.

Because the hotels all vary dramatically from one to the next, it's also nice to stay put so you don't have the emotional upheaval of loving the place you just left and not quite loving the next place.

If you are not staying at any of my suggested hub hotels, please consider arranging your travels to at least inspect the properties or dine there so you can compare price, value, and location with your current digs. All have fine kitchens and offer luncheon.

I'm big on convenience and confidence when booking hotels, so I often book through hotel associations; my two bibles for this part of the world are the **Concorde Hotels** catalogue (☎ **800-777-4182**) and the **Relais & Châteaux** directory (☎ 212/856-0115). There are almost two dozen listings for Provence and the Riviera. Do understand that the Internet plays a huge role for these small hotels these days; in some cases you must book a hotel by the name of the room you want and can only see your options once you look at the proper Web site.

Also, study your map and your needs before you book. Provence isn't that large but it's plenty big with distinctly different neighborhoods or portions of the area that may lead you to exclude other parts. Just about every time I visit I find new areas. Often I don't even return to places I've been before, simply because you are constantly forced to make choices. By choosing a hub, you begin to choose your shopping destiny.

Hub Hotels

There are more hotels listed in specific destinations; these hotels are in various corners or districts of Provence and are chosen now to help you sort out which cities and shopping experiences best fit your plans. I usually do 2 nights in an area and then move on; I'm just too old for 1-night stands. Your personal style may be to plunk down for a longer period of time. Remember that the Relais & Châteaux directory may well be your best friend, along with a very good map.

The area we call Provence includes five different French *départements;* herewith five suggestions:

HUB FOR CENTRAL PROVENCE

HOSTELLERIE DU VALLON DU VALRUGUES
Chemin Canto Cigalo, St. Rémy-de-Provence

Area & cities: St. Remy, Tarascon, Les Baux, Salon, l'Îsle sur la Sorgue, Aix

Départements: Bouches des Rhone (13) and Vaucluse(84).

Despite the fact that I cannot pronounce the name of this hotel (and to this day we still call it "That V du V place"), I originally booked it because it was listed with Concorde. Then, when I planned my assault on France, I could make all my hotel reservations with one fell swoop. I knew that Princess Caroline of Monaco lives in St. Remy when not in Monaco, so I figured if it was good enough for her, it would probably work out for a few days for the Gershman family.

In all my years of inspecting dream hotels, I've rarely found one better than this. Granted, I went with no expectations, so anything clean would have been nice. To find a fanciful and sprawling villa, rooms decorated in Provençal fabrics, and a many-starred Michelin chef (cute too)—well, *mes amis*, I might just as well send you here and retire from the guidebook business. It doesn't get much better than this.

They have their own postcards, the cutest gift shop in any hotel in Provence, and hot-and-cold running service. They even have their breakfast jam repotted into their own little jars. Every detail of life is perfected—right down to the room price. The regular rack rate for a double is about $200 off-season and $400 in season. Considering the splendor of this particular property, it happens to be a bargain.

Dinner, on the other hand, is priced according to Paris prices for a Michelin-starred kitchen. This is

what it costs, period. It's worth it, but you may have
to save up. You may not be able to afford to eat
dinner on a regular basis. And for God's sake, don't
bring the kids. The local phone is ☎ **04-90-92-
04-40;** fax 04-90-92-44-01.

HUB FOR EASTERN HIGH PROVENCE

LA BASTIDE DE MOUSTIERS
La Grisolière, Moustiers-Ste-Marie

Area & cities: Lorgues, Fayance, Moustiers-Ste-
Marie, Manosque, Digne, Forcalquer

Départements: Var (83) & Alpes de Haute Provence
(04)

There is not a magazine, a guidebook, an in-flight
piece of reading material, or anything in print that
has not already alerted the public to the fact that
the famed chef Alain Ducasse has recently opened a
small country inn (eleven rooms) with restaurant in
Provence.

Frankly, I didn't even know where Moustiers was
before I met M. Ducasse. Alain gave me all the
printed materials for the inn, including the little
English-language packet for Americans. It's an ex-
pensively produced (watercolor reprints, lavish thick
paper, fine printing) little job with an insert as simple
and charming as Ducasse himself. On a one-page
form you are asked to fill in the blanks about your
arrival and the number of people in your party. You
are asked for a 50% deposit or a credit card number, and then you can choose from a list of the seven
rooms—each is listed by name and price with the
footnote that prices do change with the seasons. In
fact, there's a baffling list of choices and prices, each
based on weekends and seasons. Mostly it costs
about $200 a night, which is affordable although
some rooms are more and some are less.

Breakfast costs 65 F ($11) (and you thought you
couldn't afford Alain Ducasse!) and dinner menus
range from 180 F to 250 F ($30 to $42), which
includes tax and tip but does not include wine or

beverage. Again, the price depends on the day of the week and the season and all that. And no, you can't dine in at dinnertime unless you are a hotel resident or unless it's out of season.

In tiny letters on the side of the fill-in-the-blanks form it says: "Extending your hospitality to others means taking care of their happiness while they are under your roof." Is there any question why I am in love with M. Ducasse?

Oh yes, I almost forgot to mention it. There is an airstrip for small planes and helicopters in Moustiers. See? The man thinks of every little detail.

A few cottages were added this past year, including the very private pigeon house, near the gift shop! The best way to book is to look at the Web page where there's a photo of each room; the rooms all have different styles in terms of use of space, showers, and bathtubs (ask for the Philippe Starck tub) and adjoining space for the kids. Each room must be booked by name. The local phone is ☎ 04-92-70-47-47; fax 04-92-70-47-48. The Web address is www.relaischateaux.fr/moustiers.

HUB FOR NORTHERN PROVENCE

AUBERGE DE CASSAGNE
Le Pontet (Outside Avignon)

Area & cities: Avignon, Carpentras, Orange, l'Îsle sur la Sorgue, Beaumes des Venis, Vaison la Romaine
Département: Vaucluse (84)

After I fell in love with the V du V in St. Remy, I began to realize how lucky I was that I accidentally found the best place in Provence. I realized how devastating it would be to leave the grounds and face the real world again, let alone hotel roulette, so I sat down with the general manager of the V du V and asked, "Are there any more like you at home?"

He recommended his other property, the Auberge de Cassagne, which also has a great location as a possible hub choice, since the hotel is right outside Avignon. You exit the autoroute at "Avignon-Nord."

The exit road (called the *sortie péage*) curves around just the slightest bit (past a golf course!), and there you are, at the inn. It is not in Le Pontet *centre ville,* so there's no need to go to town to get lost to be found.

This hotel is very similar to the V du V: A perfect villa decorated with Provençal fabric. The tables in their garden are actually set with genuine Souleiado. There are 25 rooms, all totally modern but with tile floors, Provençal prints on the bed and furniture, and classic local decor, with an additional five apartments. There's a pool, an excellent chef, and a fine wine cellar. There's everything you could dream of. Prices range from $200 to $400, depending on the room and the time of the year. The local phone is ☎ 04-90-31-04-18; fax 04-90-32-25-09.

HOSTELLERIE CRILLON LE BRAVE
Crillon le Brave

Département: Vaucluse (84)

This location is actually more central than Avignon Nord and may make it easier to get around. It's about 2 hours from Aix and a half hour from Avignon— you're more to the east and get views of Mount Ventoux.

HUB FOR SOUTHWESTERN PROVENCE

HÔTEL LE MAS DE PEINT
Le Sambuc, Arles

Area & Cities: Arles, Nimes, Salon, Ste. Maries de la Mer, Marseille

If your visit is more oriented to Provence and Camargue, this is the hotel of your dreams, available through Relais & Châteaux and sometimes even with promotional deals out of England that include airfare from London. The hotel is outside of Arles; not far from Marseille—it is very tiny and very special with just eight rooms and two suites. The property is run as part of the personal home of the owners, who also live on the estate. My friend Richard brought his teenage sons here for the family vacation; my friend Janet booked it for a romantic weekend getaway; my friend Patricia wrote about it in her book of the best hotel experiences in the world. This is a keeper! Rooms cost between $200 and $400 depending on size (suites are $400) and season. The local phone is ☎ **04-90-97-20-62;** fax 04-90-97-22-20; e-mail: peint@avignon.pacwan.net.

Provençal Style

There are tons of coffee-table books that can show you in one picture more than I can say in one paragraph. Instead, I'd like to just tell you about a photograph that I saw in a French magazine recently.

It was a close-up of two red espadrilles bound with pink grosgrain ribbon. That's it. That one photograph, of a pair of shoes designed by Inès de la Fressange, said everything I could ever expect from France, from design, from style, and even from fashion. The colors were the colors of the south; the addition of hand-stitched grosgrain ribbon to otherwise plain old fisherman's espadrilles was the whimsy of design that stands for genuine style.

That I got it all from a French magazine, and could then copy the idea in my own life, was the very essence of why we all travel and why we look at pictures in foreign magazines even when we cannot read the language.

Provençal style is about color and comfort and rustic country ties that wear and wear and have the heart of the people and their land in every stitch. Color and texture are the backbone of the look; handmade and slightly rough hewn—even when done with finesse—add to the value.

Shopping Provence

While the Riviera offers you two types of shopping—glitzy and/or Provençal—Provence offers only one: Provençal. Because all the thinking is done for you, it all costs more. But what a way to go.

In the Riviera, you have to pick and choose and take the schlock from the good goods. In Provence, everything that's for sale is sublime. Sublime is more expensive.

There are a few designer shops here and there—usually in Aix or Avignon, and yes, in Saint-Tropez—but Provence is not the place to really wear or to seriously stock up on your Chanel. Hermès ties and scarves, well yes, they work; otherwise the things to buy are either foodstuff or decorative items. What's for free are ideas and visions that you take home and translate into your own personal style.

I'm sure that everyone goes wild for Souleiado clothing at some time during a visit; my bet is that it only takes one mistake to cure you. I bought one of those fabulous tiered skirts, which people actually wear in Provence and the Riviera. I feel like a fool in it. In fact, I wear it in Mexico more than I wear it in France. Souleiado has in the past year updated some of its clothing; they still do traditional but they also do more wearable fashions. I just fell again, buying a marvelous dress that makes me look like a tablecloth.

If you insist on fashion accessories à la Provençal, go for the tote bags or the backpacks. They're chic and they're sturdy. The bangle bracelets made out of plastic-covered Provençal cottons are also nice. In markets, you can buy Provençal print leggings, which will probably fall apart in the washing machine but will give you the look for a season or two.

When it comes to gifts for others, be careful. Provençal style may not travel well out of France or have the cachet to others who don't know what it means, or costs. I bought a $100 silk tie in a Provençal print for an American gentlemen who does a lot of work in France. He had no idea what it was or who (or what) Les Olivades was, so the entire gesture was wasted on him. Stick with soap.

The best souvenirs and gifts for others are inexpensive local products: soaps, jams, jars of honey,

The Souleiado Rule of Shopping

This is a very simple premise and a very important one, so get out your highlighter or your scissors. This may be all you need to know about Provence. I am listing below some of the addresses of Souleiado shops in Provence. All you need to do whenever you enter a new town is go to the Souleiado shop. It's always in the best part of town, usually on the best shopping street. By getting to this address, you will find everything else you want to find.

olive oil, local candies (a box of callisons for $3 is a winner), a small piece of pottery, some dried lavender, perhaps a small bottle of lavender oil.

THE MARKET DAY RULE OF SHOPPING

· ·

Many villages aren't worth visiting if it isn't market day. Sunday is particularly tricky. As you decide which towns and villages to visit, mark your map for market days. Specific market days in towns and nearby villages are further delineated in the body of this chapter. This list is of overall bigger markets.

To find out about antique fairs or salons, brocante day at the local market, or general fun junk shopping, there are a few regional and national guides. *L'Incontournable du Chineur* is a tiny computer-printed free guide to fairs in the regions of Alpes-Maritimes, Aude, Bouches-du-Rhone, Gard, Hérault, Pyrénées-Oirentales, Var, and Vaucluse—in short, most of the Riviera and Provence. It includes a calendar of events as well as ads. Get it at any flea market.

MOUSTIER-STE-MARIE

. . . .

I love Alain Ducasse; I love the Bastide de Moustiers; I love Provence, and I do not want to start out with a sour note, but I loathe the village of Moustiers Sainte Marie. I can't quite put my finger on it except to say it's one of the least genuine places I've ever visited: one giant tourist trap where all the shops look alike and sell the same merchandise.

Maybe I exaggerate a tad. If you were looking for a village to photograph for the cover of your next book, this might do. If Disney were looking for a village to copy, this might do. If you're looking for heart and soul, skip it.

The village is known for a specific style of faience painting. As I already said, most of the stores sell very much the same old thing. The best store in town is called **Bondil a Moustiers** and to make it even more fun for you, there are two different shops and a separate factory that you can tour, but all three are in town. (Best shop: place de la Eglise.)

If you're here because you're staying with Ducasse, get the map to town at the front desk. Do study the map as the town has two parts to it, since there's a big gorge right smack dab in the heart of things and you might not notice this at first. (Hey, I didn't!)

Then wander around or better yet, go back to Ducasse and eat.

If you are approaching Provence from the southerly route, Moustiers is a good first stop. Soothe yourself at chez Ducasse—don't worry too much about the shopping and move on only when you are strong enough. In a year or two.

MARSEILLE

. . . .

Marseille can also serve as the gateway to either Provence or the Riviera, depending on which way you are coming and/or going. I can't tell you that I adore Marseille, that the streets are filled with charm, that I want to live here, or much else except for the fact that there's a great airport and this is a nice stop for a turnaround. Of course, while you're turning around, you might as well do a little shopping.

Sleeping in Marseille

You may need to sleep in Marseille if you are catching a flight out the next day or if you are arriving from a transatlantic flight and need a day to rest up before you start driving the hills of Provence. Despite the fact that the town is lacking in overall perfection, there are two hotel properties that are marvelous in terms of location, fantasy, and price.

Before you book, I feel compelled to tell you that the city of Aix and the city of Marseille are equidistant (25 to 30 kilometers/18 miles) from the Marseille International Airport, so if you're going into town to avoid driving and to rest up, there is a bit of a drive.

HÔTEL CONCORDE PALM BEACH
2 promenade de la Plage, Marseille

This hotel sort of reminds me of Loew's in Monte Carlo—it's that same sort of low-slung, modern zigzag sprawling hotel across a panorama of beach. This modern hotel has a pool, the ocean, and views to calm your nerves before or after travel. This is almost a resort unto itself and certainly does not reflect the real world you'll find in the Old Town. Rooms begin at less than $100 per night.

For U.S. reservations, call ☎ **800/888-4747**. The local phone is **04-91-16-19-00;** fax 04-91-16-19-39.

LE PETIT NICE-PASSÉDANT
160 promenade de la Corniche, Marseille

This is the local Relais & Châteaux property. It too is a dream and very unlike the old port or the seedy Marseille that is out there, somewhere. There's a small (14-room) villa, with a gorgeous swimming pool, dining on the terrace overlooking the sea, and a total lack of the real world. The Passédant family owns and runs the property; their son Gérald is the award-winning chef. The local phone is ☎ **04-91-59-25-92;** fax 04-91-59-28-08.

Sofitel Vieux Port
36 bd. Charles Livon, Marseille

I have become a huge Sofitel fan in the last year, especially when it comes to the Riviera and to Provence. Some insiders say their best property is their hotel in Marseille. Good chef, too. In fact, like the Sofitel in Cannes, this one specializes in fine dining with a view. Even if you don't stay here, come take a look. The local phone is ☎ **04-91-52-90-19;** fax 04-91-31-46-52.

Markets & Fairs

Markets range from daily fish markets in the old port to a very nice food market at rue Longue des Capucins, near the Canebière. This is where you'll buy all the ingredients for your fresh bouillabaisse. Also check out the heaps of spices, dried fruits, and many exotics. Aux Capucins is open daily from 7am until 2pm and from 4pm until 8pm for the after-work crowd.

There's a flower market every Monday morning at place Felix Baret and on Tuesday and Saturday mornings in the allées Meilhan.

A Provençal market selling regional specialties from Provence is held every day at la place Castellane; there's also a fresh food market Le Marché du Prado—it's extremely lively and very ethnic.

Brocante is sold at the flea market at Porte d'Aix, which is not your most glamorous neighborhood. Expect a lot of broken Edith Piaf records. There's a daily book market at Le Cours Julien.

On weekends, there's a gallery called Les Puces de la Madrague, 4 rue Neuve Ste. Catherine. The big weekend flea market is called Le Marché aux Puce de Marseille, and it's held every Friday and Saturday, from 9am until noon and 2 until 6pm, and on Sunday from 8am until 1pm (chemin de la Madrague-Ville, 15e). There are about 200 dealers at the flea market, and there are a few bistros for breakfast, lunch, or snacks.

The second Sunday of each month there's a brocante at the Cours Julien, where the daily book market is held.

There is also a daily souk for African transients. It lacks the soul of Provence.

The Santon Fair is held from November until February in the allées Meilhan. There is a Garlic Festival from the middle of June until the middle of July; check out the Cours Belsunce for tables stacked high and mighty. There's a pretty big antique salon each October.

Finds

ATELIERS MARCEL CARBONEL
47 rue Neuve Ste. Catherine, Marseille

One of the most famous makers of santons in all of France, Carbonel is known as a master. On Tuesday and Thursday you can watch him at work. The shop is open Monday through Saturday. Small santons start around 70 F ($12). Closed in August.

CHOCOLATS PUYRICARD
155 rue Jean Mermoz, Marseille

This is one of the most famous chocolate shops in France. Even though this brand was only founded in 1967, it has an international reputation. There are now several branches in various cities in the south.

Check out their seasonal molded chocolates—chicks and fish for Easter, and the like. Another local specialty is the chocolate pralines made with almond pâté.

La Compagnie de Provence
1 rue Caisserie, Marseille

Take a look at the little gift packs here: three paper-wrapped scented soaps tied with string and sealed with an old-fashioned wax seal go for 69 F ($11.50).

La Savonnerie du Sérail
50 bd. Anatole de la Force, Marseille

A real live Marseille soap factory with a factory store! Open weekdays only from 8am to noon and 2 to 6pm (5pm on Friday).

AIX-EN-PROVENCE

Aix is a very large city. Even the city center has a few parts to it, so if you are driving, you need to study a map and drive around a little to take it all in and get yourself oriented before you park. The reason you need this fine grasp on the lay of the land is that you won't find a parking place on a market day. You will probably end up in a city parking lot with a bit of backtracking to do.

Now that I've been to Aix from many different directions, I can tell you that the parking difficulties remain the same, but the ease of entry into the city is very much related to which way you come in.

Once there, you need a map.

The Lay of the Land

The main drag of the touristy part is called Cours Mirabeau. This is the street with the biggest stores and multiples (yes, Monoprix!). They even have a hair salon that features Carita-trained beauticians and Carita products.

The cours Mirabeau is a wide avenue lined with marvelous trees, sprinkled with a fountain or two here and there, and populated by many look-alike cafes with chairs on the sidewalk, so that you can have a coffee, write your postcards, and pretend you are in heaven.

The town has been attracting tourists for thousands of years; there are tons of Americans in town because of the local language school and the fact that the city has positioned itself as the capital of Provence. There are tour groups galore, and there is now even a small street of fancy-schmancy designer stores (rue Marius Reinard) and a second fancy street with more big names (rue Fabrot). There's a touristy street (rue Esparaid) with a combination of affordable shops and cute tourist traps (TTs) such as **Maison de Lucille** (no. 43), which sells soaps and stuff with the look and feel of Provence. I'm also partial to a back area around place des Chapeliers filled with multiples such as Orcanta (for lingerie, no. 2 bis) and some real-people shopping, so that you feel like you're French.

Yes, there is a **Chanel** boutique, along with **Hermès, Sonia Rykiel,** and even **Christian Lacroix.** There's also **Souleiado** and **Les Olivades,** as would be expected. Without question, Aix is the designer shopping capital of Provence.

When you study your map, or just wander, you'll see that everything interconnects and weaves together in a maze, leading to an amazing number of stores. Many are TTs and there are branches of famous French multiples, such as **Geneviève Lethu** (13 rue Aude) and **Sephora.** The rue del'Ancienne hosts branches of **Lacoste, Laurél,** and **Descamps.**

There are also a lot of shops that specialize in Provençal cute, besides Souleiado and Les Olivades, which are mostly fabric and clothing shops. Other vendors sell clay pots, earthenware, garden furniture, and sundials. You get the drift. Take a look at **Terre du Soleil,** 6 bis rue Aude, for a big hunk of the local look and more pottery than you ever dreamed of.

One block over, on the rue Fauchier, there's a branch of **L'Occitane** (no. 10), which sells L'Occitane bath and soap products, as well as other brands. There's also local soap sold for 10 F to 13 F ($1.70 to $2.20) per cube from stalls in the market.

If you cut out the back end of Monoprix, you can wander to find **Pimkie, Escada, Yves Rocher, The Body Shop, Natalys, Bally, Georges Rech,** and others. The luxury street (**Sonia Rykiel, Christian Lacroix**) is rue Fabrot—before you get there, you'll pass all these other choices.

The best antiques are found on the rue Jaubert and the rue Granet, both of which are on the other side of the Palais du Justice from the marketplace. This is a mere block from the rue Rifle-Rafle, which I love to say, and which houses the local shop for **Chocolats du Puyricard** (no. 7).

If you prefer a trip to the factory outlet (prices are not less) you are looking at about $100 for a kilo (just over 2 lbs.) of fine chocolates. You can drive from Aix to the town of Puyricard, some 10 kilometers (6 mi.) to the north (see below).

If you want to browse around antique shops, I got a list of the best in town from the guys at Villa Gallici, whom you know are the most famous interior designers in France. They suggest:

- Les Paris d'Helen (rue Jaubert)
- Brocante Ungaro (no relation; rue Jaubert)
- Mr. Bianchi (rue Granet)
- Robert R (rue Granet)

Finally, I must confess that while I rarely buy art and I don't do galleries, I was blown away by a painting in the window of **Galerie d'art Le Roman** (place des 3 Ormeaux), just past the antique area. The original work cost $500; I didn't buy it but I wish I did!

The fun thing about Aix is that it's all twisty and curvy, and you just wander in and out and pretend to get lost. There are bookshops and low-ceilinged boutiques and cafes and candy shops and everything you need to have a grand time. There's a good branch of the makeup kingdom **Sephora,** located right inside the Passage Agard but with a street address of 12 rue Fabrot—the passage is one of the alleys leading from the place Verdun to cours Mirabeau. Don't miss it.

Sleeping in Aix

GRAND HÔTEL NEGRE-COSTE
33 cours Mirabeau, Aix

I found this hotel sort of by accident, while looking for a pay phone. It is located right in the center of the main street, between Monoprix and all the cafes. It's the kind of funky little not-too-expensive three-star hotel you want to find if you are a three-star hotel kind of person. Rooms are just under $100 per night. Best yet, they have on-premises parking! Cute breakfast room. The local phone is ☎ **04-42-27-74-22;** fax 04-42-46-80-93.

VILLA GALLICI
Avenue de la Violette, Aix-en-Provence

This may be the most perfect hotel you will ever visit. It's drop-dead gorgeous and also located within walking distance of town, fulfilling all needs. There's a good chef, a nice crowd of guests, and all sorts of nice touches that make staying here your dream come true. Because the hotel is owned by a team of interior designers, it is more beautiful than you can imagine. A wing of three new rooms has just been added to the original 18. Prices are about $300 to $400 per night and this is a Relais & Châteaux property. The local phone is ☎ **04-42-23-29-23;** fax 04-42-96-30-45; www.relaischateaux.fr/gallici.

Snack & Shop

The town is filled with cafes, pizza parlors, ice cream stands, and creperies—you'll have no trouble grabbing a bite.

One of the best tables in town is Le Clos de la Violette (10 av. de la Violette; ☎ **04-42-23-30-71;** fax 04-42-21-93-03), which is located in an old house with gardens, trees, and flowers. There is a luncheon menu at 200 F ($33). Sit, enjoy, and forget the tourists. It's near Villa Gallici, where, of course, I eat most of my meals. Villa Gallici saves most of its space for hotel residents but sometimes has an opening.

At the place de l'Hôtel de Ville is a tea room and tiny restaurant with a patio. I know it from Paris— La Cour de Rohan; it's open every day.

Shopping Hours

Most stores open at 10am and close for lunch at 12:30pm. Antique dealers and factory shops open at 9am or even earlier. Stores reopen after lunch at 2pm and stay open until 7pm. **Monoprix** does not close for lunch. Most stores are closed on Monday morning. TTs are open Monday morning and during lunch. In fact, Aix is not totally dead on Monday, which is a blessing.

Markets, Festivals & Fairs

Market days are Tuesday, Thursday, and Saturday. The market is a complicated thing with various parts to it: fruit and veggies to one side, *brocante* to the other. Meanwhile, the flower part of the market is half a block away and dealers selling new clothes and cheap imports from India spill onto cours Mirabeau on Saturday.

Should you approach town this way and see these vendors first, you will wonder who in the world ever thought this town had a special market. You may even miss the good part of the market, near palais justice, because it is rather well hidden.

There's a big antique salon in November and a Foire aux Santons in December.

Finds

Lora Lune
8 rue de la Glaciere, Aix

This small shop is in the maze of fun shopping streets in the heart of town; it specializes in bath products and aromatherapy. The novelty is that Lora obviously has been influenced by Lush, in London, so she makes a Provençal version of many Lush standards, such as bath bombs and loaf soaps. The store expects to expand throughout France. I like the antistress bath oil, which you add to the bath water after the tub is filled, as running water bruises the scent and its ability to perform. There are also infusion baths in linen bags, shampoos in soap form, and big pump dispensers of cremes.

L'Oustaou
12–14 rue Granet, Aix

Although there are plenty of touristy shops selling Provençal fabrics, this one is not very touristy and sells with a secret—it is a factory store. Some merchandise is 20% off the ticketed price. Best is that the clothes are for real locals, so you find authentic styles that are really worn, not dress-up costumes.

Maison Fouque
65 cours Gambetta, Aix

Offering almost a dozen different sizes of santons, including those which are all but life-size!

Scenes de Ménage
5 rue Aude, Aix

I call this "the poor man's Genevieve Lethu." Only a few doors from Genevieve, this store looks like a TT but actually has wonderful gifts and housewares and small items at good prices.

About the Souleiado Factory

We all know why we came to Tarascon, right? Right. To buy cheap Souleiado. Ha!

The prices at the Souleiado factory are so high they are offensive. The salespeople at the Souleiado factory shop are so uninterested in your business that *they* are offensive. (Even PA, who is French, was offended. This is not just an American tourist thing.)

Since you're going to ignore me and come anyway, here are some facts you need to know:

- The factory shop opens on Monday morning at 8:30am. This means they are indeed open on Monday, and you can get in some shopping first thing in the morning when just about every other store in France is closed.
- They close at noon.
- The shop is large and gorgeous, with many interconnecting salons and lots of merchandise. There are a few corners here and there with heaps, but even things in these heaps are not cheap enough.

Slightly Beyond Aix

I've already mentioned the town of Puyricard, which sells chocolates, tiles, and wine—certainly worth a 10-kilometer (6 miles) drive to me.

Within the town of Aix, but outside the immediate tourist downtown, on the rue Gambetta—which is a main artery leading in and out of town—there is a santon maker you might want to track down. Head for **Santons Fouque,** 63 rue Gambetta, or call ☏ **04-42-46-33-38** for an appointment. The shop is open from 8am until noon and 2 to 6:30pm. He is also open some Sunday in late November and into December, for the Christmas season.

- Most of the tablecloths are in boxes that are so high even I could not reach them. You have to ask for help. And the help is not very helpful. Nor do they speak English.
- The price of the tablecloth that I bought in Cannes for 750 F ($125) was 950 F ($158) in the outlet shop. A big rectangular tablecloth was 950 F ($158) in Cannes and 1,000 F ($167) in the outlet shop.
- The salon in the far back is where fabric is sold off the bolt. Fabrics per meter are at least 150 F ($25); many of them were very old prints. Very, very old. A fabric I bought on sale at Pierre Deux in New York 10 years ago for $8 per yard was selling at the factory shop for 170 F ($35) per meter (1 meter = 1.9 yards). I do not have that good a sense of humor.
- The museum, located across the courtyard, is sensational. It's open Monday through Friday, from 10am to 3pm. The entrance fee is 30 F ($5) per person. It was not worth it for the three of us to go ($20!), so I went alone.

TARASCON

Serious shoppers have already marked Tarascon on their maps, secure in their knowledge that they only have one life to live and that they want to see the Souleiado factory before they die. Well guys, welcome to my honest opinion of Tarascon.

I love Tarascon. I welcome you to Tarascon wholeheartedly. I love the Démery family—creators of the Souleiado prints (even though I don't know them, I love them). Their little museum on the premises of their factory is worth seeing before you die.

The factory shop, however, is outrageously expensive, and the people who work there are notoriously rude. I cannot welcome you to shop there. But I do welcome you to browse. Then you can go to the museum where you'll spend your money far better than on anything you can buy in the shop.

The Lay of the Land

You will probably enter town via the N99 and find yourself on the main shopping street for real people. (See that **Monoprix?** Don't you feel better now?) It's called cours Aristide Briand before it becomes the avenue de la République. This main street will curve around the city and hit the water, and you will see a bridge. Don't cross the water unless you want to leave Tarascon. Park. Walk.

The main cute area is a cobbled pedestrian street called Les Halles. The tourist office is located here, as are a few real-people shops, such as the grocery store, the bakery, and Super Drug. Some of the stores are open on Monday morning (as is Monoprix, 2 blocks over).

Like all medieval towns, the city center is a warren of squares that dead-end into nothing. Get a map.

AVIGNON

This is the part of the book where we all burst into song: *"Sur le pont d'Avignon, on y danse . . ."* You too will be dancing when you get on Avignon, but not on the bridge. In fact, I don't know if you know this or not, but it's not really a bridge—it's half a bridge. It just sort of juts out into the water and ends. People walk to the end, look down, and then walk back and tell their relatives they've been there and done that.

I would just as soon brag to my relatives that I've been to the **Sephora** store in Avignon. Maybe it's not as famous, but it's a lot more fun than the bridge. Sephora is one of France's leading makeup and beauty stores; don't miss it!

Please remember that Avignon is to get a new train station when the TGV Mediterranee becomes a reality, around the turn of the century. This train station will change many of the realities of the town, while the main shopping will remain where it is. The orientation of the heart of the old city is connected to the old train station, not the new one.

The Lay of the Land

Avignon is bigger than you think it is and has many parts to it. Avignon proper is easily a 3-day city. If you come for 3 hours, you may not even have time to shop. In fact, you may not even have time to park.

If you're driving, head for the walls and enter the city through any of the gates. Like all medieval cities, Avignon has walls and is then built in concentric circles. There are no grid streets whatsoever, and only the teeny center of the circle has any kind of sense to it. The whole city within the walls is a warren of tiny streets and they are all one way— *bon chance*. Your bigger rental cars won't even make some of the corners. We know from experience.

Since the famous bridge is just outside the city walls, we're going to forget about it right now. It's not the Ponte Vechio and there are no shops on it, so do a drive by. Then park and go shopping. Once you get inside the city walls, get as close to the place de l'Horloge as possible and park. If you are returning your rental car, all cars go back to the train station so you can dump the car, leave your luggage at the train station, and then wander the town.

If you're lucky, you'll actually enter town through the Porte de la République (across the street from the main train station). By entering through this gate, you're on the cours J. Jaures, which will become the rue de la République, the main shopping street. It dead-ends into the place de l'Horloge.

The fancy shopping street in town is rue Joseph Vernet, which veers off to your left from the rue de la République right across the street from the tourist office. It is to your left if the tourist office is to your right, and the train station is behind you. Don't turn onto rue Joseph Vernet at this point, just note where it is. You won't head for the good shopping until you've walked clear through town.

Among the stores you'll find on the rue Joseph Vernet are **Laurèl** (Escada's less-expensive brand), **Georges Rech, Ventilo, Cacharel, Souleiado,** and **Façonnable.** There are also assorted boutiques for everything from jeans to Japanese droop. The big names are concentrated on the part of the rue Joseph Vernet that is almost directly parallel to the place de l'Horloge; get there via the rue St. Agricol.

All of the little streets clustered around rue Joseph Vernet right there, including rue de la Petite Fustiere, rue Limas, and plan de Lunel, have charming and wonderful stores. Many of them are antique shops.

All of the basic multiples, as well as **Galeries Lafayette** and **Monoprix** (what more does any shopper need?), **FNAC, Sephora, Codec** (a supermarket chain), and **Cléopatre** (a chain that sells cheap costume jewelry for teens), can be found on the rue de la République in a fairly straight parade of shops. There are also some crepe stands and some tourist traps. The big stores are open during lunch; Monday mornings are not totally dead.

On the other side of the place de l'Horloge, leading toward place Pie, is the rue Marchands, the town's second-tier leading shopping street. You'll find **Les Olivades** here as well as assorted other real-people shops, even Foot Locker. This is a pedestrian area where you can amble and browse.

One final note about neighborhoods: On the other side of the river, which you can reach by a whole bridge, not the famous half-bridge, lies the suburb of Vileneuve-lès-Avignon, which has a flea market on Saturday morning. You can get there by bus if you didn't drive to Avignon.

Sleeping in Avignon

HÔTEL D'EUROPE
12 place Crillon, Avignon

This is the hotel of your dreams right in the center of town that you wish you had booked for your honeymoon. This restored old hotel is decorated with tapestries and is just a stone's throw from everything. There are 44 rooms and three suites; prices average out to over $200 per night. There's also a nice restaurant on the property. The local phone is ☎ 04-90-82-66-92; fax 04-90-85-43-66.

HÔTEL LE MIRANDE
4 place Amirande, Avignon

I found this small hotel near the Palais des Papes while trying to find a parking place; rooms are about $250 and up. Charming, cute, and small. The local phone is ☎ 04-90-85-93-93; fax 04-90-86-26-85.

AUBERGE DE CASSAGNE
Allée de Cassagne, Le Pontet

See listing under "Sleeping in Provence" above. This is the more secluded dream come true.

Snack & Shop

CAFÉ DES ARTISTES
Place Crillon, Avignon

This was the favorite cafe of my sister-in-law, who was a French playwright and showed her work at the festival in Avignon every year. The 1930s-style bistro for the artsy crowd is chic and yet funky and elegant. There's a menu at 150 F ($25) that will be just the thing. Closed on Sunday.

NANI
Rue de la République (at the corner of Rue Théodore Aubanel), Avignon

This is the perfect soup-and-sandwich kind of cute local cafe, right off the main shopping street. You can eat upstairs or on the street level. They offer salads, quiches, potato tarts, and local fare. Warning: They don't take credit cards!

Markets, Festivals & Fairs

Every day except Monday, there's a market, Aux Halles, at place Pie. There's also a supermarket there in a small mall called Les Halles, as well as a public parking lot.

On Saturday morning there is a brocante market at place Crillon. On Sunday morning there is a *marché aux puces* (flea market) at place des Carmes, which is within walking distance of Aux Halles, but a little off center. Check your map.

The city is famous for its summer theater festival. There are also numerous big antique salons and brocante fairs during the year.

There's also a regular Saturday morning flea market across the river, Foire de la Brocante de Villeneuve-les-Avignon.

ST. REMY DE PROVENCE

St. Remy is a unique town in Provence because it's perfect, but it's not touristy and it hasn't been ruined. It's one of the few places that still has some soul left. It offers just the right combination of real-people funk and cute perfection. It does not look or feel like Disneyland, which accounts for its innate charm.

I can't tell you that the shopping here is great. I can tell you that walking around the town, window shopping, poking in and out of Souleiado, touching this and that, and buying postcards is a dream because you have the sense that, at last, you have found your own village. Even if Princess Caroline found it first.

The Lay of the Land

Like many medieval towns, St. Remy is built in a circle. Once inside the circle, the town has a semblance of a grid system, but there are still blind curves, dead ends, and alleys to nowhere. Fun, huh?

Most of the shopping is on the boulevard Gambetta, the rue Lafayette, the avenue de la Libération, and the boulevard Mirabeau. The best store in town is possibly **Le Grand Magasin,** 24 rue de la Commune. **Souleiado** is located at 2 rue d'Résistance, which is one of the main drags of the grid. **Les Olivades** is located at the place de la Maire.

The circle that encloses the town is so small, this is the perfect place to just park and ramble.

Note that the Hostellerie du Vallon de Valrugues is right at the edge of town, just outside the circle, and it is worth visiting for lunch (al fresco) or dinner and to poke into the gift shop. The gift shop is only open in season.

Markets & Fairs

Market is held on Wednesday and Saturday morning. There's a local arts and crafts fair the last weekend in July and a big celebration on August 15, which is a holiday in France (Feast of the Assumption).

There is a small brocante open afternoons only (3 to 7pm), Tuesday through Sunday, from the last weekend in November until Easter on the boulevard Gambetta (no. 19).

Finds

EBÈNE
38 bd. Victor Hugo, St. Remy de Provence

My friend Valerie from Carpentras sent me here for "The Look"—home furnishings and high Provençal style. My friend Ellen said it was the best shop she's seen in France. Photo op and a chance to really understand what French style is all about, and how to make it work for you.

Les Olivades Factory Shop

Chemin des Indienneurs, St. Étienne-du-Grès

My husband Mike, our son Aaron, and I have just left our gorgeous hotel in St. Remy, and we're on the road to Tarascon, headed west on the D99. I am in the back seat, reading a French fashion magazine and not paying attention. Suddenly Mike says, "Do you want to follow that sign for the Olivades factory?" Brakes screech and we make a French-style U-turn on a one-lane road.

The shop is a freestanding building out in the rear of the factory with its own parking. It is open on Monday morning, which totally shocked (and delighted) me. The shop is open Monday through Thursday from 9am to noon and 2 to 6pm. They will gift wrap, and they accept Visa. They will also fetch an English-speaking salesperson if needed.

The selling space is compact, neat, and filled with color and merchandise of all sorts and all prices. The best bargains are in a few bins and baskets with things crumpled into them. My steal of the day, from just such a bin, was a circular printed

L'ASSIETTE DE MARIE
1 rue Jaume-Roux, St-Remy-de-Provence

No, this is not a shop about a little donkey but is a home furnishings, design, and gift shop with all the magic you want from a town like this. Many flea-market finds in a fabulous jumble. You can also eat here and there's a relationship with the Hôtel Le Mirande in Avignon, mentioned above.

LILLIMAND
5 av. Albert Schweitzer, St. Remy

My friend Cindy Brown sends me e-mail about her finds in France; St. Remy is one of her regular haunts, and her kids swear by this source for candied fruits.

form for a tablecloth—you must cut along the dotted lines to get the circle and then hem the tablecloth yourself. It cost 100 F ($20) and was marked down three times, mind you. I used red blanket tape on the hem; it took 20 minutes on my sewing machine and is spectacular.

Not everything was such a good buy; some things were good buys compared to regular retail for Les Olivades, but this is an expensive line to begin with, so you need to understand that you are paying for a status brand. Fabrics ranged from 60 F to 110 F ($10 to $18) per meter. Borders at 20 F ($3.30) per meter were a good buy; an oven mitt for 50 F ($8.30) made an excellent gift. Generally speaking, the goods are priced 30% less than regular retail.

If you are waiting for the Souleiado factory outlet (located just a half hour away) or want to know which of the two competing firms offers the best buy, there is no question about it: Shop at the Les Olivades factory (☎ **04-90-49-19-19;** fax 04-90-49-19-20.

They also like the part about being washed off with a hose when they get too sticky. It seems their feet stick to the sugar on the floor in the very old factory. The firm was founded in the mid-1860s and is famous throughout France for its product.

LES BAUX DE PROVENCE

Les Baux, as it is called, is one of the most famous *Provençal villages perchés*. No cars are allowed in the village; you'll see why when you get there. The village consists mostly of one curvy upward shopping street and an enormous cliff side. During a mistral one February, a gust of wind caught my coat and I thought I was Mary Poppins. It was not funny.

The town has a few of the more famous cute retailers, but is mostly made up of TTs and locals selling the usual handcrafts and souvenirs. There are some bistros, cafes, and a crepe place or two.

L'ÎSLE SUR LA SORGUE

. . . .

If it's *dimanche,* this must be l'Îsle sur la Sorgue, so *bon dimanche* everyone and welcome to the best Sunday in Provence. *Note:* This is a Sunday that needs to be carefully planned because towns that are open on Sunday in France are few and far between, and you wouldn't want to sleep late and miss all the action. If you are staying anywhere in central Provence, your choices for Sunday flea markets are Marseille, Avignon, Le Muy, and l'Îsle sur la Sorgue. So welcome to a very good choice.

Please note that l'Îsle sur la Sorgue has a flea market and food market on Sunday only; on Saturday and Monday the dealers are open, but there are no markets. It is hard to understand the difference until you see it all in action.

Don't forget:

- Parking in this town is very difficult; get there early and use the **Marché U** (a local supermarket) parking lot.
- If you are planning on doing your grocery shopping, don't forget to bring a tote bag or your own little French string bag. This is France, remember? Each package will be wrapped in its own small fashion, but you will not be given any carrier bags.
- Not all toilets are up to American standards. Have tissues in your handbag and be prepared for stand-up bathrooms.
- Learn your shipping options early in the game.
- Carry a notebook and pen, take notes and memorize this phrase: *Je suis marchand.* It means "I

am a buyer" and it entitles you to an automatic 20% to 25% discount off the asking price. Taking notes is the most convincing part.

- Speak some French; it's not essential but it makes everything work better, including discounts.

The Lay of the Land

For a village you've never heard of, l'Île la Sorgue is surprisingly big and stretches along the banks of the Sorgue River, hence the name.

The high street runs alongside the river. The village is on the other side of the river from the main road, so you really have two parts of town to explore. You might want to do a drive through first, although finding parking will be hard, so you may need to grab any available space and trust me.

The main part of the flea market, which is held every Sunday no matter what the weather, lies at the far end of town along the riverbank. Antique shops, some cafes, and some antique warehouses line the high street on the nonriver side. The name of this street changes frequently but is most often written as the avenue des 4 Otages. There are some 200 dealers in permanent digs; there are about 50 more vendors who set up for the flea market. Many of the dealers are in buildings that are behind buildings or in little villages set up over tiny bridges on or around a courtyard. The scene is far deeper than you can imagine at first glance, and the shopping is also far more serious than you can imagine.

The heart of town (*centre ville*) lies on the other side of the river from the antique shops. The main shopping street is called the rue de la République. A fruit, vegetable, and food market runs along the quay side on the centre ville side of the river. This is called the quai de Jean Jaures.

Numerous bridges—some for cars, some just for pedestrians—connect the two parts of town. The river is not very wide. In fact, in my notes I wrote down that it was a canal.

Here's a tip: The Marché U has a huge parking lot in the rear. And it seems to be free.

Sleeping l'Îsle

Although every now and then I do clip out little tidbits on in-town hotels or inns, I end up going for my creature comforts and book with fantasy in mind. This means pull out your Relais & Châteaux directory.

Hostellerie Crillon le Brave
Place de l'Eglise, Crillon le Brave

I chose this from the handful of possibilities in the Relais & Châteaux book partly because it has a wonderful reputation, and partly because the Crillon in Paris is part of my life and this hotel is in the ancestral home of the duke de Crillon. The drive to l'Îsle sur la Sorgue is about 20 minutes.

The hotel turned out to be a brilliant choice for me, because I fell in love with the people here; they packed all my things for me, I found a house I wanted to buy, and I discovered a part of Provence I didn't really know before. The location is also about a half hour away from American cooking expert Patricia Wells's home in Provence, if you're thinking about stopping in or taking her cooking classes. Local phone is ☎ **04-90-65-61-61;** fax 04-90-65-62-86; www.relaischateaux.fr/crillonbrave.

Shopping Hours

Things get going around 9am on Saturday and Sunday. Dealers start to set up at 8:30am, but that first hour is sort of lazy, so no need to rush. Just about everything in town is open on Sunday morning. The food market closes at 1pm on Sunday, as do most of the local shops, but the dealers and the flea market go on until 6pm.

Note: The flea market is on both Saturday and Sunday, but the combination of food market and flea market is only available in this particular town on Sunday.

I wouldn't bother with this town anytime except the weekend, and then maybe I'd come for a weekend. Then you spend Saturday with the regular dealers (many of whom are only open on weekends) and Sunday with the market and those dealers you missed or want to visit one more time.

If you're just in town for a Sunday, arrive by 10am and shop all day, but plan to buy your Sunday dinner as a picnic before the market closes at 1pm. They'll put your rotisserie chickens in hot-bags for you. Just store in your car, as you will make many trips to the car during the day anyway.

While you roam the streets, choose your luncheon spot and reserve a table, so that you can return by 1 or 1:15pm. You'll probably want to stop by your car to drop off the groceries and the loot before you sit down to lunch. Many places have regulars who know the drill. (I was belittled in French for not knowing the routine at the place I chose for lunch on my first day.)

Dealers are open on Monday. And many are open "*sur rendez vous.*" That means you call ahead and make an appointment for a time and date other than when the store is open. You speak French.

Markets & Fairs

Brocante day is Sunday. Market days are Thursday and Sunday (mornings only). There are two big antique fairs during the year: one at Easter and the other during the few days before August 15, which is a holiday in France (the Feast of the Assumption). Last year this fair was held August 12 to 15. You can call the fair organizers at ☎ **04-94-03-40-72** for the exact dates (fax 04-94-31-27-25).

There's a big marché provençal toward the end of July. A local country fair is held in September.

Price & Selection

I went so wild and crazy for the food market that I immediately began buying things and didn't stop until my husband, Mike, and I couldn't carry anything else. I did find that prices for foodstuff were most expensive in the center part of the market and least expensive at the outer reaches of the market. There can be a differential of up to 5 F for similar merchandise and foodstuff.

Prices in the food stores, which are also open on Sunday morning, are the same as market prices. Prices on small items, such as soap and T-shirts, are very good. You can't beat a great T-shirt for 30 F ($5). Most vendors were generous with the notion that you should taste their goods; only the soap vendor was nasty, because it was raining and she was afraid her hard work would go up in suds.

While the brocante is marvelous to look at and stimulating to dream about, I found the asking prices to be high the first time I visited. I liked the market a lot better the next time; it's very hit or miss.

There is very much a system in place: Stores and dealers have the good stuff and brocante is brocante. Because the selection and the quality of the goods is so high, particularly in the shops, if you are willing to pay good prices for good stuff, this is a weekend you will never forget. Serious shoppers will probably have to make shipping arrangements.

Finds

Many of the dealers in town are famous and are sought after by buyers from all over the world. Perhaps the most famous is **Michel Biehn** (7 av. des 4 Otages), who is an expert on textiles and Provençal fabrics and costumes. Biehn's shop is in a freestanding house; they even have their own printed paper bags—it is one of the best stores in France and sells far more than regional textiles. Francine of La Boutique de Francine is also big on fabrics and lace (1 rue Julien-Guigue).

There are numerous buildings that are marked as if they are brocante fairs unto themselves. Take a look at **Brocante 11** at 11 av. des 4 Otages. Also check out Îsle Aux Brocante (no. 7 and 4), where you can shop and eat lunch (see below). Rives de Sorgue is another building filled with dealers.

Not all of the finds are antiques. This seems to be a serious town for food, especially with that market going on. I found two gourmet food shops, a bakery, a wine shop, and a grocery store, *Marché U.*

LA CAVEAU DE LA TOUR DE L'ÎSLE
12 rue de la République, l'Île sur la Sorgue

Wine shop specializing in wines of Provence.

LES DÉLICES DU LUBERON
Avenue du 8 Mai, l'Île sur la Sorgue

More food; they have their own stand at the market and parking at their store just over the bridge.

SOUS L'OLIVER
16 rue de la République, l'Île sur la Sorgue

Grocery.

YVES & DOMINIQUE CHALAVAN
38 rue de la République, l'Île sur la Sorgue

Special breads.

Snack & Shop

CHEZ NANE
L'Île aux Brocantes, l'Île sur la Sorgue

The Îsle aux Brocante is a 50-dealer complex in the heart of town. They suggest a reservation (04-90-38-51-05). This restaurant is open only on

Saturday and Sunday and serves the dealers and the in-crowd of shoppers. Entrées begin at 100 F ($17). There is a daily menu at 95 F ($16) offered at lunch only.

L'OUSTAU DE L'ÎSLE
21 av. des 4 Otages, l'Îsle sur la Sorgue.

This was my first choice for lunch. It's the cutest place in town. Tons of Provençal fabrics and wood and charm and high prices. To reserve, call ☎ 04-90-38-54-84.

About Shipping

There are several shipping agents in town, you just wander in and have a chat. Essentially it's easy but expensive—price is determined by cubic measurement not weight, so you can buy a large piece of furniture and fill it with stuff and it will cost no more to ship it than the same large piece of furniture. That was the good news. The bad news is that prices begin at $500 per 1 cubic meter and that does not including packing, insurance, or clearing U.S. Customs, let alone getting from the port of entry into your dining room. My advice? Excess baggage costs less!

CARPENTRAS

. . . .

Carpentras isn't on the regular shopping road through Provence, but when you live in Crillon le Brave, as I plan to, it's town, so you might want to poke in, but not on a Monday because just about everything is closed on Monday, especially in the morning.

Nonetheless, the town is not without charm, or shops. There's our old buddy **Genevieve Lethu** (105 rue d'Inguimbert) and there's **Souleiado,** 3 place Charles de Gaulle. The town sort of goes in circles so you might want to drive around a little bit before you wander; I did get thoroughly lost and confused on my first stab at it. You might also want to stay at the Hostellerie de Crillon le Brave just because they hand out super little printed maps with the stores already printed on them. Oh yes, also carry your hotel phone number with you: I was forced to make an emergency call home (to Hostellerie de Crillon le Brave again) because I made the wrong choice on one of the ring roads in downtown Carpentras and was lost in no time at all. Finally, for secret sources in Carpentras, you must get the list from Valerie at Crillon le Brave, who suggests **Les Olivades** and **Souleiado** and **La Tonnelle,** 28 rue des Halles.

Chapter Thirteen

· · · · · · · · · ·

SHOPPING ATLANTIC FRANCE: BIARRITZ TO ROUEN

CRUISE NEWS

· ·

While traditional cruises may be Mediterranean bound or based, more and more lines are adding Atlantic French ports in cruise visits that include Lisbon, a few ports in Spain, and many in France. The new Guggenheim Museum in Bilbao, Spain, is a mere 2-hour drive from Biarritz, and it has increased the interest in this part of France.

Historians will tell you to ignore physical borders and go with the flow, therefore this chapter does include some parts of Spain. *¡Ole!*

THE OTHER COAST

· ·

Biarritz, which was once enormously chic (its heyday was 1890 to 1930), is just now being rediscovered, along with the surrounding Pays Basque—the French and Spanish Basque country. The sprawl of beach and splendor leading from Spain into France was known to local aristocracy and royalty, but it never really made it to the American tourist agenda, until now. Although Biarritz was put on the map when Napoléon III built his Spanish empress a summerhouse there, what the world doesn't remember is that Biarritz was firmly located on the medieval pilgrim path to Santiago de Compostela. This prime location certainly meant something to the Empress Eugenie, and it also means a lot now, in terms of the centuries of culture and trade that have followed the path you are about to explore.

Biarritz isn't really in the middle of nowhere. It's been in the middle of somewhere since, well, the Middle Ages.

Santiago de Compostela is one of the most special places in the world, and while it's a bit far to be considered a day trip from Biarritz, it is part of the hidden layers of secrets that await you in this corner of both Spain and France.

Because of the Schrengen Convention laws, the border between Spain and France has "disappeared." You can cross without your passport; no stopping at immigration. In fact, the immigration stalls have been abandoned. *Vaya conmigo.*

BASQUE STYLE

· ·

Southwestern France has a warm, Spanish country tradition. Colors move away from the dark blues you associate with seafaring design or the warm blues you associate with the Mediterranean and into warm yellows, golds, and baked earth tones. The fishing influence is found, of course, in everything from espadrilles to striped T-shirts. Think Picasso.

Espadrilles, berets, and Basque linens are three of the most important stylistic ingredients that have come from the Basque region. They have permeated not only French style, but international chic. If the Pink Panther wears a beret to signify he's French, it's because the beret has become a visual signature for the Frenchman, when, in fact, few people in Paris wear berets.

Indeed, all of France is now shrugging off its old attachment to Provençal and southern looks and is suddenly going for the simplicity of west coast chic. Provençal is old hat; southwestern is the new chic. The pottery manufacturer Poc A Poc sells a look they call *l'esprit Catalan*. Jean Vier, a local linen maker, has become master chef Alain Ducasse's choice for the linens and bathrobes at Ducasse's new bastide in Provence, and all of France is embracing the simplicity of western-style country wares as a complement to other French country designs.

While I still love the colors and patterns of Souleiado, I see the future and it is simple. I see the future of French taste in America and it is Basque; the antithesis of Souleiado. The return to elegance and simplicity makes room for the toned down chic of the Basque look.

Basque linen, as seen in Jean Vier shops all over France and assorted regional shops in Biarritz and Bayonne, comes in two varieties—either bleached hard white or natural unbleached beige with a small line of color woven through the final inches of fabric toward the selvage. Pascale-Agnes has explained to me that originally, the colors that were woven in meant something: red meant you owned the property and green meant you rented or were the guest. Thus, the napkin at your place would be color-coded.

BIARRITZ

For as long as I can remember, I have dreamed of visiting the Hôtel du Palais. When we sat in our suite—the Winston Churchill Suite—with the big glass doors opened to the crash of the Atlantic Ocean on the rocks below, and raised our champagne glasses, I got all teary-eyed as I proposed the toast.

"Here's to your dreams; if you wait long enough and you work hard enough, they can come true."

So I toast each and every one of you who has ever dared to dream, especially those of you who have dreamed of grand hotels.

The Lay of the Land

To actually understand Biarritz, we are talking location. The town has always been a resort city, a place for royalty and aristocrats. It's situated at the edge of the rocky Atlantic coast, and while there is a big, beautiful beach, it's the ragged edges of the rocks, the pounding of the sea, and the rugged land that help make Biarritz such a magical place.

The Riviera stands for calm seas; Biarritz is made of energy and waves.

Biarritz also has a second city a few miles away— Bayonne—where many of the people who work in Biarritz actually live. This becomes the shopper's trick of the century: Some of the goods sold in Biarritz are also sold in Bayonne, only much more cheaply.

Biarritz is also near the coastal fishing village of St. Jean de Luz, which is a lovely day's outing; it's not far from the Spanish border and it's an easy day trip to San Sebastian. More importantly, Jean du Luz is conveniently located near the Jean Vier (maker of fine Basque-style country linens) factory, which has its own bargain store. I do not suggest Bilbao as a day trip, but it can be done.

Centre ville (the town center) in Biarritz has a surprising number of neighborhoods; this is not the one-lane town you may think it is. The city has layers and levels to it, with the main street winding down to the sea. This city was designed for the promenade, so you'll have plenty of wide sidewalks to browse.

You have to love any town that has a big Hermès sign on top of a biscuit-colored stucco villa; a town where you can turn a blind corner and suddenly see the sea shining between the buildings or the enormous wrought-iron gates at the foot of the shopping street. The gates are welcoming you to the Hôtel du Palais and a town with far more glamour than you can stand.

Getting There

You can fly from Paris to Biarritz, or arrive by train
(TGV service). There are 14 trains a day.

Or you can drive. We drove from Cannes, by
way of Provence. It is a long drive from the Riviera;
do not make the mistake of thinking you can do it
in 1 day or that France is a small country. France is
a big country with small roads.

Getting Around

The town is easily walked; the Hôtel du Palais is
right in the heart of things. To get to the nearby
villages (or Spain) you will need a car. There is an
autoroute, so driving is relatively easy.

Sleeping in Biarritz

HÔTEL DU PALAIS
1 av. de l'Impératrice, Biarritz

Surprise, surprise. You too can afford the fanciest
hotel in France. Because Biarritz is a little away
from the swing of things, prices—even for the
grandest of life's little dreams—are moderate and
less than comparable hotels in Paris, the Riviera, or
Provence.

That means room rates of about $255 out of sea-
son and $295 in season, guaranteed in dollars
through the U.S. offices of **Concorde Hotels** (☎ 800/
888-4747). This isn't inexpensive, but if you consider that you are sleeping in the private home of
the emperor and his empress, with the ocean outside your window, in the resort town that ends all
questions about chic, then you actually have a bargain. The hotel is also a member of Leading Hotels
of the World; the local phone is ☎ 05-59-41-64-00;
fax 05-59-41-67-99.

Use some of the money you've saved to dine overlooking the sea at the hotel's Café de Paris, where
the chef has some Michelin stars.

Shopping Biarritz

This is an unusual town for shoppers. There are plenty of stores and lots of places to roam, as being out and about is part of the local etiquette. Most of the interesting shops are related to food and/or candy. There are some designer shops, but not an overwhelming number. There are no big malls or commercial centers, especially downtown. It's a very low key kind of place.

There's a small business in antiques, with shops scattered here and there; a few discount stores (one for clothes without their labels and one resale shop) in the main part of downtown; and a very good bookstore. There's a nice New England feel to the shopping, but there's no pressure to buy and no pressure to be incredibly chic, like on the Riviera. The look is very much jeans, espadrilles, blazers, and Hermés scarves. And very good jewelry.

SHOPPING NEIGHBORHOODS

PALAIS Along the avenue de la Reine Victoria there are shops on both the left- and right-hand sides. There are more stores on the avenue de l'Impératrice, such as Cerrutti 1881 and Alain Figaret, which is well known to the French for men's ties with a certain type of silk design. Alain Figaret is also known for his dress shirts for both men and women.

HIGH STREET: AVENUE EDOUARD VII If you didn't know better, you would think this is the only main drag in town. This is where the branches of the big names are located (Hermés). It leads to the place Clemenceau and the center of town, which is anchored by the department store Nouvelles Galeries, which has a supermarket in the basement. Should you be driving across France, or simply spending time between Biarritz and Bordeaux, you might want to note that this could be your last convenient time to do your French grocery shopping. Load up now!

HIDDEN HIGH STREET: RUE GAMBETTA

Who would have thunk it? Biarritz has a second high street. This one is not so easily found and is a little more real-people oriented. Yet it's laden with enough seaside tourist traps (TTs) and linen shops to make you really glad you came on down. There's everything here from La Degriffe (no. 19) to branches of Chipie, Façonnable, and the Scottish Wool Shop.

REAL-PEOPLE UPTOWN Leading in and out of town is yet another high street, avenue Marechal Foch, which has more shops for real people and a tiny strip mall with a few multiples such as Rodier and Cacharel. There's also a *marché* for everyday, and more food and gourmet shops one street over on Victor Hugo. These include two or three that are mentioned by foodies the world over, Mille et Un Fromage (no. 8) and Maison Arosteguy (no. 5).

REAL-LIFE NEEDS

There's a branch of Jean Louis David and Jacques Dessange, should you need your hair done. Parfumerie Frimousse, right in the heart of town, will sell you the basics. Nouvelles Galeries is the local branch of Galeries Lafayette; it's a low-end department store but it does have a grocery store in the basement, and it carries many health and beauty aids you may need. It's also a place for cheap thrills for the kids.

If you need a guide, my friend Wendi (who has a tour agency in Biarritz) works with a group of American young women who speak French and will drive your rental car for you and take you shopping. You'll pay 1,200 F ($200) per day. If you prefer to do your errands with the guide in a Mercedes with a driver, it's 2,500 F ($417) per day. Call Wendi Abeberry at ☎ 05-59-41-09-03; fax 05-59-23-34-14.

FINDS

AU BUFFLE D'EAU
8 av. Edouard VII, Biarritz

I think the name of this shop is a pun in French, although none of their leather goods seem to actually be made from buffalo. They are made with such elegant style that you won't be able to sleep at night until you've conquered the large-size Kelly bag.

DAURY
2 av. de la Reine Victoria, Biarritz

This is resort chic at its best, the kind of store that sells beautiful gifts, tabletop designs, and some antiques in such a way as to make you want to move into the store. Everything is displayed so beautifully that the magic of Biarritz becomes more real because you get to shop in places like this. Whether you buy anything or not, don't miss a trip here. It's almost directly across the street from Hôtel du Palais.

HELENA
33 rue Mazagran, Biarritz

One of the many linen stores in Biarritz, this one works for me because the color palette is different— Helena has natural linen, which is beige, trimmed with coral. Most shops sells a hard white trimmed with primary colors. Prices are also rather reasonable. I paid about $75 for a gigantic tablecloth. There are bathrobes, slippers, bedroom slippers (a nice gift at 48 F/$8), aprons, oven mitts, and all sizes and shapes of table linen. The staff does not speak English but is very friendly about opening up the linen and spreading it so you can see the true size. Wash the first time in cool water so the color doesn't run.

HENRIET
Place Clemenceau, Biarritz

As funky as Paries is (see below), this store is fancy and formal and just across the street. They sell fancy pastries, homemade chocolate candy, fruit and nut candy, their own candy bars (great gifts at 13 F/$2.20 each), and these adorable little chocolate cakes. Henriet is a local status brand. At 250 F ($42) for a kilo of the califruits, the price isn't bad considering the quality and the subtext that come with the gift.

JEAN VIER
58 av. Edouard VII, Biarritz

Considering that you are now in Jean Vier country, this shop is no more grand nor special than other branches around France. Hold out for the factory.

PARIES
27 place Clemenceau, Biarritz

In a town filled with candy shops, this one stands out as my favorite and is the maker of a local treat called a *kanougas*. For those of you who have tasted your way across France, loosen your belt. Kanougas is a Basque regional gooey treat, sort of like fudge meets taffy, but not as hard or crunchy as nougat. In fact, they are flavored caramels. I've gone flat bonkers for the chocolate ones, which are made by the shop owner's family recipe, handed down through the generations.

You can buy kanougas in a bag of mixed flavors (the colors of the wrapping paper indicate the different flavors), or you can just buy a kilo of the chocolate and get it over with.

The shop also sells candied fruit rinds, traditional Basque regional candies, and even tourons, which are Spanish-style candy loaves. They are cut to suit. Oh yes, they also have pastries and local *gâteaux* as well as macaroons and other yummies, like their own homemade black cherry jam.

BEYOND BIARRITZ
. . . .

BAYONNE   It's certainly not New Jersey, although it's sort of the same idea. Bayonne is the other town where you live, because you can't afford

Biarritz. We did a quick tour and found parts of it pleasing to the eye; we didn't spend a longer amount of time because of that old French problem, no parking.

I made the requisite visit to Berrogain, one of the local icons of Basque linen, and found them so expensive that I left in despair. Note that the store is on a side street, on the wrong side of a divided road so that if you are going into Bayonne from Biarritz, you should visit on your way out of town, when the store will be on your right-hand side.

Although I had dreams of chocolate shops and hocks of ham and cute linen stores, I didn't get to any of them. But my fellow travel writer Alexander Lobrano did.

My only notes: Market days are Tuesday, Thursday, and Saturday morning at the newly renovated Les Halles de Bayonne; great hams from Pierre Brillant, 24 av. du Marechal Foch. The main shopping street is Pont Neuf. Everyone raves about Cazenave chocolates and Daranatz for tourons; both shops are on Pont Neuf. If you cross the bridge over the river, you've gone too far.

ARCANGUES I remember this town quite well because it is little and charming and quaint, and I explored it with the delight you reserve for the kind of towns you'd like to visit and not live in. There is not a lot to do (or buy) in Arcangues. But Alec recommends a shop called Loco for Basque antiques; it's in a restored stable at Maison Achtal.

FERME BERRAIN Yep, it was my husband who spotted the Jean Vier linens factory. Actually, spotting it wasn't hard; getting there was not so easy. Ah Jean Vier, how could your retail business turn to *merde?*

If you are driving from Biarritz to St. Jean de Luz on the N10, you pass the factory on your right, but there is no road. You have to turn around, go back, get off at the next exit, cross under the highway at a trestle, and then circle around on a small road to the farmhouse showroom.

But it's worth it! The showroom is utterly and divinely gorgeous; each room of this restored farmhouse has been done to the nines with "the look." The place is filled with fabrics, linens, towels, gifts, little chairs for kids, and millions of things you never knew you needed until you saw them here.

Part of the factory is a museum, part is a glass wall so you can see the work going on, part is a showroom, and then, toward the rear, is the bargain basement. You actually shop while you hear the *clack, clack* of the machines. It's wonderful.

Everything in the showroom is for sale at the regular price; everything in the outlet store is discounted by about 40%. This means that a sheet that was 699 F ($117) is reduced to 419 F ($70). This is still beyond my budget. Did I forget to mention that all this big-name charm is not cheap?

However, there are many small items in the outlet. The baby bibs were adorable. They have a massive display of *porte-serviettes* (the linen holder that you keep your napkin in at your place each day) with names already embroidered on them. If your name is Jean-Louis, you're in luck. Otherwise, it's catch as catch can. Still, at $10 per, they are quite a bit of fun. And you can always rename your friends back home.

One of the most charming things to buy here is sold up front, but it's still affordable: a tiny container with flax seed and the explanation that people from the region always traveled with the seeds to protect them and bring them luck. They're about $5 per package.

Now then, for the basics. The Jean Vier factory is open Monday through Saturday from 9am to 12:30pm and 2:30 to 7pm. It is also open in the afternoon on Sunday and holidays! They take credit cards, and they'll do complimentary on-the-spot embroidery if you want your purchase personalized.

ST. JEAN DE LUZ I think this may be the French version of Puerto Vallarta. It's a yummy little

Bayonne Buys

by Alexander Lobrano

Locals know that the prices for beautiful, traditionally woven Basque linens (from dish towels to sheets and bed covers) and Basque woolens (berets, sweaters, blankets) are best in Bayonne; stop by Berrogain for an excellent selection, carrefour des Cinq-Cantons. Bayonne is also famous for producing some of the best chocolate in France. Sample some at Chocolaterie Cazenave, a charming cafe that serves what may be the most delicious hot chocolate in the country, 19 arceaux du Pont-Neuf. Garcia is the only place to buy espadrilles, Pont Baskutenea; they offer 52 different colors.

fishing village with plenty of shopping and lots of beautiful people.

Those who want to do some real-people shopping may want to pop into Monoprix in the *centre ville*; others may prefer Elise, down the street, for Basque linens. There are a lot of pizza parlors and places for paella, plenty of beachy TTs, and a few artisans who sell Spanish-style (make that Basque-style) arts and crafts and, yes, tiles. Try La Fonda, 8 quai de l'Infante, for Spanish-style ceramics and *azulejos* (tile). Don't miss Adam for chocolates or macaroons, 6 place Louis XIV.

Size Conversion Chart

Women's Clothing

American	8	10	12	14	16	18
Continental	38	40	42	44	46	48
British	10	12	14	16	18	20

Women's Shoes

American	5	6	7	8	9	10
Continental	36	37	38	39	40	41
British	4	5	6	7	8	9

Children's Clothing

American	3	4	5	6	6X
Continental	98	104	110	116	122
British	18	20	22	24	26

Children's Shoes

American	8	9	10	11	12	13	1	2	3
Continental	24	25	27	28	29	30	32	33	34
British	7	8	9	10	11	12	13	1	2

Men's Suits

American	34	36	38	40	42	44	46	48
Continental	44	46	48	50	52	54	56	58
British	34	36	38	40	42	44	46	48

Men's Shirts

American	$14^{1}/_{2}$	15	$15^{1}/_{2}$	16	$16^{1}/_{2}$	17	$17^{1}/_{2}$	18
Continental	37	38	39	41	42	43	44	45
British	$14^{1}/_{2}$	15	$15^{1}/_{2}$	16	$16^{1}/_{2}$	17	$17^{1}/_{2}$	18

Men's Shoes

American	7	8	9	10	11	12	13
Continental	$39^{1}/_{2}$	41	42	43	$44^{1}/_{2}$	46	47
British	6	7	8	9	10	11	12

INDEX